Praise for *We Are All in Shock*

"This is a book that is engaging intellectually and well worth the read from cover to cover for the many useful and practical exercises and tools, so that we may be strengthened in our minds, bodies and spirits. It is a book for our times."

—Peter A. Levine PhD, author of *Waking the Tiger*

"In a world of constant debilitating shock, Stephanie Mines offers skillful means to resolve personal and collective wounding in ways that illuminate as well as heal."

—Jean Houston, PhD, author of *The Wizard of Us* and *A Passion for the Possible*

"Uncover the deepest treasure of who you are and why you are here by connecting to your own body. Weaving applied neurophysiology and traditional medicine, *We Are All in Shock* will show you the formula and tools for sustainable health."

—Anita Sanchez, PhD, author of *The Four Sacred Gifts*

"*We Are All in Shock* is a landmark book. Reading like a novel but informing like a text, it edifies that psychological shock is a universal malady of modern and technocratic cultures and teaches us practical ways that shock can be self-managed and treated. It's a 'must read' for anyone who wishes to self-heal or to heal others."

—William R. Emerson, PhD, president emeritus of the Association of Pre and Perinatal Psychology and Health

"Stephanie Mines moves through the complex territory of healing with refreshing grace, candor, and immense wisdom."

—Pat Ogden, PhD, director of the Sensorimotor Institute and author of *Sensorimotor Psychotherapy*

"Stephanie powerfully embodies the teaching she is offering. As a healed healer she is a catalyst and a nurturing guide. Her work navigates the delicate terrain caused by shock and trauma. It is grounded in the body, sophisticated in its thinking, and delivered in love. My development as a creative woman has been inspired by Stephanie's caring presence in my life."
—Melissa Michaels, EdD, author of *Youth on Fire*

"Stephanie Mines infuses warmth, compassion, and wisdom into her approach to healing. Her design not only regenerates the human body and spirit. It also regenerates the planet's well-being."
—Spring Cheng, PhD, author of *The Resonance Code*

"Dr. Mines has gifted us with simple, yet profound and empowering techniques for the resolution of shock and trauma."
—Carmen Freeman, MS, CHT, health activist and recipient of the National MS Society Achievement Award

"This book is a treasure! It is of special importance to every prospective parent as well as to all those who have survived trauma."
—Suzanne Arms, author of *Immaculate Deception*

STEPHANIE MINES, PHD
Foreword by Donna Eden and David Feinstein

We Are All in Shock

ENERGY HEALING FOR TRAUMATIC TIMES

Disclaimer—

The information and practices described in this book are designed to support a holistic approach to healing from the effects of shock and trauma. Nothing in this book is presented as a cure for disease or intended to be applied as a substitute for appropriate advice and care from trained practitioners. The healing process should be undertaken with the advice and guidance of trained professionals who are best suited to address the needs of each individual.

The case histories described in this book are based on the experiences of people who have provided consent to the author for inclusion in this work.

Dedication—

For the children of the future

Acknowledgments—

Without the insightful editorial comments of Marsha Kerley and Bob Yuhnke, this book would be much more discursive. They not only kept me on target, they also shared my commitment to service and to how readers would benefit from a focused document.

My gratitude to Drs. Peter Levine and William Emerson are in the text of this book, but I want to reiterate here that their mentorship was, and continues to be, inspiring. Similarly, I am touched and invigorated by the tireless warriorship of Suzanne Arms, who never stops crusading for the children of the future.

Others who found time for my manuscript in their overburdened schedules, such as Lawrence Germann, Selma George, and Nashalla Gwyn, will always be dearly remembered for their commentary and their energy. I would also like to commend Michele Stein not only for her exquisite artwork, but also for her loving nature. I am honored to have her as my friend and colleague. This is equally true for Monica Edlauer, who models the treatments in Chapter 4.

The names of the people who trusted me to serve them are also inscribed in my heart. Their persistence in thorough healing and their belief in the intended joy of life continue to motivate me.

I am deeply indebted to the Dom Project for supporting and sustaining the TARA Approach and to Naropa University for its research grant.

—Stephanie Mines
Eldorado Springs, Colorado
January 2003

Contents

Foreword

Most people do not think of themselves as being in shock. *We Are All in Shock* suggests that if you live in a human body within an advanced technological society, your body probably reverberates from shock. The level of stress in modern cultures has direct and profound impact on the human energy system. Studies that have evaluated shock levels in infants, children, and adults found that 65 percent of Americans carry traces of psychological shock of which they are largely unaware. Though you may not be aware of them, echoes of past and present stress and shock are nestled in your biochemistry, and they limit you. They limit your adaptability, flexibility, creativity, judgment, and capacity for joy. You can do a great deal to change your biochemistry in ways that will heal you and free you.

At one time, shock was the body's response to severe physical trauma, threat, or loss—a tiger enters the cave, a limb is lost, a child dies with fever, a neighboring tribe threatens the clan, a hunter's spear does not stop a charging rhino. But shock isn't only what it used to be.

As we have moved further from our natural roots, other kinds of shock have become part of our lives. This—as has been persuasively demonstrated by William Emerson, Ph.D.—begins before birth. The medical management of pregnancy and birth have, without question, decreased the infant mortality rate. However, even a relatively routine diagnostic test such as amniocentesis (100,000 women in the United States will go through this procedure this year) carries a risk of infection, physical trauma to the fetus, and, in one case of 200, loss of the baby. We can only speculate about the shock to the 99,500 each year who will survive the procedure. The fetus and its developing brain are particularly responsive to the pollutants the mother breathes and to toxins in the fluids that provide nourishment. Some 10,000 human-made chemicals that we did not evolve to process have been identified in our food, and their harmful effects on the unborn baby are beginning to be catalogued. Meanwhile, efforts to keep labor brief and on schedule, the use of drugs during the birth process, unnecessary cesarean deliveries, forceps, harsh lights, and cold surfaces all compound the trauma of leaving the womb.

The infant then grows up in the most complex culture in history. We are faced not only with the physical threats to which every human body is vulnerable, but with the unprecedented challenge of finding an identity in a society where the rules are changing far more rapidly than any previous generation could have imagined. More stresses pour on us with the need to master unfathomable amounts of information, being cut off from traditions and extended families, marriages that do not last, multiple career changes, residing in many homes and geographies in one lifetime, increasing dangers regarding world stability and terrorism—you know the adventure. And that is under the best of circumstances. Add violence, accidents, child abuse, incest, and natural disasters. In a lifetime, there are many shocks. Each one that is not properly managed may dull or oversensitize the nervous system. And, as this book demonstrates, the effects are cumulative.

The contemporary treatment of shock has generally been under the auspices of the medical profession, dating back at least to "shell shock" during World War I. The strategy has been to approach psychological shock in terms of the mind, and treatments have included psychiatric medication. Another of the author's teachers, Peter Levine, was one of those who helped shift this focus to an understanding of how shock becomes lodged in the body and is most effectively treated at the mind-body level, using methods that integrate primitive survival responses, emotions (whose chemical correlates are distributed throughout the body), and the brain's highest functions. Dr. Mines' book makes two distinct contributions to the emerging field:

1. It demonstrates the subtle, insidious nature of shock and the importance of recognizing its pervasive nature.

2. It shows how energy medicine can be applied in the healing of shock and trauma.

Energy medicine recognizes energy as a vital, living, moving force in the body that is at the foundation of our physical and psychological well-being. It is a very new field with very old roots. It borrows from 100 traditional healing methods, integrates them into 100 types of modern settings and perspectives, and is practiced in 1,000 different ways. Quality varies. The field is still finding itself, its standards, and its efficacy studies. Yet even in this early stage, commentators, such as the renowned physician Norman Shealy, are making statements such as "Energy medicine is the future of all medicine."

Energy medicine works directly with the electromagnetic and more subtle energies that orchestrate health, emotions, and behavior. It is proving to be an effective, powerful, and surprisingly precise way of improving health, enhancing performance, and increasing the joy in one's life. This book will show you how Dr. Mines has applied the Japanese healing art of Jin Shin to trauma work, and it shows how you can as well. It offers a decidedly accessible self-help approach. It does not suggest that there is no role for professional intervention in the aftermath of severe shock or trauma, but that there are certain perspectives and tools that can benefit everyone in their recognition of and response to the residue of the shocks that are part of modern life.

There are many questions that I would encourage you to let this book address for you. What is the difference between shock and trauma? What is the biochemistry of shock? What are the varieties of shock? What is meant by the "layers of shock"? Does the book make the case that we are all in shock? How does shock based in the sympathetic nervous system plays out like the opposite of shock based in the parasympathetic system? How does shock disrupt our normal neurological and endocrine responses to threat? How do touch, attention, and stimulation play into the treatment of shock? Does an energy approach make a significant contribution to the existing repertoire of methods available for working with trauma and shock?

In my own reading of the manuscript, I was impressed with several things. The ideas are accessible. The biochemistry is relevant, authoritative, up-to-date, and reads more like a fascinating account of nature's handiwork rather than a scientific treatise. The approach it teaches involves, in the author's words, "gradual and self-empowering care... that reminds the nervous system of the capacity it has to respond [to shock] in a balanced way." The techniques are easily applied and are effective. As one who has worked in the field of energy medicine for over 25 years and trained thousands of students, this is probably my most important assurance to you, the reader.

—Donna Eden, and David Feinstein, Ph.D.,
authors of *Energy Medicine*

Note from the Author
for the 2020 edition

The global burdens of psychological stress or allostatic load have trebled since Donna Eden and David Feinstein wrote the foreword to this book. In the spring of 2020 alone, mental health vulnerabilities have accelerated exponentially. The United Nations Department of Mental Health and Substance Use, the World Health Organization, the Lancet Commission on Global Mental Health and Sustainable Development, the Johns Hopkins Bloomberg School of Public Health and the World Mental Health Survey Consortium all agree that there has been a marked upswing in people's exposures to traumatic events, and those who may have coped well before are now severely challenged. This describes the case in developed countries. The situation in developing countries is dramatically worse.

All the statistics included in the foreword were alarming then and now they have increased. In both popular and academic literature the word "shock" has come to replace "trauma" indicating that magnitude of overwhelm occurs more and more frequently. This makes the resources in this book of even greater value.

Antonio Guterres, the UN Secretary-General, declared in May 2020 that mental health is at the core of our humanity and that support at the community level is essential to address what is unquestionably a growing crisis. He pointed to the ramifications of isolation, fear, physical distancing from loved ones and peers, economic turmoil, misinformation, and uncertainty as factors contributing to this prediction. Effective practices that calm our nervous systems heighten immunity and allow us to naturally project hope wherever we go. That is the intention of these practices.

All the interventions in this book are safe and can be shared; indeed I encourage you to be enthusiastic and generously share what you learn and experience. In promoting readiness and preparedness Antonio Guterres, from his statement to launch the UN Policy Brief on Action for Mental Health, concludes his comments with a sentence that I echo here: "My hope is that we can be ready for this. People need us to be."

Introduction

*"You are the beginning of the trans-
formed world."*

—*Eckhart Tolle*

Throughout this prophetic book I speak to the innate capacity in everyone to heal from even the most overwhelming experiences, regardless of age or background. In the time since it was first published, I have never, not for one moment, lost faith in what I describe as "the power and skill of the average person to treat and resolve shock." If anything, my research since writing *We Are All in Shock* has underscored that faith. The impacts of pandemics and global crises include but go beyond specific symptoms. The human nervous system is the physiological mechanism driving each individual's holistic response to shock. The intention of this book, and everything I do, is to be of service on that same comprehensive level.

The general public is depicted, in virtually all media including film, as emotionally unprepared for catastrophe, panicked and chaotic when confronted with it, desperate for a leader to show the way. That superficial story obfuscates the much greater though less publicized reality that innovation, competence, and altruism are both our collective human history and our greatest hope. This applies to health perhaps first and foremost. We saw that in Puerto Rico, for instance, when authoritative, agency-driven healthcare services were cut off by Hurricane Maria. Determined to be of service, villagers came out to help one another apply the original medicines they learned from their grandparents. They saved lives, sustained well-being, and healed in community without equipment, pharmaceuticals, or medical doctors.

The renowned anthropologist Margaret Mead said that what marks the beginning and assures the continuity of civilization is compassion. She was referring to healthcare delivery at the grassroots level. The illustration she proffered was the discovery of a healed broken femur. This was proof that someone took the time to stay with the person who fell, bind up the wound, carry the person to safety, and tend the person through recovery. "Helping someone through difficulty is where civilization starts," said Mead. She spoke pointedly of aiding someone in physical distress and pain, using innovative, practical intelligence with the essential ingredient of compassion. As we approach what threatens to be the end of civilization, compassion for one another is what we are called upon to reclaim and re-member, to bring back into the members of our bodies.

The resources collected in these pages will help you tap your authentic wellspring of compassion. This happens organically through the process of uncovering the treasure of who you are and why you are here in a refreshing new way. The compass is somatic. Even under enormous stress the body can be trusted to lead in the direction of health, alignment, and balance, if you know how to decode its messages and follow them. Connection to our own physicality along with connection to the body of the Earth is the formula for sustainable health. The applied touch energy medicine protocols that are a significant part of the formula are based on traditional medicine synthesized with the mechanics of the nervous system. These instill the sensory experience of belonging that is your birthright. They root you firmly in the present. They re-ignite the flame of original purpose.

Without denying, avoiding, wishing away, or rejecting the crises surrounding you, you can come out of shock into a compassionate relationship with yourself, humanity, and the natural world. This is what these times call for in order for humanity to thrive. They call for a rewilding of inner consciousness and the uprising of somatic intelligence that directs a heart centered, embodied way forward. Your body is your wisdom keeper. It reveals the stewarding intelligence our children and our children's children need to assure their futures.

By diving deeply into your origins and the ways in which the elements of nature move through your body, you come home to yourself and your unbreakable bond with being. This is the moment when compassion is ignited and brings with it a cascade of neurohormones that irrigate synaptic pathways of creativity and visionary, innovative problem solving. You wake up to the miracle of life that lives in your cellular matrix. The way forward becomes known as biological imperative; sensory and indigenous motivation awakening in a time without precedent. It is true liberation—to not wait for solutions to be discovered by someone else but to feel them forming within you. That is the potential if not the certainty of this book's promise for you. By using these resources consistently, you become your own teacher and an unprecedented leader for yourself, your family, and your community.

This promise is based on the evolution of life itself. Life unfolds and evolves at every stage of existence, but the stages that reveal this the most dramatically are embryological. There are two aspects of human experience that are available to everyone equally: organic development and relationship with the natural world. Both stimulate emergence as well as unity or interbeing. Both are systemic and while they have been deeply impacted by accelerated stress, they endure and shift harmoniously because humans and the forces of nature are innately resilient. As we move towards birth from within the bodies of our mothers, we learn from the compressive forces around us. We harness enormous courage that is instilled by our commitment to life. We keep softening, opening, reorganizing, moving, expanding, and evoking the space we need to come forth. We can continue to do that throughout life. That physiological capacity is always available. It is elected; it is a choice. This book shows you how to make that choice consciously, uniquely, and actively. In these pages you will be reminded of how you, in fact, made this choice before, and that is what will assure your confidence that you can do it again and again.

As you read these pages, as you reflect and select the practices that match your needs, you will reconnect to the ecstatic ignition of your own life-force. You re-member; return to your somatic truth. This is not a memoir of facts, photographs, or events though these may flash before your inner vision. Rather what you will experience most irrevocably is a memoir of sensation. You will re-member your greatest love story through sensation. Claiming your innocent and original victory song, the epic saga of your prenatal life and your birth, certifies your capacity to define your own truth. It gives you the potent agency to tell your story for yourself and actuates the voice that stakes this claim without hesitation. You become what you were always meant to be: a force of nature.

We Are All in Shock provides ten steps to resolution. These remain essential for this present moment in which we are privileged to be alive.

Ten Steps to Resolving Shock

1. Identify the lesson in the overwhelming experience.

2. Sustain this awareness.

3. Establish a strong relationship with your body.

4. Develop an inner witness.

5. Make a bond with nature.

6. Know that laughter is the best medicine.

7. Use language as a healing tool.

8. Use touch to heal.

9. Separate past from present.

10. Address shock immediately.

The practices in this book turn on the capacities to take these steps. One of the significant differences between when I first wrote *We Are All in Shock* and now is the combination of the advancing climate crisis and the Coronavirus pandemic, which has illuminated the lesson of our global, overwhelming experience. The urgency to find whole-body, heart-centered intelligence is unavoidably, unquestionably upon us. The future of humanity depends on it. My teacher, Mary Iino Burmeister, who imparted to me many of the applied touch protocols recorded here, said that we need to come out of the order of the disorder. It is your body that leads you to the order of the universe. The somatic practices that allow you to surrender to your own indigenous wisdom, your unique genius, are in this book. The discipline to utilize them is the discipline of love. As my friend Charles Eisenstein says, "True discipline is really just self-remembering." That discipline heightens your attention. Experience the practices of presence and active mindfulness that move you into your center, initialized by touch.

These times also call for the end of secrets. Life-saving, strengthening, and mind-expanding wisdoms have, throughout history, been kept secret to protect them, insure their correct usage, and sometimes to deny them to others. We need them all right now, and the people most capable of using them appropriately are those who mobilize a groundswell for the continuity of human civilization. That is why I have included an appendix with new material that specifically addresses the challenges of these times which I had previously reserved for advanced students. Tapping into the roots of compassion, which have deepened in my years of service, eradicates the need for proprietary secrecy and elevates my abilities to reach into the minds and hearts of others to cultivate skill and somatic understanding. Energy medicine is medicine for the people.

The modalities, protocols, and interventions assembled in these pages translate readily into online formats that allow therapists and service providers to be available for everyone in need. The mental, emotional, and spiritual consequences of climate change and the Coronavirus pandemic are expanding rapidly and will outlast the pandemic itself. The inner climate shifts propagated in these pages promote essential resilience and adaptation as life alters unpredictably in every sector. This is a trend that will only continue. Simple hands-on practices that down-regulate panic and stress within seconds are a gift of great worth, allowing us to evolve fearlessly. These applications translate to every age group, culture, and demographic, further increasing their value.

This book was written for these uncertain times. When the title originally came to me I was not conscious of the magnitude of its prophecy. I accept now the destiny of being a messenger. It is a privilege and a responsibility. I am humbled by the former and loyal to the latter.

Section I

Understanding Shock

1 A Shock Primer

The movement is so violent that it arouses terror. It is symbolized by thunder, which bursts forth and by its shock causes fear and trembling.

—*I Ching*, Hexagram 51, Shock

The need to develop a comprehensive approach to the treatment of shock evolved out of my years of trying to unravel the effects of shocking experiences on my own body and life, and then translating everything I was learning for those I served. In this regard, completing graduate school was hardly the end of my quest to understand the nature of overwhelming experience and its resolution. It felt more like the beginning.

I went in search of more information and a mentor. I heard about Peter Levine's program, Somatic Experiencing. This was before the publication of Peter's groundbreaking book, *Waking the Tiger*, which Peter was writing as I studied with him. Peter's information on how the body responds to trauma was like the parting of the Red Sea for me. Everything stood still as I saw a pathway people could cross to get to the other side of trauma. Peter's research became a source of encouragement to me about the health that was possible, especially for those of us who could identify the relationship between nervous system damage and trauma.

Peter's theories about titration (the careful pacing of interventions), the body as healer (using sensorimotor sequencing to create recovery), and the role of fevers and anesthesia in trauma launched a wave of new understanding. My life, my practice, and my writing changed dramatically, not only because of what I learned from Peter, but, much more importantly, because of what I experienced as I applied his insight to my own unfolding and in my practice. As I owned a new dimension of healing within myself, I saw how significant it was to broadly redefine trauma treatment.

What this meant in terms of application was that everything slowed down as I inquired into titration, or "right rate." What was the right rate at which one emerged from traumatic repetition? It was, of course, highly variable, depending on the individual and their particular history. But one thing was certain: the use of subtle energy medicine, and in particular Jin Shin, always assured that this right rate would be honored. This was because the energy medicine I taught and practiced was based, in large part, on energy pulse or energy rhythms that were felt in the fingertips of the practitioner (this is discussed more in Chapter 4). This pulse always reflects an individual's true response to change. It is like using biofeedback, only your hands are the instruments that "read" the bio-information. It was a great boon to be able to teach trauma survivors how to treat themselves and thus become self-regulating and self-pacing. Peter's paradigm emphasized the cultivation of both internal and external resources almost above all else. One of the best resources available for recovery is Jin Shin Tara.

At the same time, my curiosity about resolving the consequences of overwhelming experience was even further stimulated as I realized there was much more to discover now that the physical body was such a thoroughly acknowledged participant in the conversation. Gloria's experience was a watershed case in pushing me in the direction of further exploration and not stopping with just an understanding of trauma.

Gloria had survived a horrendous accident as a teenager. She fell from a subway platform and was run over by a train. She lost the lower part of her foot, and one side of her body was maimed. Months in a hospital and numerous painful skin grafts followed. Of course, she had received an enormous amount of anesthesia and had lived for a long time on painkillers, which she still reverted to from time to time. Despite all this, she felt very lucky to be alive.

Gloria was extremely soft-spoken and withdrawn. After her recovery, she married and had two children whom she cherished. Her husband, however, could not handle his wife's special needs and abandoned the family. Though she still had intermittent pain, wore a prosthesis, and suffered from ongoing exhaustion, she never complained. Gloria was thrilled with Jin Shin. Once she began to use self-care regularly, her pain diminished substantially. She had frequently been threatened with infections where her prosthesis met her flesh, and advanced energy medicine applications that I taught her succeeded in warding off these infections each time.

Somatic Experiencing helped Gloria on numerous occasions to step out of the trauma vortex (cycle of reenactment) into the healing vortex (a resourced lifestyle that builds slowly upon the release of held traumatic memory in the body). Nevertheless, Gloria's previous struggles with depression resurfaced and were increasing as her daughter neared adolescence. A question that had occurred to me before now reared its head again. Perhaps this was something more severe than trauma that played out in different neurological and physiological ways.

It wasn't until I met William Emerson, however, that I first heard the word shock used precisely and definitively. "Shock recapitulates globally," he said. "The shocks we have experienced remain after therapy has been concluded, and frequently reveal themselves in recurring discomforts for which it is very difficult to find a solution."

William Emerson is a pioneer, having carved out new territory by clearly differentiating shock from trauma and identifying prenatal and birth experience as the most likely settings for completely overwhelming experience. William spoke emphatically about the role of the adrenals in shock and about the differences between sympathetic and parasympathetic shock.[1] It was because of what I learned from William that I began to pay attention to how the word "shock" had been misused (using it interchangeably with trauma, for instance) and how important it was to carefully point out the unique considerations of treating shock.

It was unquestionably true that Gloria's adrenals had been utterly drained by the shock of her accident, followed by her husband's abandonment of his family, and then her struggle to support her children. But Gloria had also talked about the stressful nature of her early family life. Her father had been extremely punitive, though that had changed drastically after the accident. I wondered if the more recent stress actually was an additional weight on a foundation already compromised by earlier shock. Perhaps there were additional precursors. I spoke with Gloria about this and we shifted her use of energy medicine to focus more strenuously on adrenal regeneration. (See the chart on page 42 for more information on adrenal treatment.) I encouraged her to receive an intensive five-day series of treatments designed specifically for this purpose, and I asked her to rest deeply and to avoid work for the duration of this series. I also suggested that she do everything she could for the health of her kidney-adrenal system, such as not ingesting caffeine. The change was remarkable!

Gloria had always been extremely pale with dark circles under her eyes despite the fact that she went to bed each night right after her children, and sometimes before! Now her skin took on a rosy glow, her eyes sparkled, and she shifted from being reserved to being much more expressive. She gained a resiliency she had not previously had. She gathered strength and began to focus more on her own life and growth. I took the cue and became a student of William Emerson's.

As I read, researched, and undertook nearly seven years of experiential learning about shock, I saw that there was, in fact, a substantial difference between shock and trauma, though shock could be referred to as extremely severe trauma. The language is less important than identifying the distinguishing characteristics, such as the actual levels and magnitude of adrenal activation and debilitation. The study of shock also inspired me to become more of a detective in my inquiries into the sources of suffering. Believing so completely in the "healer, heal thyself" wisdom, I pursued this detective work heartily in my own life. The results were astounding. By discovering, through my own internal investigations and then later in validating conversations with my family, some of the almost insurmountable difficulties of my mother's pregnancy with me and the threats to my survival during that time, I was able to have a much clearer understanding of myself. The long-term effects of these discoveries were extremely calming, despite the fact that I was learning about my own profoundly shocking experiences. Knowing that my life had been so severely endangered made me realize that I must have truly wanted to be here because the obstacles to my birth were enormous. This realization continues to nourish my commitment to life. Indeed, it has shaped my clear perception that shock is the defining experience of our time and that few are left untouched by it.

As I listened to more extensive histories, sometimes going as far back as conception, prenatal life, and birth, I saw how shock that happens at the most vulnerable times of our lives persists and is reactivated unless it is resolved. I noticed that domestic violence was common during pregnancy and had a devastating impact on the children born under these circumstances. When I worked with people with AIDS, I heard story after story of childhood sexual abuse compounded by experiences of ridicule and exclusion for many years prior to infection. These were not single event woundings; these were lives of shattering, compounded, and overwhelming shock. In Mexico and Hawaii, I became aware of long lineages of repeated and horrendous violations to entire groups of people and factored this into my understanding of shock. Gradually, a picture came into focus for me, with a message of stunning urgency. We are all in shock. We are living in the whirlwind of an ongoing, albeit unseen epidemic. Countless babies born under anesthesia, separated from their mothers at birth, delivered with forceps, and with memories of stress, begin life conditioned by shock. This was true for me and for most of my generation. Without an awareness of this epidemic, we perpetuate it, becoming depressed and dysfunctional, and unable to protect ourselves, much less the children of the future.

I knew, in my heart, that it was shock that had to be addressed at this point in history. Current events in the world that I could never have anticipated have corroborated this over and over again.

The purpose of this chapter is to further clarify the use of the word "shock" in this book. A refined and current definition of shock is necessary, along with an understanding of previous designations. I also want to make it known that the use of subtle energy medicine (which in this book is restricted to Jin Shin Tara but has many forms), is exceedingly beneficial, specifically for the treatment of shock. My work with others, as well as my own experience, has demonstrated this to me without question, as has recent scientific research.[2]

Shock: An Historical Perspective

Shock is part of human experience and always has been. We carry, within our larger though sometimes unconscious memory, the history of shock as it has happened in our lives, our families, and our culture. Shock is cumulative, and this accumulation is its danger. It becomes less threatening to our health and well-being when it is exposed, addressed, understood, relieved, and released. This is true on a collective as well as on a personal level.

The oldest reference to shock is in the *I Ching* (or *Book of Changes*), which has been called the most ancient book of wisdom on Earth. Its origins are in China, at least 5,000 years ago. Carl Jung is responsible for bringing awareness of this text to the West a century ago. Jung wrote the foreword to the first classic translation of the *I Ching*.

The *I Ching* can be read in two ways: as a book of oracles, or as a book of philosophical and spiritual wisdom. These two uses are, of course, not mutually exclusive. To serve both these functions, The *I Ching* provides poetically concise and thorough descriptions of all the patterns of life. These are put into the form of hexagrams, which are consulted for guidance. Number 51 is named "Shock."

Ron Masa is an expert on the *I Ching,* so I asked him to tell me something about this hexagram. "Shock is one of the archetypal principles of the Cosmos and hence one of the 64 basic hexagrams. It is part of the natural cycle of existence. It is that aspect of experience in which the magnitude of things overwhelm our normal function," he replied. The ancients, Ron told me, identify shock as "one of the harder paths of human evolution."

The *I Ching* offers thunder as a symbol for shock. Stop for a moment and, using a combination of your memory, visualization, and time travel, slowly replay your response to hearing the sudden clap of thunder overhead. The sensations you experience exemplify the physiology of shock. Shock comes unexpectedly, out of nowhere. It moves quickly and violently. It stuns and shatters.

For me, and for most of the people I have seen in my years of practice and teaching, shock has occurred not just once, but time and time again. Unless older shocks are resolved, when the new ones happen, the resources that should meet them are not available or are in such a state of depletion that they cannot function well. If, however, shock is understood and addressed, it is possible to be fresh and ready when and if another shock should occur. It is to this preparedness that the *I Ching* speaks.

Because the *I Ching* is a book of wisdom, it provides shock's remedy and spiritual function. "There is a path of development in shock," says Thomas Cleary, the translator of *The Buddhist I Ching.*[3] This development links threat with transformation. Shock, by virtue of its unavoidable and dramatic force, demands that we become wise beings or be undermined by it completely. That is why, as Ron pointed out, shock is such a difficult teacher. "Only by virtue of a lifetime of development can you go forth into emergencies that 'startle those afar and terrify those nearby,' from which all other people flee, and stand up to them with a steady mind," says Cleary.[4]

The *I Ching* thus suggests that the experience of shock can catapult us into going within to understand the purpose of the very experiences that undermine us. The end result of this, according to the ancients, is the maturity and wisdom that allows us to heal ourselves and to serve others. This is the wisdom about shock that the *I Ching* offers.

The actual etymology of the word shock is from the French "choc" or "choquer," which means violent attack or striking against. The Dutch word "schokken" (to jolt) sometimes is referred to as the source of the French word. A subsequent definition, "to offend," emerged in 1694. In 1706, we find the first association of shock with electrical current. During World

War I certain responses were described as "shell shock" because of their association with explosions. This was the first diagnostic use of the word shock, and "shell shock" later became what we now know of as PTSD or posttraumatic stress disorder.[5]

The use of shock to treat shock, as in the electroshock therapy that was used to treat shell shock in World War I and is still in use in some places today, is the polar opposite of what is suggested in this book, which is gradual and self-empowering care. Even catharsis could be seen as being based on a "like treats like" concept. Exposing the nervous system to something as overwhelming as the original disorganizing experience is not really effective, according to my observations. The recipients of this radical intervention, who are not often consulted, report a variety of responses to this intervention.[6]

A subtle energy medicine approach reminds the nervous system of the capacity it has to respond in a balanced way. The recommendations that I make for self-care treatment in this book allow you to be at home or wherever you are most comfortable, and to follow the guidance of your own inner direction in knowing which areas of your body to hold or touch. This utter and complete safety stimulates the organic arousal of crucial neurotransmitters, such as dopamine and serotonin, that free us of the distress associated with both shock and trauma. It also invites the kidney-adrenal system to be totally at ease. Subtle energy medicine takes your adrenals to the spa, where they can relax, refresh, and renew!

While I have been talking about the physiology of shock and the adrenal glands in particular, when I speak of "systems" affected by shock, I am also referring to emotional, psychological, spiritual and, of course, energy systems. Whether you think of these as energy bodies, chakras, states of being, or an aspect of self is unimportant. What is important is the acknowledgement that when shock occurs, it demands a thorough engagement of *all* these systems.

Let's look now at some of these landmark references to shock and see if they add to what we know about the treatment of the overwhelming and shattering experiences of today.

From Shell Shock to PTSD

One of the first diagnoses to address shock arose during World War I, and led to the second, which arose from the Vietnam War. Shell shock and post-traumatic stress disorder grew out of the extreme conditions that throw the nervous system into total chaotic disarray—a characteristic of shock. Reconstructing the nervous system after war is much more difficult than reconstructing destroyed buildings.

Shell shock was applied as a diagnosis to all soldiers who became withdrawn, paralyzed with fear, and unwilling to return to battle. The diagnosis noted marked physical trembling, often to the point of convulsive seizures. This trembling is one of the threads that tie together all references to shock. It is characteristic of panic attacks. Even when it is deeply internalized, it usually accompanies shock. It is the physiological demonstration of shock's global impact on virtually all bodily functions, particularly the immune system. Journalists like Philip Gibbs described men during World War I as "shaking with ague" and "shaking in every limb."[7]

When this trembling is allowed to complete, the body is restored from overwhelming experiences. In cases of repeated shock, this completion can take much longer than in cases of single event trauma. Condemning the physical expression of shock, of course, makes it virtually impossible for this trembling to successfully sequence through the body. Therefore, shock remains unresolved and contained physiologically, creating residual shock that continues to impact all systems until it is resolved.

Soldiers, however, were not the only ones experiencing shell shock. Most people subjected to the sights and sounds of war found themselves highly adrenalized, trembling and overcome with fear. The stigma of shame has stuck to the word shock, as if this panic and freezing should actually *not* be happening. Shame continues to be affiliated with both trauma and shock.[8]

Other Uses of Shock Terminology

Toxic shock and septic shock are names for massive and multisystem dysfunction and, therefore, they accord with the definition of shock that I propose. Both conditions are evidenced by overwhelming infection in which many systems malfunction simultaneously, one of which is always the kidneys. Recovery is dependent on one major factor—the degree of adrenal reserve. As discussed previously, adrenal reserve is a reflection of exposure to shock and the capacity to regenerate after such exposure. The depletion of the adrenal system is frequently, though not always, evidenced by trembling or shaking. Unresolved shock can make us more vulnerable to infection because of adrenal debilitation.

Toxic Shock Syndrome is a reaction to toxins, especially dioxin, which, because of decades of pollution, is everywhere and therefore can be present in anything. When young women who used tampons started having incident after incident of toxic shock syndrome, an investigation into the fabric in tampons revealed a barely detectable amount of dioxin. Nevertheless, reactions continued. One conclusion is that the tolerances for dioxin are far less than regulators want to admit. The impact in these cases is extremely severe, even fatal, and the responses are always multi-system.

Another form of toxic shock syndrome occurs following a streptococcus infection. Again, the kidneys are always involved in broad-spectrum debilitation. In both forms of toxic shock syndrome there is not a clear understanding of how the illness initiates, and this mystery seems to accompany all forms of shock. Solving the mystery, as I venture to do in this book for some instances of shock, is an endeavor intended to contribute to our human evolution.

Culture shock may seem an anomaly in this camp, but it too is omnisystemic in its impact and can recur, like other shocks, with certain reactivating stimulation. Culture shock is what happens for people when they move from one culture to another and feel overwhelmed by the transition. Estrella, who you will meet in Chapter 3, experienced culture shock during her hospitalized labor and delivery. My grandparents, who came to America from Eastern Europe, were never able to master the English language and experienced culture shock. The loss of a skill such as communication upsets so many life functions that behavior is radically altered. This dramatic impact creates a vulnerability or feeling of being without resources that fits a more current definition of shock or extremely severe trauma.

The common threads in the uses of the word "shock" help us to substantiate usage now for this category of human experience. By naming the characteristics and conditions of shock, we can more clearly address not only its assessment, but, more valuably, its specific requirements for attention.

Having taken a look at some of the historical uses of the word "shock," let us turn to a definition of shock that applies very pointedly for the time we are living in right now.

What Is Shock?

Shock begins the moment when we are confronted with an experience so stunning that our body/mind system is overwhelmed. A baby separated from his or her mother at birth; a child in need of attention who is ignored by busy parents; witnessing the death of a friend or a loved one; losing a body part in war, a child at birth, or all your possessions in a natural disaster—these experiences are the settings for shock. When trauma occurs, it strikes and wounds, but when shock occurs, it shatters us into a million pieces and it takes some time to find them all.

Shock occurs as the result of any experience that overrides all our healthy coping mechanisms. The shocking experience confuses our nervous system with its extraordinary demands and disrupts our normal and balanced neurological and endocrine responses to threat. Lacking any resources to cope, we feel as though our nervous systems are failing us. In a micro-instant, we are overcome with utter and complete vulnerability, and this seems to silently seal the experience in the very cells of our being.

Trauma, on the other hand, primarily stimulates the limbic brain, which accesses resources to respond. The overriding and extreme nature of shock is an all system alert. Trauma, by comparison, is more orderly, sequential, and developmentally specific. For those who are unfamiliar with both brain structure and developmental psychology, this can be said more simply. You could say that the difference between the two experiences is a matter of degree, with trauma being the less overwhelming experience. The issue of magnitude is significant because it affects not only the physical consequences of the experience, but also the duration and expression of those consequences. This difference in magnitude requires differences in treatment. Chapter 2 will amplify these distinguishing characteristics.

Before we go any further, I'd like to broadly address the whole issue of terminology so that we are not waylaid by it as we proceed. The terminology regarding shock and trauma is in flux. This is promising because this flux represents growth, evolution, and needed change. Though "trauma" and "posttraumatic stress" appear to have temporarily become entrenched definitions, new language has already started to emerge. Refining the use of the word "shock" is part of this process. Both words also have medical definitions apart from their psychological applications, with trauma relating primarily to a wounding or bodily injury (trauma to an area of the body) and shock relating to a nervous system condition that radically lessens or even eliminates the ability to feel sensation. Even from a purely medical frame of reference, trauma is specific whereas shock is global.

The most recent and developing literature reflects the growing number of variables in the trauma-shock continuum, including unique conditions of socioeconomic status, heredity, previous exposure, cultural differences, and personality structure. This is a wonderful transition and is already expanding our capacity to treat both conditions with enhanced respect for the courageous survivors of shock and trauma. Terms like "posttraumatic thriving" and DESNOS (disorders of extreme stress) are part of this fruitful refining that considers, in addition to the factors mentioned above, the many variations in physiological response, with each variable having relevance.

Through the true stories told in these pages, I will portray the broad spectrum of experiences that I have categorized as shock. This includes major and minor shock, early shock, immediate shock, conditioned shock, and residual shock. My primary point at all times is to demonstrate how shock can be thoroughly resolved by the very individuals who experienced it. The transmission of these tools is the centerpiece of this book.

I am convinced that resolving shock is the missing link to empowerment today. I see the empowerment process as one of attuning the body and clearing out the cobwebs from our brains, nervous systems, tissues, and joints. When primitive responses, both physiological and emotional, no longer rule our behavior, we are liberated into a spacious spontaneity that directs all our movements and expressions. As we do this clearing away, we begin to know what it means to truly live. We feel both our inherent buoyancy and our earthiness. Life becomes a celebration when we step into the present and the shocks that occur, whether large or small, are wisdom teachings to expand awareness. This is what it means to come out of shock.

We are all in shock today because we have not been able to make a choice to be shock free. Ironically, our inability to make choices is directly related to the fact that we are in shock! We must heed the *I Ching* and use the repetition of shock that has afflicted us to go within and find the wisdom teaching for each of us personally and for our time. If we continue to see ourselves as choiceless, we will condemn our children to a choiceless future. By tracing the etiology of shock and pointing out its distinguishing characteristics, I hope to awaken your own awareness of shock so that you can choose to come out of it. Only you can make that choice. If you want to come out of shock, this book will give you the fundamental support to do so. You can bring yourself out of shock with the information in these pages. Then, when overwhelming events occur, you will not be so shattered. You will know, from the core of your being and the behavior of your nervous system, that shock is in the moment and healing is forever.

By the time you finish the next chapter, you will be an expert in identifying shock. By the time you finish Chapter 4, you will know how to use
subtle energy medicine. This will grant you the capacity to be of great
service to this world at this time, whether you choose to serve yourself,
your family, your neighborhood, or the world.

2 The Physiology of Shock

We shall not cease from exploration
And the end of all our exploring
Will be to arrive where we started
And know the place for the first time.

—T.S. Eliot

Everything in this book is built on the powerful belief that even the most severe and earliest shock that undermines neurological development can be healed and that you are the primary healer. The keys are:

◈ The consistent use of self-administered subtle energy medicine.

◈ Noncathartic, carefully paced repatterning of experiences.

◈ The use of language as a healing vehicle.

◈ Holistic integration. This means taking the time to fully own the changes in your body and your nervous system that occur when you are resolving shock.

◈ The neurobiology of love. This describes the fluid and appropriate release of neurotransmitters that stimulate and enhance creativity, self-confidence, contentment, and focus. This neurobiology can only occur when the primitive brain is at rest and for this reason feelings of safety and comfort are necessary to launch this neurochemistry.

Self-love is not just a feeling or a thought. It is a wonderful physiological experience that results, in part, from a neurological shift that you could call the neurobiology of love. This shift is identified by new and more positive thoughts, inspiring and practical problem-solving skills, and love for others, as well as yourself. These are the signs of higher brain engagement. You will also feel the neurobiology of love in your body in a variety of ways, including less lower back and shoulder tension, deeper breathing, and greater flexibility. This is a transformation out of vigilance or defensiveness into presence. It is a thorough change in consciousness.[1]

For the survivor of shock, consciousness is the ultimate victory. The silencing of self-criticism and other forms of negativity that deter the neurobiology of love is the refreshing result of the practices recommended in this book. The entire process of resolving shock is a rebirth. We may even revisit our physical birth experiences in this quest. To comprehend how repatterning our neurology can bring us out of shock, it will help to have a deeper understanding of the neurological developmental process.

To fully grasp the physiological impact of shock on neurology consider cranial evolution. The primitive, reptilian brain develops in the first trimester in utero; the mammalian or limbic brain develops in the second trimester; and the neocortex, the uniquely human brain, begins developing in the third and final trimester of pregnancy. The prefrontal lobes, humanity's most recent neurological achievement, develop in the final stages of the last trimester and during the first two years of life. They then have a second growth spurt during mid-adolescence.[2] In Chapter 6, I will thoroughly explain how prenatal and birth distress interrupts this evolution.

Neurological development is carefully sequenced. First one window of opportunity opens, then the next, and then another in a precise order wisely predetermined by nature. When a particular window (developmental sequence) is not fully opened (nurtured until completion), it remains in a limbo state, neither fully open nor fully closed. Shock is the culprit that prevents these windows from opening completely. We can, given awareness and opportunity, revisit these developmental stages, clear off the cobwebs, pull out the cotton that is stuffed into the opening, and raise the shutters on each and every neglected developmental window of opportunity.[3] In so doing, we have cleared the way for our entire brain to function at its optimum level, and we become fully conscious beings.

We are most vulnerable when the networks and structures of our neurology are rapidly forming and before we have the self-regulatory mechanisms to respond to overwhelming experiences. The assessment of shock depends on one essential measurement—the quantity and quality of resources available. This is true for both of the two central purposes of this book: prevention and treatment. The equation is simple:The fewer the resources, the greater the impact of overwhelming experiences. At no time in our existence are we more resourceless than during our prenatal life and infancy. For this reason, actively preventing shock (or alternatively resolving shock quickly and thoroughly), is essential for our greatest treasure, the children of the future. Preventing and resolving shock is no less important for us.

Brain Development, Evolution, and Shock

The brain is the flower of human development, a towering bloom of learning poised on the stalk of the body. We are ecstatically curious, alert, and brilliantly present for our entire lives—unless our windows of opportunity are stuffed with cotton. Authors speaking from various neurological perspectives have come forth with new research, new terminology, and new brain maps. These influence our understanding of the effects of overwhelming experience and the language we use to talk about them. I am confident that this is just the beginning of an even bigger wave of awareness.[4]

The chart on page 38 is my simple brain map. Of course, what is behind it is much more complex. It illustrates a triune structure that I will use for simplicity's sake, though I also wanted to include the newest information. It has been suggested, for instance, that the prefrontal cortex is a fourth brain, not part of the neocortex, or third brain. I am generally going to incorporate the prefrontals into what I refer to as "the higher brain," though I will allude to its distinguishing characteristics. Some researchers also suggest that the brain can reside elsewhere in the body, other than in the head. The heart, for instance, is referred to as a brain. The intestines have been called "the second brain." There is also another question that deserves exploration, though not here: What is the difference between the brain and the mind?

No matter how many we think there are or what we call them, the brain is a marvelous demonstration of Nature's profound handiwork. It is sculpted both to receive (learn) and to manifest (create). It is intended as a work in progress, and indeed Nature is still sculpting us. The interaction between brain development and environment must never be forgotten. For additional discussions of this theme, please see both Chapter 6, which focuses on prenatal life and birth, and Chapter 8, which focuses on environment.

The most primordial brain is the basal ganglia—nature's initial neurological design, constructed for continuity and survival. It is the network where sensory-motor action originates. It is located at the top of the neck, at the entrance to the base of the skull. It is the receiving station for the

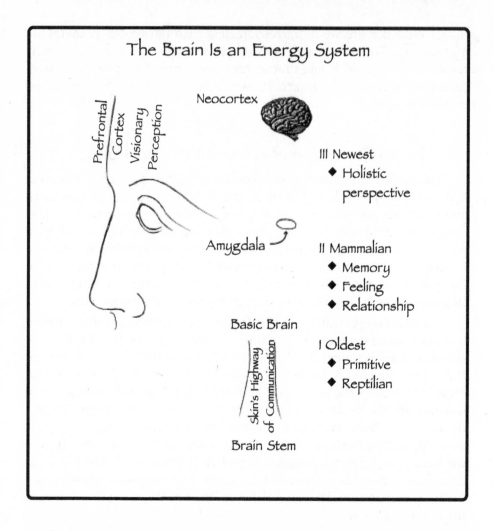

The Brain Is an Energy System

Prefrontal Cortex
Visionary Perception

Neocortex

III Newest
- Holistic perspective

Amygdala

II Mammalian
- Memory
- Feeling
- Relationship

Basic Brain

I Oldest
- Primitive
- Reptilian

Skin's Highway of Communication

Brain Stem

sensory messages transmitted from the skin via the spinal cord. It sends its information directly into the reptilian brain. The basal ganglia and reptilian brain, which together form the primitive brain, use only the present tense and speak through behavior. They contain the neural machinery for preservation. The words "unconscious" and "instinctual" belong to them. Witnessing your reactions to stimuli reveals critical data about your primitive brain. The evaluation of this data allows you to consider new options that go beyond survival. Repatterning the conditioned impulses that arise from the primitive brain not only enhances your perspective, it also increases the healthy functioning of your spinal column and neck.

You can have fun if you position yourself as a witness and watch how your primitive brain responds. Here's an example. I love to dance. One day I was in a class at my favorite studio. About midway through the class a man entered and stood in the doorway and just watched. The longer he stood there the more my insides began to churn. I grew extremely agitated. I glanced around the room and everyone else appeared to be unaffected. I moved out of the man's range of vision and then I felt much better. However, whenever the movement propelled me so that he could see me, my heartbeat increased and my movement decreased.

It turned out that the man was the teacher's boyfriend and he came to watch her teach a new routine. He had unwittingly created a great opportunity for me to observe the activation of my basic brain. I was threatened, frightened, and confused, so I never confronted him directly; I tried to avoid him or become invisible. This is basic brain recapitulating shock—using the same protective techniques it has used for decades. By paying attention to and learning from this experience I could see how shock was driving my neurology and my physiology. This awareness allowed me to make different choices the next time this happened. The experience became part of my databank about my particular shock-conditioned patterns. The new options are the ones I create by choosing to evolve from my primitive behavior to a higher level of consciousness. In this case, when a similar event happened again, I told the spectator that I would prefer that he leave, being that he was not in the class. He did so very respectfully. I also asked my teacher to let me know if he was coming again, as I felt that was only fair to the class, and to me in particular. She understood completely and honored my request.

Changing conditioned shock behavior provides real-life differentiation between the past and the present. All the brains get the message of change from the immediate and repeated experiential feedback that they receive from body sensations. This ongoing interactive dialogue between brain and body ultimately leads to one conclusion—you are out of shock and you are in the present. You no longer respond with unconscious habitual reactions, but take action with conscious intent and understanding of your current situation.

The limbic, or mammalian, brain is the intercranial territory of feeling and memory. In its geology we find the amygdala, the thalamus, the olfactory bulbs, and the hippocampus. All mammals have this brain. Here is where we find "emotional intelligence." The keyword for the mammalian brain is "relationship." Relationship is what shapes the evolution from primitive being to sensitive being. Reptiles leave or eat their babies; mammals stay with them and nurture them. Everything having to do with personal, intimate relationships is in the mid-brain, including sexuality, affection, desire, and attraction. The unconditional, spiritual experiences of compassion and impersonal or universal love are higher brain expressions. Memories of relationships are stored in the limbic brain and direct our behavior with others. This brain interacts directly with the higher brains, frequently using the forms of dreams and intuition to converse. This means that our personal experiences in relationships contribute to the evolution, or lack thereof, of higher brain activity.

The neocortex was long considered the newest brain, but the prefrontal cortex has just won this distinction. Neuroscientist Paul MacLean first presented the possibility that the prefrontals were a fourth brain. He called them the "angel lobes," referring to them as the territory of love, compassion, empathy, and understanding. In this regard, they reflect our most advanced intelligence and our capacity to regulate our behavior for the highest good. If we prevent shock for babies, we enhance the possibility of increased prefrontal development. Untreated damage to any other part of the brain, on the other hand, inhibits the successful evolution of the prefrontals and prevents us from becoming fully conscious individuals. Treatment of overwhelming experiences, no matter what age we are, will allow the awakening of prefrontal development.[5]

As this map of the brain becomes part of our common knowledge, our awareness increases along with responsibility. This book invites your participation in using the brain's great bounty of plasticity (motility, flexibility, and the capacity for change and growth) and interaction. This means cultivating the intention and the tools to relax the reptilian brain, allowing it to work in the service of the higher brains. I am suggesting that we consciously claim the gift that is ours for the taking—the capacity to be compassionate and holistic, and clear and focused all the time, up to and including the moment of death. "Wonderful," you say, "but how exactly is this done?"

What we need in order to open developmental windows are touch, attention, and stimulation that we can provide to ourselves and to others. We must be as attentive to ourselves as the best possible caregivers. In fact, we probably have to be more attentive than this, channeling love-infused touch into our connective tissue, flooding the heart (which is sometimes considered the highest brain) with nourishment. Deliberate, personalized self-engagement with healing whenever possible and each time shock is reactivated will result in its complete resolution and disappearance from the whole mind-body system.

The Adrenal System and Shock

The second region of our body-mind complex that is dramatically impacted by shock is the adrenal system. The adrenals are two small glands, each weighing 3–5 grams. They are located above the kidneys (see illustration, page 42). Each adrenal gland is composed of two separate functional entities. The outer zone, or cortex, accounts for 80–90 percent of the gland and secretes adrenal steroids such as cortisol, DHEA, and aldosterone. The inner zone. or medulla, comprising the remaining 10–20 percent of the gland, secretes adrenaline and catecholamines (epinephrine and norepinephrine). Cortisol, DHEA, and adrenaline are the three adrenal stress hormones.

The adrenals secrete their hormones in cycles called circadian rhythms. This 24-hour clock awakens us with vibrant energy in the morning light and surrenders us to the moon and rest at night. Abnormal adrenal rhythms influence all bodily functions. This includes not only sleep, but immune system activity, tissue repair, bone health, joint function, responses to inflammation and bacteria, skin regeneration, thyroid function, allergic response, and stress tolerance. You can see why shock, which imperils this system, has an extensive multisymptom impact.

The medulla of the adrenal glands is essentially an extension of the sympathetic nervous system. The hormonal secretions of the medulla functionally increase heart rate, constrict blood vessels, dilate the bronchioles, increase blood glucose, increase metabolic rate, inhibit gastrointestinal activity, and dilate the pupils of the eyes. These distress signals are designed for use under threat. If overwhelming experience is a constant or if it occurs before we have consciousness of how to regulate sympathetic activation (such as prenatally), the result is hyperactivity, hypervigilance, and an inability to rest at appropriate times. This is sympathetic shock.

Parasympathetic shock is the repression of these secretions, a diminishment of glucocorticoids, and an inability to deal with stressors. This takes the form of withdrawal, fatigue, isolation, and an overall appearance of lowered vitality. This condition also impacts immune response and shapes metabolism. In particular, inflammation can go unchecked when there is parasympathetic dominance. Some secretions increase in parasympathetic shock, such as mucous and tears.

The parasympathetic response is resistant and defeated. It resembles depression. The sympathetic response is active, aggressive, and extremely physical. Sympathetic responses mobilize reactions and emphasize them.

Adrenal Regeneration

1. Hold both right and left Points 23.

2. Hold Point 24 and opposite Point 26, three times on each side.

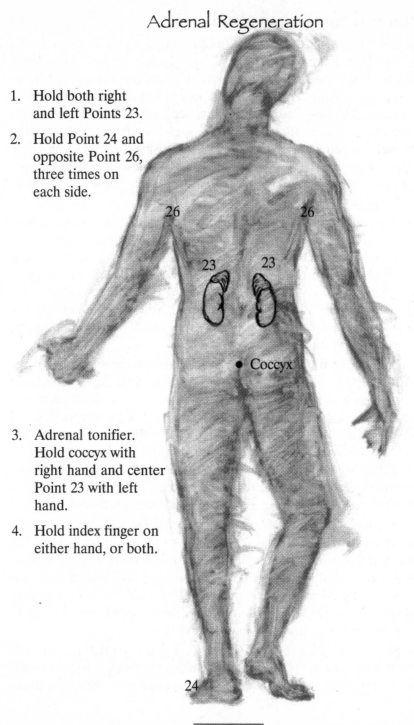

26   26

23   23

● Coccyx

24

3. Adrenal tonifier. Hold coccyx with right hand and center Point 23 with left hand.

4. Hold index finger on either hand, or both.

Parasympathetic responses are designed to keep things away and reveal little or nothing. See the chart on pages 59 and 60 for more information on differentiating sympathetic from parasympathetic appearances and behavior.[6]

The stories that follow are included here specifically to expose you to the differences between sympathetic and parasympathetic shock. Read them and absorb the physiological information through real-life healing experiences. This will allow you to make the necessary clear and discerning judgments to treat each form of shock appropriately. The chart on the adrenals on page 42 includes energy medicine treatment that addresses both sympathetic and parasympathetic shock. The information in Chapter 4 increases this knowledge.

I'd like to introduce these case studies with a story that demonstrates why it is so worthwhile to proceed on this healing path. Resonant and affirming encounters like this one, which validate the direction of the heart occur repeatedly for those who choose to heal. The parasympathetic response is frequently the only avenue for a baby who cannot articulate with words and whose action is limited. Please remember this as you read what follows.

One of the high points of my life was treating Amelia, an eight-week-old baby girl, born with one eye swollen shut and leaking pus. Her doctor had already scheduled surgery. One week before surgery, her mother brought her to me at the suggestion of a friend. I asked her mother to tell me about her pregnancy and Amelia's birth. As she spoke, I stayed in contact with Amelia and, the child, sensing my focus, returned my gaze and retained our bond throughout the session.

The pregnancy was fraught with hardship, tension, and turmoil. Amelia's parents had fought constantly, separated, filed for divorce, and became involved with new partners. Alcohol and drugs were pervasive. Amelia's father virtually disappeared until the moment the mother went into labor—two weeks early and on the day the divorce papers were to be signed! During the birthing process, Amelia's parents had remarkable insight into their dilemma. By the time Amelia was born, they were reunited. Both committed themselves to providing a safe and sober home for their daughter and themselves.

As Amelia's mom told her difficult tale, I asked questions related to her awareness of the impact of this chaos on Amelia. Each time I drew attention to this child's experience of grief, despair, and abandonment, Amelia responded with a plaintive cry and reached her arms out to me.

Her mother commented on our communication, which I felt with great certainty. Tears began to pour out of the baby's suffering eye and became more and more profuse. I did simple subtle energy medicine (Jin Shin Tara), putting my emphasis on the consciousness and intention of my touch. I wanted my touch to communicate validation, awareness, compassion, and acceptance. I instructed Amelia's mother in treatment she could do and underscored the quality of touch and the importance of frequent treatments. Amelia's mom really heard her daughter in this session. She knew that Amelia needed to express her grief to her, and that her mother's touch would be her way of listening and responding.

On the day after Amelia's scheduled surgery, her mom phoned to tell me that the doctor had cancelled it after examining the baby. Both Amelia's eyes were wide open and clear, and the surgery was no longer necessary. This was, for all of us, a profound demonstration of the power of authentic contact and touch to resolve shock and its physical manifestation.

My hands spoke directly to Amelia's reptilian brain, telling her it was no longer necessary for her to hold back her tears in order to survive. She could cry and open up now because her parents were ready to listen to her. This experience filled me with awe and gratitude for the gift we all have to end suffering with awareness and presence. Amelia was waiting to be heard and seen, and once this simple need was met, she became whole and healthy.[7]

Parasympathetic Shock: The Mirror of Ice

The young woman who sat directly opposite from me in the university classroom where I was teaching was exquisite. Her mother was from India and her father was from the Philippines. She carried both these tropical lands in her slender body and exotic face. How could someone so beautiful look so sad, I wondered? Ultimately, Kamala wrote the story of her sadness in painful detail in a paper she turned in to my class on the treatment of shock and trauma. Her minister had sexually abused her. What stood out in her story was the way she completely froze during the abuse. She recollected it as going into a deep sleep. When she finally awoke she was determined to forget the entire experience. She succeeded—or at least she thought she had until she took my class. Even when we talked about it later Kamala froze, her eyes remaining wide and unblinking, the look common to parasympathetic shock.

Edith was in the same class, as was Jeremy. All of them, including Kamala, were able, before the course was over, to determine that they had been thrust into parasympathetic shock at some point early in their lives and that this shock could be evoked again by specific kinds of circumstances. Additionally, they discovered the origins of their shock-conditioned patterns, and through that knowledge, they were able to heal themselves.

Kamala, Jeremy, and Edith had at least one important thing in common. Intimacy exacerbated their parasympathetic shock. They all noticed the same syndrome: a feeling of being cold, disconnected, speechless, and breathing shallowly. At the possibility of real closeness with another human being, they became temporarily frozen, cold and stiff reflections of themselves.

Edith was a strong, independent, and deep-feeling woman who nevertheless froze and became mute when anyone, man or woman, came too close. At these moments, her usually clear voice changed dramatically to an almost inaudible whisper. There were very few people with whom Edith felt safe. I was fortunate to be one of them, so I could help her demystify the behavior that kept her lonely.

Jeremy, the third figure in the parasympathetic triumvirate, had been afflicted more than once with cancer and was on a path of resurrection. In remission now, Jeremy was determined to get off the roller coaster that repeatedly put his life at risk. Yet it wasn't until he understood shock that he could open a new chapter of his life.

Kamala, Edith, and Jeremy had formed a small practice and study group during the semester that they were in my class. They shared their investigations into healing with me and occasionally asked for my commentary. In their practice, they focused on strengthening adrenal and overall energy to heighten their responsiveness in a generalized way. They could do this with different subtle energy techniques. One was to place one hand at the base of the spine and the other in the center of the chest. Doing this would, dependably, bring them out of the trance-like state that is parasympathetic shock. Another technique was holding either the right or the left index finger. This was an unobtrusive approach to building adrenal strength that could be utilized anywhere at anytime. Another option was to place the palms of their hands directly over their adrenal glands, or on Point 23 (see chart on page 42). This served to balance adrenal function and simultaneously lessen their resistance to change. In all cases of resolving shock, overcoming resistance is essential because the tendency most humans have is to retain coping mechanisms, even when they are outmoded or ineffective.

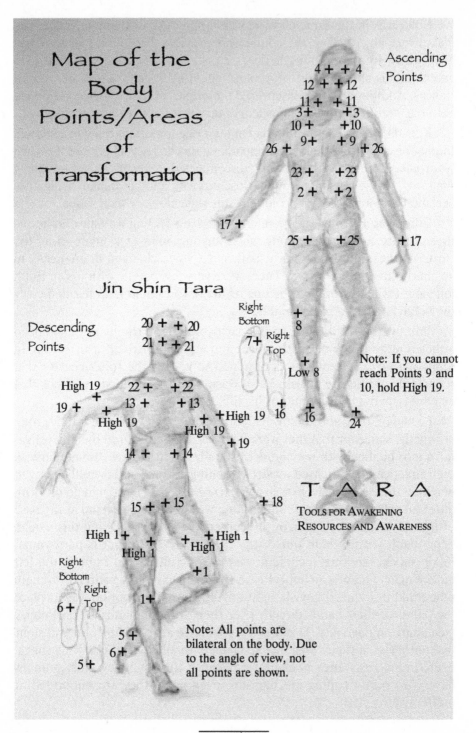

Map of the
Body
Points/Areas
of
Transformation

Jin Shin Tara

Ascending Points

Descending Points

Note: If you cannot reach Points 9 and 10, hold High 19.

T A R A
TOOLS FOR AWAKENING
RESOURCES AND AWARENESS

Note: All points are bilateral on the body. Due to the angle of view, not all points are shown.

ONE	Awakening—Walk Your Talk
HIGH ONE	The Mover's Support—Confident Legs
TWO	Wisdom—Soft Focus Is True Seeing
THREE	Release and Receive—Breathing From an Open Back
FOUR	Clear Consciousness—Shamanic Gateway
FIVE	Fearless—Self-Support
SIX	Balance—Androgeny-Center of Compassion
SEVEN	Peace—Death and Rebirth
EIGHT	Alchemy—Clarity
LOW EIGHT	The Dispeller—The Purgative
NINE	Transition—Anger Makes Space for Itself
TEN	Transformation—Your Voice Tells Your Story
ELEVEN	Unloading—Coming out of Codependency
TWELVE	Surrender—Acceptance of Body Truth
THIRTEEN	The Mother—The Calm in the Storm
FOURTEEN	The Sustainer—Nourishment and Assimilation
FIFTEEN	Wash Your Heart With Laughter—Joy in Everything
SIXTEEN	The Foundation—Muscular Joy
SEVENTEEN	The Connector—Nervous System Healer
EIGHTEEN	The Pathmaker—Walking on Your Path
NINETEEN	Being in the Center of Your Own Life—Good Boundaries
HIGH NINETEEN	Selfhood—Really Good Boundaries
TWENTY	Conscious Awakening—Allowing Intuition
TWENTY-ONE	True Security—Freedom From Worry
TWENTY-TWO	Adaptation—Wholeness in the Moment
TWENTY-THREE	Destiny—The Energy Underneath Anxiety
TWENTY-FOUR	Peacemaker, Relationship Counselor—No More Jealousy
TWENTY-FIVE	Regeneration—Reserve Energy
TWENTY-SIX	Completion—Self-Love

The second group focus for Kamala, Edith, and Jeremy involved taking risks, particularly in terms of their responses to other people. They agreed to support one another in new behavior that would invite closeness with others, even if it was just being encouraging and making gentle suggestions. In this way, they would repattern the reptilian survival strategy of isolating themselves, allowing new options to be fully sequenced in their minds and bodies. Their mutual support was crucial, as it was something they had never known in this arena.

They kept track of the changes they observed in each other in terms of skin and voice tone, pulse, quality of sleep, and overall health. Because they were interested in reversing parasympathetic dominance, they were especially keen on tracking the connection between sensation and expression. This link is buried in parasympathetic shock, and they wanted to uncover the "missing link" that would allow them to feel and express more.

Kamala was deeply ashamed of the fact that she had not fought off her minister or reported him. What could have caused her to be such a willing victim? Sharing her story with Edith and Jeremy was a huge risk for her. She was surprised when they did not condemn her. They helped her search for the source of her parasympathetic dominance. One day, when Edith was treating Kamala with subtle energy medicine, Kamala saw a picture in her mind's eye. It was from the bible story in which two women claim they are each the mother of the same child. King Solomon has to settle the conflict, and he does so by saying the child should be cut in half. Kamala's image zeroed in on the baby. The baby she saw was absolutely still, frozen, expressionless, and silent. Why was she having this image? She was stunned and confused.

Then Kamala remembered something her mother told her and that she now knew was certainly true. When Kamala's mother was pregnant, her parents fought intensely about where they should live. "Perhaps I thought they were going to chop me in half, so I stayed absolutely still, in terror," Kamala said out loud to Edith when she was sharing her experience of the session. Then she sobbed, long and hard. She had found the "missing link" source of her freezing response and her pattern of parasympathetic shock. The compassion she felt for herself once the whole picture was clear before her completely eliminated her feelings of shame and humiliation.

Edith's mother had never wanted to have children. Nevertheless, she had three daughters, of whom Edith was the eldest. Edith became the surrogate mother, particularly when the youngest daughter was diagnosed with epilepsy. The shock of not being wanted was compounded by the shock of too much responsibility at an early age. Edith's competency became her identity, and anything that threatened that identity was suspect and had to be defended against. What was striking was how rapidly she abandoned that competency when a relationship asked her to be vulnerable. How she longed to stop this and have a *real* relationship!

When Kamala had her awakening, which gave her the key to her parasympathetic freezing, she thanked Edith profusely and even threw her arms around her as the tears of awareness streamed down her face. Edith was stunned. She hadn't done anything! She had just been there as the midwife to Kamala's discovery. Later she realized that this was *her* "missing link." She had never been valued for just *being*, and she had steeled herself throughout her life to avoid this very need. Though she was resentful for the burdens her mother had imposed on her, she had always wanted a mother who just enjoyed her. Because she trusted me, Edith asked me how she could connect this "missing link" into her life to balance herself. I suggested that she find a good mother to surrender to, like Mother Nature or Mother Earth, to let in the pure acceptance she deserved.

Jeremy, who was adopted shortly after birth, searched for his birth mother in the course of the semester and found her. She wanted no communication with him, but the investigation revealed that she was a drug addict when she conceived him. The discovery itself was an enormous shock to Jeremy and intensified his parasympathetic behavior. He could sense himself shutting down so much that he felt as if he was turning to stone.

Verbal expression had always been close to impossible for Jeremy. In conversation or when he had to present before a group, he stared for long uncomfortable periods before saying a word while his audience waited, unsure and confused. Though he was an excellent writer, writing was an agonizing process. He would have to stay awake almost all night drinking coffee before he would burst forth with page after page of extremely well articulated information on whatever subject he was addressing. Now these empty spaces were elongated even further. Kamala and Edith not only gave Jeremy treatments, they also encouraged him to practice consistent self-care so that he could experience empowerment by bringing himself out of shock. They recommended that he hold the 19 and High 19 areas on his upper arms (see chart on pages 46–47). These points support verbal expression, articulation, and movement forward.

When Jeremy revealed his history of adoption, Kamala and Edith were available to hold him while he cried. He told them that he felt cursed, turned to stone by a wicked and taunting Medusa. "Push that haunting out, honey," feisty Edith suggested. Kamala and Edith found out about an interesting purification ritual and performed it for Jeremy. Then they discovered a cleansing diet that would help protect Jeremy from the recurrence of cancer. They supported him in being strong enough to say no to whatever toxins threatened to invade him. In all of this, Jeremy discovered one of his "missing links"—permission to rebel and to refuse. Having been rejected so early in his life, he thought the only way he could survive was to accept whatever came his way, including poison. His mother said no to him, but he couldn't say no to his mother...until now.

When Edith declared that she did not want to be the caretaker of the group who organized all of their meetings and their agenda, Jeremy and Kamala agreed to share that responsibility. When Kamala determined that she would confront her minister through the church hierarchy, Jeremy and Edith were thoroughly behind her and helped her with logistics and supportive treatment. By working together and using subtle energy medicine, they found a way to discriminate between the past and the present. Learning that they did not have to do everything by themselves was one of the biggest awakenings in their magnificent learning process. Much later, they realized that just by banding together, they were transmuting the parasympathetic necessity for withdrawal and removal, despite the fact that their union was based on their parasympathetic similarities. Each of them made the amazing discovery that they were actually not withdrawn people at all, but loving, engaged, and committed human beings.

They each wrote about the outcome of their collective and personal processes. Of course they received excellent grades, but what was most compelling for all of us was seeing the potent truth of finding original cause and repatterning survival-based responses. After this, it was impossible for any of them to return to their parasympathetic dominant behavior. They knew too much now. They were physiologically changed and prepared to share what they had experienced with others. They had escaped the hold of their reptilian brains and were firmly ensconced in the relational realm of the limbic brain.

Sympathetic Shock: The Dance of Fire

One of my favorite movies as a young girl was *The Red Shoes*, based on the story by Hans Christian Anderson about a dancer who was so impassioned by movement that she gave all her power to the dance rather than to herself. Eventually, she could not stop her shoes from dancing, and they danced her to death. This is the driving, relentless force of sympathetic shock. The burning heat consumes like a fever, and it seems as though nothing can stop it. While parasympathetic shock is the suppression of adrenaline, sympathetic shock is the repeated firing of adrenaline under all circumstances, even at the slightest suggestion of anything resembling the original threat.

If, in fact, the original threat can be determined, the firing process can be appropriately tempered and redirected with the profound support of subtle energy medicine and other healing resources. For the person dominated by sympathetic shock, the most important first step in healing is a willingness to not be so stimulated. Sympathetic shock brings with it a deep, obsessive bond with action and a resistance to rest. You might say that sympathetic shock can be characterized as a raging fire that cannot be controlled and parasympathetic shock can be characterized as a frozen body of water.

While parasympathetic shock waits for the awakening of authentic responsiveness, sympathetic shock longs for calm. One of the most remarkable interventions for shifting both sympathetic and parasympathetic dominance involves contacting the center of the hand. By bringing the palms of the hands together with a very slight pressure, as in prayer, adrenal firing is balanced. Other options include holding the little finger of either hand and holding just under the collarbones (this is point 22 and you can locate it on the map of the body on pages 46–47) on both sides of the body. These simple acts of self-care awaken the option to respond authentically rather than with effort. (See the chart on the adrenal system in this chapter for additional ways to balance adrenal function.) This is a clear demonstration of how easily the reptilian brain can be given new information.

Leticia was in the same class as Kamala, Edith, and Jeremy. She hotly contested the theory of shock entirely, and her beet-red face and bright eyes flared whenever we debated the subject. She had a variety of troubling and disabling physical problems, including chronic lower back pain and intense headaches. Her life, she said, had always been relatively stress-free and she saw no indications of shock in anything she had ever experienced. She was sure there was no link between her physical discomfort and the events or experiences in her life. When we were just over the halfway point in the term, she asked me if I had any energy medicine suggestions to help her with tremors that she was having in the night. She was newly married, and her husband had woken her several times since their marriage.

He was concerned that she might have a severe disorder because she was shaking so thoroughly. In the course of further discussion it became clear to me that Leticia simply did not have any way to calm down that worked for her. It was as if a flame inside her kept rising and had no way to be put out.

I asked her if she was willing to let the class share in her healing. The answer was an instantaneous yes. I then asked her if she would invite her husband to be involved. Again she said yes, and smiled brightly. Leticia was very pleased to have found a successful relationship. She knew she was not an easy woman to live with because of her driving energy. Many people liked her and admired her, but few people could tolerate her twenty-four hours a day. Insomnia was a common theme in her life, and she tended to snap back if challenged. Ben, her husband, was the perfect balance for her. He was patient and caring, and capable of holding his own space and integrity with quiet and certain confidence.

What I wanted to demonstrate was the power not only of subtle energy medicine and shock resolution, but also the role of relationships in the healing process. Energy medicine can be a miracle worker in families and in interpersonal relationships. Everyone in my family has learned Jin Shin Tara, and we all treat each other at times of need. This has not only saved us enormous amounts of money in healthcare costs, it has done something else for our family life. It has given us a connection with each other that is unique and useful, no matter what else may be occurring. I first learned Jin Shin to help my first daughter and myself when we were building a new family life together. That foundation has never been shaken. Even to this day, when she is a full-grown adult with her own life, she will ask me for treatments when she is distressed. The treatments link us together repeatedly at different junctures in our lives and renew our bond as mother and daughter. In treating family members, please note that there are usually fewer words spoken. Even when, for instance, my husband and I are furious with each other, we can support one another with energy medicine and it always dissipates the fury in a silent sweep of unconditional caring administered by intentional and educated touch.

Shock isolates us from each other. It also separates us from the natural world and the resources available outside of our own minds and bodies, including community. This is quite evident when you observe sympathetic nervous system activation. The activated individual plows ahead relentlessly, unable to stop or notice avenues of help. There is a driven quality to movement and expression. Sympathetic activation can appear to be a powerful force to be reckoned with, and sometimes help is deflected by the velocity of the fiery drive forward. That is why it was so momentous for Leticia to seek my aid and to be willing to let others witness her process.

Ben seemed reserved standing next to Leticia in the center of the classroom when I described her seizure-like nocturnal behavior, but he was thoroughly present. He said he had a good feeling about what we were about to do. I asked him to hold the base of Leticia's cranium (Point 4 on the right and the left sides, see chart on pages 46–47) while I sat at her feet and held the base of her big toes (Point 7). Leticia was lying on her back on a massage table that we had placed in the center of the classroom and the other students were seated in a circle around her, giving the process their full attention.

I asked Leticia to imagine that there was a wave of gentle energy moving up from the soles of her feet, along her legs, back, over her head, and down the front of her body. I told Leticia that I thought the problem was that her energy rose up repeatedly from her adrenals, and that it was blind as to how to descend and needed some direction, which the points we were holding would provide.

They both laughed a little as I said this, acknowledging that they had noticed something like this themselves but they had not used the language I was using. I asked Leticia to help the class participate by describing any of her sensations.

Leticia focused on the oval energy wave (see page 54) and after just a few moments her face contorted, furrowing deeply in her brow "What are you feeling?" I asked her. "I feel a lot of pressure in my head," she said, "and it hurts."

"Stay with the wave of energy," I said, "but tell me anything else that you notice."

Then Leticia began to cry. "I can really feel that Ben wants to be here," she said, and more tears gushed forth.

"Let Ben's caring in, little by little." I said. "Keep focusing on the wave of energy, breathing and feeling all the way down to your toes."

"You mean it's not over?" Leticia asked, and the whole class laughed. "I thought this was it," she said.

"Oh, no. It's just beginning," I replied, and I couldn't help from laughing myself. Leticia stayed with her experience of being held and witnessed,

Oval of Energy

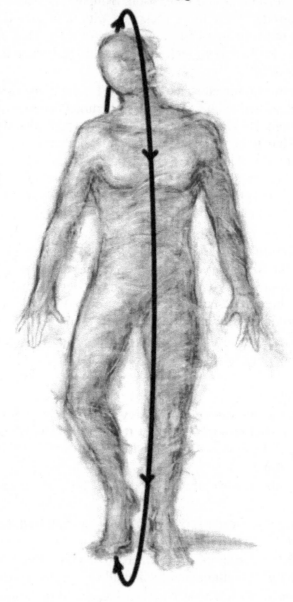

not having to do anything else. Eventually the tears stopped flowing but her breathing deepened and began to even out. It continued to originate from her belly, which rose and fell in steady undulations, indicating that her primitive brain had relaxed.

"I can feel my feet," she said.

"That's great," I immediately responded. "If Ben can hold first the base of your cranium (Point 4 on both sides) and then the bottom of your big toes (Point 7 on both sides) until you can feel your feet, your energy will learn a new pathway and you won't have the shakes when you finally lay down to rest."

The cranial base is frequently compressed and painful for people whose energy tends to rise more easily than it can descend. This was the source of Leticia's headaches. The base of the big toe, on the sole sides of the feet is a potent energy center. They drive the oval of energy that I was asking Leticia to envision. This fluid oval is like a transparent shield of protection and harmonious energy flow. (See illustration on page 54.)

I showed them a few more things they could do to bring Leticia's energy down the front of her body, such as holding inside the knee on Point 1. This point focuses primarily on drawing energy down into the body. Another option was holding the base of the buttocks (Point 25) and the top of the shoulder (Point 11) on the same side, holding first one side and then the other. These two points, especially when held together, also encourage energy's descent into the body.

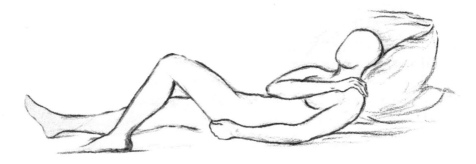

Holding Points 11 and 25

I asked the class members if they noticed the change in Leticia's coloring. Instead of her usual extremely reddened face, she had a pink glow. I gave Leticia a mirror and asked her if she noticed this too, and she acknowledged the difference.

"But what's the shock part?" she asked. "I didn't resolve any shock, and I still don't know what shock there is to resolve."

"I don't know either," I answered honestly, "but you don't slow down easily and the energy in your head was so intense and excessive that you were trying to shake it loose."

"Well, for some reason, this reminds me of something my mom and dad talked about when I asked them about my birth," Leticia said, looking very much at ease. "They said I came out of my mom so fast she thought I was going to tear her apart, but that it was probably because they gave her some drug so she could hurry up and have me. The doctor wanted to go home or something like that. I don't know. Could that have anything to do with it?"

There is evidence to support the possibility that stimulants given to mothers to increase the speed of delivery can have long-term effects on the adrenal functions of the child. Perhaps this was the elusive shock that Leticia could not think of earlier in the semester. The pain in her lower back might well be the strain she felt in the area of her kidneys. Could it be that what had happened so long ago would still be disturbing her now? These were questions we could explore in the class as a way of understanding the nature of shock. Leticia could choose to further explore these questions further at her own pace as her life directed her.[8]

The following week, when the class met, Leticia wanted to report on the results of our demonstration treatment. Ben had been treating her regularly and her "seizures" were on their way out. They had been reduced to occasional trembling in her sleep, but even that had diminished. The best news for Leticia was that a pain in her neck that was so chronic she had not even mentioned it, had mysteriously disappeared after the demonstration treatment. Finally, she was realizing that she did not have to "hurry up and do it" all the time.

The Condensed Guide to the Resolution of Shock

The physiology of shock resolution is, from one perspective, really quite simple. This is not to minimize the intricacies of neurobiological sequencing and neurochemical reorganization, which we are learning about more and more and in increasing detail. This literature, however, is not always accessible for the lay reader. It is my belief that we lose nothing of importance with a simplified understanding of neurobiology and the tools that allow us to feel the physiological benefits of healing. The heart of shock resolution is achieving thoroughly balanced human function, increased brain capacity and fluidity, and enhanced vitality. If we find a way to provide this for ourselves, then it matters little how precise our knowledge is.

From my vantage point, both as a survivor of shock and as someone who aids others in its resolution, the understanding of the following physiological components are both central to and sufficient for the healing process:

1. Adrenal function.

2. Sympathetic and parasympathetic responses.

3. The structure of the brain.

4. The communication network comprised of skin, spinal cord, and brain (see Chapter 4).

5. The role of the spinal cord in reporting on the central nervous system (see Chapter 4).

I recommend that anyone interested in recovery from shock and trauma provide themselves with a basic education about these physiological functions. This chapter addresses the three items above and the remaining two are addressed here and in Chapter 4. If you want to go deeper with this learning, there are references and resources in this book to provide you with additional education.

The insight derived from new research in neuropsychology can be captured in a few concepts:

◈ The brain is an interactive system. If you engage in its dynamic process for the purpose of healing, and if you lovingly focus on the balancing of reptilian or primitive responses, you will create the necessary stimulation for the nurturance of the cortical brain and the prefrontal lobes. These evolved structures will bring you into your own future with grace, dignity, and compassion.

◈ Take good care of your adrenals. If they are either overactive or extremely hesitant, notice and attend to them. This can mean avoiding coffee or other stimulants if your nervous system is sympathetically dominant. It can mean going to bed when the sun goes down and waking up when it rises to support natural biorhythms. It can mean encouraging yourself, gently, if your nervous system is parasympathetic, to find healthy outlets to express your anger or excitement, and express your desire for space and boundaries in relationships.

◈ Honor your sensory wisdom by faithfully witnessing and reflecting on your sensations and noting how your skin, your spinal cord, and your gut instincts speak your own unique truth. This, in itself, will send a message to your reptilian brain that you are ready to move on from early shock conditioned habits.

From a physiological perspective I want to encourage you to enjoy your healing process as much as you possibly can. This will benefit both your adrenals and your brain chemistry, and it will also speed up the overall healing process. The way to heal from shock the fastest is to laugh as much as possible. See Chapter 5 for more on this subject, including the way that words function to stimulate neurology.

One of the reasons why I have complete confidence in the veracity of simplicity is that it is thoroughly empowering, and it is almost impossible to heal from anything unless you are empowered to do so. In addition, I know that we, and by we I mean all of us without exception, are entitled to thoroughly inhabit our own bodies, our own intelligence, and our own unlimited potential.

Differentiating Shock From Trauma

Some Indications of Shock to Consider Are:

1. Sympathetic Dominance:

Reddening of the skin.

Rapid blinking.

Edgy laughter.

Fidgeting.

Profuse sweating in social situations.

Compulsive talking.

Hypervigilance.

Muscular hypertonicity.

Emotional outbursts.

Exaggerated startle with long duration.

Laughing when describing a charged situation.

Sudden heat in body.

Darting eyes.

Environmental hypersensitivity.

Over-responsiveness.

2. Parasympathetic Dominance:

Whitening of the skin.

Very little blinking (staring).

Sudden flattening of affect.

Amnesia of events.

Loss of affect in describing a charged situation.

Paralyzed speech when stressed.

Coldness of limbs.

Agorophobia.

Needing to stand far away from others to feel safe.

Unresponsiveness.

Hypothalmic (bulging) eyes.

Hypotonicity (flaccidity) in muscles.

Interventions That Are Helpful for Sympathetic Dominance

Key Intention: Interrupt Obsessive Discharge of Adrenaline

1. Be a strong presence.

2. Direct attention to sensation, emotion, and cycle.

3. Separate past from present.

4. Encourage quiet, focusing, stilling awareness practices, such as journaling and walking. Invite nature as a healer. Slowing down helps.

5. Encourage clarity about the fear that lies behind the activation.

6. Bonding eye contact can be approached slowly and gently.

7. Encourage the articulation of boundaries.

Interventions That Are Helpful for Parasympathetic Dominance

Key Intention: Being Seen

1. Notice withdrawal.

2. Make empowering suggestions for creativity—the reclamation of self through expression.

3. Encourage the articulation of feeling.

4. Sort out the repressed history of feeling.

5. Avoid flooding from catharsis and too much regression.

6. Focus on uniqueness and individuality.

7. Mirror, using language.

3 Picking up the Pieces: Stories of the Successful Resolution of Shock

*If we believe that our greatest wounds are
in fact our greatest gifts, we can embrace
the idea that the hardships we experience
in our families of origin are no accidents.
Whether we are born to loving parents, born
by natural childbirth or by Caesarian, born
into or without a community, born with
disabilities, or found in a trash yard, we all
have unique gifts to bring to the world.*

—Sobonfu E. Somé

Estrella Linda Feliz Muñoz: Star of the Heart

*You that grew well here in the arroyo by the dampness
of the river, we lift you to make you good medicine.*

—The prayer of the curandera in Rudolofo Anaya's
Bless Me, Ultima

Estrella's eyes were spirit fires, burning above her remarkable smile. Her true beauty surfaced in the flash of that smile, an ageless illumination. Estrella's warmth and magnetism helped bring her success in the career she finally chose in her middle years after her children were grown. As a therapist, she could now draw freely on the life experience that had brought her true wisdom and compassion. Her rich saga that began in another land and another time was, to her amazement, bearing fruit in her maturity.

In the seaside Mexican village where Estrella was born, domestic violence was a way of life. Nevertheless, she could never accept this tradition. Estrella loved her father and mother deeply, but she did not love what happened to her father when he drank and vented his dissatisfaction with life on his wife. Her mother, her grandmothers, her great-grandmothers, and all of their line as far back as could be remembered, had endured this, and it was expected that she would as well.

Estrella felt great tenderness and loyalty for her village and the people in it, especially her own large family. The community and its daily honoring of nature created a lifestyle that Estrella trusted. Simple people, sharing life honestly with one another despite poverty and hardships—this was what she had always known. But the way in which women were abused and the agreement to deny this cruelty was intolerable, even nauseating. Estrella felt alone and enraged in her repudiation of what no one else wanted to protest—domestic violence.

She knew what to call it because she had educated herself, going beyond the village resources to become fluent in English so she could read books and articles from other places. She did not understand how or why her mother hardened against her when she spoke out. It was as if she and all the other women of the village could not imagine that change was possible. Things had to remain the same. The conflict between her love, her loyalty, and her fury was unbearable.

One day, Estrella knew that she could no longer live with this conflict. Though she was only 17 years old, she decided to flee her village and her family. She believed she could find a life without violence somewhere. Leaving her family was the most difficult thing she had ever done. The melodious early morning sounds of her village, the colors of the marketplace, her friends, the small zocolo (town center), the smell of the ocean nearby—she treasured all these aspects of what she had always known as home. But something had cut into her soul. The only word she could find to describe it was betrayal. She had to leave.

Estrella went first to Mexico City where she learned about San Miguel de Allende, a popular town in the mountains near Guanajuato that drew tourists from all over the world. It was renowned for its international atmosphere and for the well-known artists who lived and worked there. There were jobs in San Miguel for waitresses and maids in the hotels, and because of her obvious intelligence and fluency in English, Estrella had no difficulty finding work as soon as she arrived.

Her first foray into the world outside her village was extremely positive. It was evident to Estrella that her bright mind was a great asset. It allowed her to quickly rise to the top wherever she was. Soon she was a supervisor and then a manager, serving as a liaison between English-speaking guests and the hotel staff.

In San Miguel, she fell in with a group of freethinking Europeans and Americans—philosophers and artists who talked into the night about subjects Estrella had dreamed about, such as literature, politics, sociology, and economic theory. She was stimulated and excited by this group and the books they discussed. This was the kind of world she had always wanted—a world of beliefs and ideas that led to real change.

A central figure in this group was a charismatic American named David deYoung. Estrella enjoyed David and his appreciation of her thinking. Their long conversations stayed with her and fueled her days. Their relationship became more and more passionate until it meant everything to Estrella. In her village, Estrella had surprised her family because she had so little interest in the local boys. Now she had found her first romantic love. David, in turn, was captivated by her enthusiasm for him and her dark beauty. They got married and left Mexico together, freeing Estrella from dependency on her homeland. She continued to work as a maid and waitress to support them because David was a writer, an artist, and an activist, and this left him little time for employment. She stood out in the United States, just as she had in Mexico, as an efficient, competent worker. She consistently got promotions and better pay.

Nearly every woman has at least one central, passionate love in her life, and if this lover betrays her, for a while it feels as if all is lost. David was this kind of love for Estrella. He embodied all she had ever wanted to be and thus, she adored him. When he became infatuated with another woman, and she discovered them together one day when she came home early from work, she thought she would go insane. She was four months pregnant. Recovering from the betrayal of love frequently puts a woman on a new path—a path of self-love. For Estrella, this duplicity had actually already occurred, though she had not yet acknowledged it. It had, in fact, happened twice, once with her father and once with her mother.

For a child, domestic violence is inherently a double loss and a double shock. One shock is the perpetrator's aggression. The second shock is the victim's weakness. While Estrella's father never beat her, Estrella was the witness to his rage and her mother's capitulation. In each instance of domestic violence that she saw, her heart tightened more, and her anger was driven deeper and deeper into her spirit. This accumulation of shock postponed the time when Estrella would fall in love with herself, but like the precious rain that saves us from drought, it would come in its own time.

Alone now in a foreign country, Estrella faced the delivery of her first child without the companionship of her mother and grandmother, who were parteras in their village—midwives who attended to all the needs of a pregnant woman and her newborn. She prepared herself for what was called in America being a "single mother." But what she wasn't prepared for was the difficulty of her labor and the ultimate Caesarian delivery of her son, Ignacio. The double disappointment of not being able to have her child naturally and of facing this alone hurt even more than Estrella was aware.

When David returned to her after Ignacio's birth, begging to be reunited with his new family, Estrella gave in. Her love for him had not diminished, and she had longed for him night after night during their separation. Her reluctance to differentiate from this abusive relationship was evidence of the deeply rooted shock she carried. Within a year, she found herself pregnant again. Their daughter, Aurora, was also born by Caesarian, but this time David was there to share the experience. But when Aurora was two years old, David became involved with another young woman and after horrible arguments, many tears, and bitter battles, Estrella found herself the single mother of two.

I met Estrella after these years of repeated shock were over. She was well known for her artful integration of Western psychology and Mexican curanderismo (healing), which she had learned directly from her mother and her grandmothers when she was very young. She came to study with me and learn what I knew about the nervous system and how to repattern injured neurology. She wanted to offer innovative opportunities to her clients as well as refine her own evolution. Like everyone else who encountered her, I was happily seduced by the brilliance of her smile. Let it be clear—this smile was not superficial. It came from the depth of her heart, so to be seduced by Estrella's smile was to be seduced by inner starlight—the kind that is crystalline in the night sky after the storm has passed and the air smells clean. Her smile was the star of her heart.

Deciphering Layers of Shock

As Estrella proceeded to study the TARA Approach, its contribution to her healing became clear. What the TARA Approach offered her was a perspective on how all the shocks in her life were linked to one another.

Therefore, they could be unraveled slowly and carefully by addressing shock itself as neurological and physiological conditioning with an energy body correlation. The process was like opening a bag that contains a jewel inside, but the bag is kept closed by knotted strings. Once you find the main knot, the strings untie easily. The undoing of one knot leads easily to the loosening of the next. Then, the bag opens and the jewel is revealed, to the viewer's delight and amazement.

We traveled together, metaphorically, to her village in Mexico. Ironically, Estrella discovered that her quest for truth was born from living with the deception of domestic violence. Seeing where and how her passion originated allowed her to understand herself much more thoroughly. Her choices made sense once the source shock was revealed. She stopped blaming herself for her enmeshment with David, and instead, felt waves of self-forgiveness. Now she could really make choices from a non-shock consciousness. Her new perspective also allowed her to see her own survivor qualities—determination, love of justice, compassion, and quick, clear intelligence. She had always deeply admired these characteristics, and now she realized they were hers. This was the first sign of self-love.

What Estrella had also forgotten until now was that her father had functioned as a village leader. Everyone, including the young Estrella, looked up to him in the same way everyone had looked up to David deYoung. When Estrella saw her father beating her mother, she lost her hero. When she saw her mother succumb to her father's attacks, she lost her hope. She had wanted David to restore all this, but he simply repeated the betrayals. He, she discovered, was not the one who could or ever would repair her disappointment. *She* was. And only *she* could ensure that she would not be disappointed again by the actions of others.

Estrella was learning that she carried her memories in her body. She also carried the memories of her mother, her grandmothers, and her great-grandmothers. Just as she had learned from watching them take care of pregnant women and their babies, she learned from watching them being beaten and humiliated. She, despite her intelligence, had allowed herself to be repeatedly abused, albeit in a somewhat different way, by her own husband. This was a learned behavior that she wanted to "unlearn."

The body uses the language of symptoms and sensations to articulate what it knows. How else can it communicate? Estrella had watched her mother and her grandmothers ignore their own bodies, even as they attended to others. Now, she wanted to change this inheritance and not perpetuate it with her own children.

Estrella acknowledged that she felt constriction in her chest. We talked about this and I told her that I called this area of the body (Point 13 in Jin Shin Tara) "The Mother." Trying out the view of symptoms as metaphors, and with the intention of listening to her body, Estrella focused her awareness and her touch on the 13 area of her body. This region encompasses the heart, the lungs, the diaphragm, and the thymus. In Ayurvedic, Vedantic, and Hindu philosophy, this would be referred to as the fourth chakra, or the heart chakra. In the West we simply call it the chest.

Estrella

Estrella felt pain in her chest whenever she was stressed, as if her heart was skipping a beat. She had consulted her doctor about this, and he told her that her heart was fine. Her doctor's response did not reassure her because the sensations continued, even increased, sometimes creating a feeling of pressure in her chest, particularly when she felt insecure, frightened about the future, or lonely. She could not ignore these sensations. I suggested to Estrella that her awareness was accurate, but her perceptions were preventive and too subtle to register on a test. Her heart was talking to her, trying to get her attention.

The area regarded as the territory of Point 13 is where breath initiates. Like going to talk to a good mother, the 13 area is where we go to sort things out and gain perspective. When this area is overburdened, it protests. This emotional center of the body is also an expressive center. Estrella's heart center was saying, "I am carrying too much." Luckily she heard the message before her heart started screaming.

Through her contact with the 13 area, Estrella was able to take apart the layers of shock in her life that had attached to one another. These layers were like geological strata, depicting different times in her history, now fused by suffering. The relevant images from her life arose of their own accord as she held Point 13 on the right and left sides of her body (see illustration on page 66). She separated the first time she saw her father beat her mother from the realization that her husband was unfaithful to her. She separated the day she left her village, tears streaming down her face, from the day she became a mother for the first time without the support of anyone she knew. As she distinguished these events from one another and acknowledged her needs from facing their respective challenges, her burden lightened.

Estrella began to notice that her posture was changing. She was sitting and standing with more dignity, collapsing less and less over her stomach. She had always been full-breasted and after nursing her two children she felt she had to cover her more mature body by slumping. Now, however, she felt quite differently.

Being peers, Estrella and I talked about these transformations, sorting them out like examining clothes from a laundry basket to decide what to wash in cold water, what to wash in hot, and what to throw away because it is too old and ragged. Some moments of Estrella's life were prisms, reflecting all the patterns that she had accumulated. Some were pure pain, calling for expressions of anger, forgiveness, acceptance, or deeper understanding. I encouraged and supported all of these outpourings.

As each moment of resolution found its own ground and perspective, Estrella entered the present. She stepped with power into her own life, and she was able to identify her remarkable accomplishments. She celebrated her dark skin, her lilting language, her beautiful children, and her indomitable determination to learn and grow and to be of service to others. She fell in love with herself and with life. This is recovery from shock.

Lonnie Delaney: Love and Survival

Love is not just the avoidance of pain. It is the key to survival.

—Arthur Janov

Lonnie Delaney was born in a small town in upstate New York. He was the fourth and last child of Maura and Joe Delaney. Joe came from a family so big that when they came together for their yearly reunions they took up the whole campsite or filled the complete hotel. What was remarkable about Joe's family was that everyone seemed to agree with each other about all the important things: politics, religion, sexuality, and work ethic. They all were certainly united about sticking together, eating the same kinds of food, telling the same kinds of jokes, honoring the family, and always being polite.

Maura, on the other hand, had no religion and very little family. Her father died when she was five and her mother struggled after that to support the family until she died at the age of 57. That same year, Maura gave birth to Lonnie. Maura grew up knowing one thing: You had to work hard to exist. Survival meant struggle. Her marriage to Joe served only as a brief respite, in the very early months, from this belief. Once Maura started having children and Joe had to carry the entire burden of financial support, the work ethic was thoroughly reinstated with a vengeance. The relentless demands of parenting consumed them both, but in very different ways.

Joe's family had been deeply disappointed when he introduced Maura as his bride-to-be. It just didn't fit with the family contract. Maura was not one of them, not of the same religion, and certainly without the required background. No one in their family had ever married anyone like Maura. Their suspicions made a deep mark on Maura's already tenuous sense of self. By the time she gave birth to Lonnie, though, there was some acceptance of her. After all, she had adopted their religion and tried her best. Joe's mother, Anna, as a demonstration of acceptance, came over from time to time to help with the children.

Maura was exhausted from having three children, one after the other. One daughter was in preschool for two hours a day, one was still in diapers, and the other one just barely out of them when her first son made his presence known. When she discovered that Lonnie was inside her, Maura felt immediate dismay. Forbidden feelings choked her in the night. Maura's youngest daughter was turning out to be extremely demanding, usurping every waking moment of her life. And now there would be another one tugging at her, robbing her of sleep, competing for her attention, and needing her. It was too much. She sobbed secretly. There was no one to confide in. When Joe returned from work at 8 or 9 at night, he had no desire to communicate. Every ounce of his energy went into building the business that he was creating to sustain his family. Ultimately they would all reap the rewards of his labors, but for now that was just a promise. Maura was indebted to Joe for his efforts and completely inhibited from imposing on him. She remained silent, and relentlessly busy. The fragile beginnings of Maura's connection with her mother-in-law would be destroyed if she revealed how she felt about this new pregnancy. Large families were part of the contract in the Delaney tribe.

One of the tricks of survival that Maura had learned from her mother was pretense. She masked her terror, her fury, her anxiety, and the hope she harbored that perhaps she would miscarry. It isn't easy to deny overwhelming emotion, but Maura believed her life depended on it, so she found a way. It would take a long time before her repression caught up with her, but when it did, it was like a narcotic trance. By the time Maura was 75 years old, she was a widow who lived her days blankly. She remained, like a corpse, stationed in front of the television screen, smoking cigarette after cigarette. The cigarettes and the TV were all she trusted to witness the truth she had never learned to speak. It was a poor reward for all her hard work.

When I met Lonnie, Maura's son, he had just turned 50. A serious, inconspicuous man, Lonnie might escape notice if you didn't pay attention. He, like his mother, had almost mastered the art of making himself invisible. Unlike her, however, he found opportunities for expression in a few carefully selected relationships and in his writing and recreation. He had created a multimillion-dollar business and he oversaw every detail of it, from personnel management to product shipment. He survived on very little food and sleep. He had never married and never intended to. "I don't believe in it," he said. He had fathered several offspring but all had been aborted, save one who had been given up for adoption.

Lonnie's placid exterior masked a powerful drive. He was driven in everything he did. He pushed himself to the limits—the limits of time, hunger, success, personal relationships, sleep, feeling, and sensitivity. He was an anomaly in the corporate world where he experienced unprecedented success. His eccentricities were tolerated because of his wealth, though rarely appreciated.

Lonnie was uncomfortable in almost all social situations. In fact, most interpersonal relationships were an uneasy affair, except for those that were the most intimate. He craved those, though he could not sustain them. This, combined with his troubling and chronic skin ailments, brought him to the study of health.

Bright, irritating rashes had appeared suddenly on Lonnie's skin, particularly on his legs, torturing him with their burning. They persisted in making him itch and scratch at all hours, distracting him, and forcing him to pay attention to his body. Having found no relief in anything his doctors recommended, Lonnie sought a more holistic possibility and he consulted me.

The skin is a great highway of tissue that grows with us from birth until death. Like all our other organs, it communicates with us. In astern medicine, it is said that the skin is articulate about sadness, even anguish. It reveals what has been abandoned, neglected, and rejected. Every time Lonnie scratched his tormented skin, he etched deeper into his wounds. He couldn't leave those rashes alone. No chemical, cream, salve, or balm stopped their proliferation. These wounds screamed their history and Lonnie scratched until he bled.

Lonnie loved to work all through the night. Alone in his home, without wife or child, he focused and attended to everything, searching through the long empty hours for answers: How to solve problems at work? How to solve health problems? How to solve spiritual problems? How to solve the problems of the world? How to solve family problems? This solitude was completely familiar. Now, however, his outraged skin interfered, punctuating his time with need.

The Way We Are Born and the Way We Live

I always ask my students this question: "Do you know anything about your birth or your mother's pregnancy with you?" I ask the question primarily to stimulate inquiry, reflection and, perhaps, memory. It is astounding how little information most people have about their prenatal environment and their birth. Many have heard surprisingly similar non-sequitors from their mothers, such as:

"I don't really remember."

"I was so out of it, I don't know what happened."

"It was horrible."

"It went fast."

"It took a long time."

"I was glad when it was over."

"It hurt."

"It wasn't so bad."

"Everything was fine."

Lonnie, quite unusually, had given both his prenatal life and his birth a lot of thought. He had asked questions and received some useful answers. Because his family was so large, so close, and so enmeshed, everyone knew just about everything about everyone else. "Dr. Hamilton delivered you," his aunt said, "and he had to use forceps. Your mother just wasn't cooperating. It was as if she didn't want you to come out, so they had to pull you out."

Lonnie not only had external data, he also had his own memories and experiences, some of which were incredibly detailed. Dr. Hamilton had been the family doctor, and he had delivered all of Maura's children. Lonnie remembered Dr. Hamilton's oft-repeated commentary on his birth and how difficult it had been to extract a big baby from an anaesthetized, recalcitrant mother. Lonnie even remembered seeing Dr. Hamilton's detached expression at his birth, though few believed him when he said this. Neither did people tend to trust his comments on how lonely he felt as a newborn without his mother. That she was anaesthetized for his delivery and preoccupied thereafter were indeed memorable disappointments for this astute, alert individual.

As he shared his surprising wealth of information with me, Lonnie's forehead furrowed deeply. It is almost as if the forceps were still in place. His eyes were moist when open, but then he characteristically squeezed them tightly shut as if he did not want to see something or couldn't. He looked tortured.

From the perspective of resolving shock, the dominant issue in Lonnie's life was loneliness. As I had done with my student Leticia, I asked Lonnie if he was willing to bring his girlfriend, Diana, into the healing process. They both agreed. So, as a team of three, we proceeded to explore the energetic avenues that might link Lonnie's painful and chronic skin condition with shock, and therefore, not only tell us the original cause, but also give us a route for healing.

The Turnaround

I first suggested that Diana do something quite simple. I asked her to place the palms of her hands on the calves of Lonnie's legs. (See the illustration on this page.) He lay down on his back on the massage table I have in my office, and Diana positioned herself at his feet. It was a hot July afternoon and Lonnie wore khaki shorts that exposed the many severely irritated and angry skin rashes on his legs. From time to time, a flicker pecked at the wooden shingles outside, making a rat-a-tat drumbeat, and the dog next door interjected a yelp. Otherwise, it was completely peaceful, and all of us sighed as we let the serenity in.

Palming the Calves of the Legs

First, Lonnie fell into a very deep sleep. Then, as Diana and I gazed at the rawness of the skin on his legs, we saw the bright red of the irritations change—first to a subtle pink and then to Lonnie's skin tone. Almost instantly after that, Lonnie opened his eyes. "I see them all," he said.

"Who?" we both asked, mystified.

"All of them," answered Lonnie.

"Who are they, Lonnie?" I said. "Please tell us. We're very curious." Diana continued palming the calves of Lonnie's legs. From time to time she reported feeling enormous heat in her hands.

"I see everyone who rejected my mother. It was so hard on her. She felt so lonely. And I see Dr. Hamilton. You know, if anyone would have just talked to mom and helped her to relax, I bet she wouldn't have needed those drugs and then I could have come out without forceps." It was hard to tell if Lonnie was angry or sad. His face was clenched tight as a fist and tears were pouring out of the corners of his eyes. As Lonnie continued to talk, Diana and I listened, allowing him the time and space he needed. Lonnie needed to distinguish between his own experience and his mother's, and to not carry the burden of *her* loneliness as well as his own. As a small child, there was so little he could do to help her, though he had wanted to with all his heart and soul. She had set the stage for noncommunication, and Lonnie wanted to stop reading from her script. He experienced life as exhilarating, not as a death sentence.

By the end of the session, Lonnie was letting in a lot more of the love that was emanating from Diana's hands and gaze. He expressed his appreciation to her for being present for him and participating so palpably. Diana told me later how unusual this was. She had almost exhausted her hope that Lonnie would ever really make space for her in his busy life. The rash on Lonnie's legs was noticeably calmer, looking more like a wound that was healing, rather than raw. Lonnie looked at Diana lovingly. She, in turn, was grateful for his trust. She was especially pleased that Lonnie's rash was fading and that she had been part of the recovery.

I taught Lonnie and Diana many more ways to share energy medicine. They learned about the energy pathways that rule the skin. In astern medicine, when skin conditions are severe and chronic, these are the Lung and Large Intestine Meridians. The Stomach and Spleen Meridians are the pathways to attend to when the skin condition is more on the surface and infrequent. The beginning and ending locations of these meridians can be held to release the obstructions in these meridians. (See Chapter 8 for the beginning and ending points of all of the meridians.) These, combined with palming the calves, can always be relied upon to help any skin condition. Holding the ring finger of either hand is another simple approach to treating both the skin and loneliness.

When Lonnie and Diana got married, I was invited to their wedding. It felt good to have provided some resources to end a lineage of loneliness. At the wedding, it was touching to see how carefully Lonnie related to each guest out of his genuine desire that they all feel included and wanted as part of his extended family.

Rebecca Loveland: The Real Revolution

love is not concerned
with to whom you pray
or where you slept
the night you ran away
from home

love is concerned
that the beating of your heart
the beating of your heart
should harm
no one.

—Alice Walker

Whenever we do harm to each other, we perpetuate the cycle of shock and violence. When we find a way to *not* do harm, we *end* the lineage of shock and violence. It is much more challenging to find a peaceful avenue than it is to lash out. We are usually forced into the lessons of peace. Like Rebecca Loveland, many of us have to experience shock in order to make a commitment to never repeat it.

Rebecca had always been idealistic. She was a quiet, thoughtful, and studious young girl and adolescent. She surprised everyone with the scope of her concerns and the degree of her courage. While other girls her age talked of boys and makeup and vied for each other's approval, her interests were political, literary, and humanistic. It mattered little to her what her peers thought of her unusual pursuits, marking her even more clearly as unique. She felt drawn to do things that, regardless of their danger,

were statements of protest against the ways in which suffering was ignored. As she matured, she made decisions to march, carry signs, stuff
envelopes, and write letters to the government. Then, one day, when she
was in her early 20s, Rebecca fell in love with another activist, which
deepened her commitment considerably.

She became someone whose whole life revolved around activism. She
was so identified with the cause for which she fought that she no longer
had a personal life, personal needs, or personal goals. *Everything* was political; everything was activism.

She even stopped doing things she enjoyed, such as writing in her journal and reading poetry. Her job, earning a living, cultivating a career, continuing her education—all of it became irrelevant. She stopped
communicating with her family and ended all her nonpolitical, personal
friendships. What happened to her personal needs? They were suppressed
and outlawed as inconsequential. As an activist, there was no time for
self-involvement or even self-inquiry. It took torture and its unavoidable
aftermath to alert her to her own internal struggle.

The turning point came on a lovely summer night—a night that would
haunt her. The day had been so still and uneventful that it felt odd. Rebecca
had become used to the intensity of nonstop action, constant excitement,
and continual vigilance. A lazy afternoon rarely happened for her, but on
this day she luxuriated in it with her boyfriend Donald. They were two
freedom fighters on vacation.

Returning home from that afternoon, she knew she had found something she had been looking for her entire life—real love. The only problem
was that the man she adored was African and she was not. This was made
more complex by the fact that they were in the middle of a national political upheaval about race relations and he was a central figure. Nevertheless, they were still just a man and a woman in love, and she sparkled with
the joy inherent in this.

Donald liked to call what was happening a "revolution." Rebecca
wanted to believe him, but what they opposed had such long and established strength, she feared that rather than a revolution, they would become part of a tragedy, or, worse yet, annihilation. Eventually, as a result
of her involvement, she would find herself turning this question over and
over in her mind: "What is the *real* revolution?"

But that was not her focus on this afternoon. The surprising day of
love had wiped away her questions. Their love was the central reality and
it had nothing to do with skin color. It had only to do with Rebecca and

Donald, two human beings who found joy in each other. She gathered the day's exquisite memories on her bus ride home, forgetting, for a liberating moment, how dangerous it was to be on the side of change.

Rebecca got off the bus and walked slowly through the streets. Her sleeveless dress was neat and professional, a kind of disguise. She smiled, glancing down at the black and white design on the dress she wore. She wanted to look as if she was just coming back from work or church, so that her clandestine pursuits could not be detected. Thus far, she had been completely successful in keeping her political activities unknown to her neighbors, or so she presumed.

She opened the door of her home and instantly her reverie was shattered, splintered into a million shards. They were waiting for her—four men and two women, waiting to torture her for her beliefs, waiting and prepared to exert real physical pain on her until she told them everything she knew about Donald—what he was doing and with whom. They wanted names and phone numbers. They wanted to know Donald's plans and his allies. Or did they? Maybe they just wanted to hurt her. They had nothing but disgust for her and what she was doing. They had no respect for Rebecca's humanity. Her life was irrelevant, worthless to them. They could, perhaps they would, kill her. They wanted to break her, but they would not. They sat her in a chair in the middle of the room. They tied her hands behind her back and formed a semicircle around her.

She had no hope of rescue or escape. The phone rang repeatedly in the other room, underscoring her helplessness. If only she could grab it and scream for help. But she couldn't. No one would come to help her. She carried Donald in her heart so strongly it was as if he were God. She could never betray him. Even though she was tied and trapped, she was invincible. He was her courage, her spirit, all she believed in. It would take Rebecca many years to realize that this was not true. It was *her* strength and *her* spirit that carried her through this night of torture. She was a woman of unshakeable power and intention and this defined her own personal essence.

Somehow her tormentors knew this. After beating her, after seeing her blood stain the wooden floorboards of the room, after watching her face swell, her tears burning their way into the cuts they had made, after torturing her and abusing her every way they could, they realized she would never reveal anything.

Why didn't they kill her? Rebecca would never know why. For some reason, the leader of this entourage of abusers had mercy on her, and threw her out of her own house into the streets. She remembered thinking, for an instant, how strange it was that her neighbors' homes remained dark and no one came out to help her, despite the noise. She was told never to return, to leave everything behind, and to face the world in her beaten condition. The leader, shouting into the strangely silent street, told her they would do worse to Donald and that if she wanted, she could go to him and show him what they had done to her. "See if he wants you now," the leader leered.

He did. Torn, she returned to him, but they both knew that this was the end. To survive, she would have to go into hiding. Thus, she became a fugitive, but the true torture was that she would never see Donald again. The one love, the love for which she believed she was born, would disappear from her sight on this awful night. The loss was excruciating, far beyond what her skin was experiencing, far beyond what her muscles and her bones felt as they ached and burned from the beating and the violation she had endured with such courage and dignity.

Rebecca cleaned herself as best she could, washing the blood from her black and white dress, putting makeup over her bruises. She covered herself with one of Donald's old coats, and put a kerchief over her head like an old woman. Slipping a gun into her purse and a knife into her pocket, she left through a basement window and moved stealthily into the shadows behind the house. She tensed every muscle in her body to keep from sobbing. Someone had agreed to hide her in a home in another town, across the bridge. When the car drove up, she quickly slid into the backseat and dissolved at last into her pain and exhaustion.

She hid for months, sleeping long hours, crying uncontrollably upon waking and before drifting into an often interrupted slumber. She thought this was probably how drug addicts felt when they quit cold turkey. Her head ached and she couldn't hold food down. Her cuts and bruises healed, but not her heart. It was shattered in so many pieces she wasn't sure she could ever put it back together again. She longed for contact with Donald—a word, a touch. Like a junkie kicking the habit, she craved any sign that she would see him again. But she never would. She had no choice but to give up her addiction.

The people who hid Rebecca were very kind. They gave her the time and space she needed, but they checked on her, offering food and their company. Did she want them to call anyone? "No," Rebecca said repeatedly, "No one." She joined her protectors in the evening to watch the news. This was how she learned that Donald, with some of his cohorts, had left the country. Rebecca cried in relief that he was safe and also because the news deepened her loss even more. But tears run together, and no one can decipher their source or their cause.

I met Rebecca many years later. Within time, she came out of hiding, of course. The revolution had indeed become a tragedy, as she had feared. Whoever had not escaped was dead or in jail, or gone over to the other side. With the revolution squelched, Rebecca was no longer a threat. After all, her relationship with Donald had been brief and he had revealed very little to her in order to protect them both. Luckily, she was forgotten. News of Donald would occasionally resurface in a broadcast. Frequently, his name would be linked with a woman's. But he would never return and she never heard from him again, all of which enhanced her safety. Eventually he would die in exile, and Rebecca had to get on with her life. Or did she?

The analogy of the addict returned often to Rebecca. The thrill of life with an active and all consuming outside purpose was hard to replicate. She found a job and a place to live on her own. She became part of the throngs who marched to work and home again. At night, she wrote about her life, but she was afraid to show these writings to anyone. She couldn't be sure that the danger was really over. She flinched at sudden movements and sounds. Each time she entered her apartment, it was a test of her courage. She didn't want to live alone, but at the same time she didn't want to inflict her idiosyncrasies, such as screaming nightmares, on anyone. The thing that frightened her the most was luxurious afternoons, so she avoided them altogether by working all the time, adding volunteer work to her schedule to assure a busy routine. And then there was falling in love. Oh no, she would never do that again. That scared her to death.

I met Rebecca because one of her volunteer jobs required training in the treatment of trauma, and the TARA Approach did the training. It was while I was explaining the difference between shock and trauma that Rebecca began to see her history from a new perspective, and this caused her to eventually share it with me. The most effective way to learn the power of resolving shock and trauma is to experience the change in your body and your own life. Whenever I facilitate agency programs, I encourage the staff to open to this healing. Not everyone feels ready for this, but for Rebecca, the time was ripe.

There were two areas of the body that I brought to Rebecca's attention as sites where deep healing could be initiated: 19 and 26 (see illustration on page 79). The first is for personal boundaries; the latter is for self-love.

Opening the Back Door to the Heart

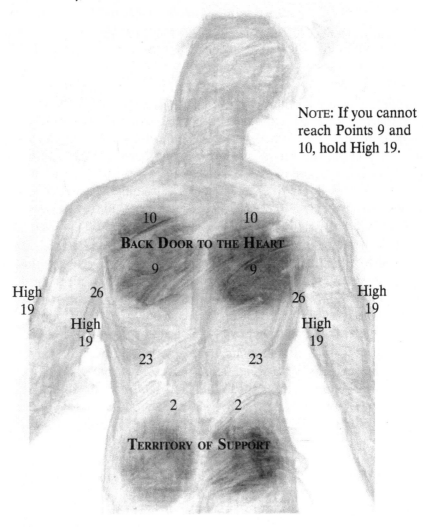

NOTE: **If you cannot reach Points 9 and 10, hold High 19.**

These are two sides of the same coin. While all the world touts love as a loss of self, in order for love to endure, individuality and selfhood is essential. While it appeared as though Rebecca had strongly individuated from her family and her peers, she had in fact lost herself in the causes she took on.

Boundaries and Really Good Boundaries

Eventually, Rebecca would research her early life for the deeper motivating forces for the choices she made. But for the moment, shock of great magnitude in her adult life had paralyzed her, so we had to focus our attention there.

The 26 area, on the back perimeter of the armpits when held, creates, appropriately, a self-embrace (see illustration on page 81). When Rebecca first reached for this area, she felt awkward. After holding there for just a short time, her arms ached. She tried different positions, but still could not be at ease. She was not used to loving herself. Finally, after many experiments, she settled into a satisfying posture and allowed herself to feel her own touch of love. The intimacy of this quiet, deep connection was almost embarrassing at first. She realized that not since she was very young, perhaps seven or eight years old, had she been so focused on herself.

Her face began to feel warm the more she held the 26 area. Indeed, when she looked in the mirror later, her face was rosy. Rebecca had been pale, even grey, for a long time. Since the night of torture, she had remained a tortured woman. Pools of black stained the territory under her eyes like the bruised remnants of her tears. Now, in her self-embrace, she sensed a heat rising up to her eyes, penetrating her losses.

When she touched the points in the crease of her elbows (the 19 area), she felt strong. Again, the weight of her losses lifted and she had a glimpse of a future. She swelled with breath and had a vision that there was a back door to her heart and that it was opening. Indeed, the 19 area does, energetically, release the upper back, just behind the heart (see illustration on page 81). Shadows fled through that exit—the ghosts of those who had abused her. Rebecca simultaneously felt a deep release in her lower back, the territory of support. She thought of her poetry and was determined that she would make more time to write. As she continued touching the points of self-love and empowerment, the fear of solitude diminished until she actually began to treasure her time alone because she could fill it with her creativity. Rebecca allowed herself to indulge her passion for language. She substituted busyness with writing classes, reading, and, ultimately, completing a book of poetry that she considered trying to publish. Like a phoenix, she rose from the ashes of torture, and while this was a prolonged process, her steady ascent was clearly her path from the moment she began to feel comfortable making contact with herself.

Point 26–The Self Embrace

The boundaries that Rebecca began to build into her life created time to heal and time to write. She discovered that she was resilient and remarkable. Little by little, she became a crusader for her own development. This was very new for her. The value of her time with herself began to dominate over the memories of torture and loss. Of course, it wasn't only holding the 19 and the 26 area that did this. It was coupled with other energy medicine healing that Rebecca learned, such as treating the areas where she had been the most severely beaten.

At first, this was very difficult because contact with these areas reawakened flashbacks to the night of torture. The gentleness of her touch, though, and the fact that she was in charge of the treatment and its pace, gradually mitigated the fear of flashbacks and then the flashbacks themselves. Rebecca's head and pelvis had suffered the most. For her head, the following areas stimulated profound relaxation: 4, 20, 21 and 22 (see body map on pages 46–47). To relax her pelvis and stimulate hormonal balance, she held the 15 area together with the 6 area, first on one side, and then on the other (again, refer to the body map). This stimulated the sensation and the neurochemistry of hope that she would be whole again—a complete woman.

There came a time when Rebecca Loveland could walk into her apartment alone without feeling a terrorized catch in her heart. This was the beginning of what she later referred to, in a poem, as the springtime of her new life.

Earthquake and Evolution: The Gordon Family and the Northridge Earthquake

Why are we afraid of dramatic or devastating
change in our own lives? In ourselves? Is it possible
to recast what we perceive to be negative as
something beautiful, something sculpting our lives,
our psyches, and our souls? Aren't we, like the
Grand Canyon, made new again and again, yet
always infinitely whole?

—Kathleen Jo Ryan

Everyone in the Gordon household was thrilled; they just couldn't stop smiling. They were going on an extended trip to Hawaii! Mom had arranged it all. She had managed to get special rates because they were going after the holidays. They would leave on the morning of January 16. Christmas was just the prelude to their real celebration.

It was hard to tell who was the most excited. Seven-year-old Aaron was practicing surfing in their Colorado living room. His mother, Nedra, had always dreamed of living in Hawaii. Born in a cold land—Denmark— she loved to feel warmth! She was busily fantasizing that she would find her dream house on this trip. Father, Fred, was trying to be organized and reasonable, but deep down inside he felt like a teenager. He planned to go scuba diving, having just completed his certification. It was the vacation of a lifetime for each of them!

The morning of departure arrived, bright and cold. They smiled at each other knowingly as they rode the shuttle to the airport. They wouldn't be cold for long! Mom was thoroughly organized. She had found the perfect carry-on. It held everyone' s preferred snacks, books, toys, as well as overnight necessities. Nedra prided herself on being prepared for anything. She always expected the worst, so they had everything with them that they would need...just in case.

Their enthusiasm wasn't even daunted when they arrived in Los Angeles and, after waiting an hour, learned that their flight to Lihui, on Kauai, was delayed. Mom, however, didn't get grumpy until they were told the flight was cancelled and they would have to spend the night in a hotel by the airport to be ready for an early morning departure. In the hotel room, Aaron rushed to jump on the huge beds and watch the big television. Dad went down to the gym, and Mom worried about the luggage.

When night came, they were all tucked beneath their crisp sheets. The lights from planes coming in for a landing stroked their slumbering faces like transparent feathers. The air conditioner hummed dependably, soothing them as they dreamed of sunsets and ocean waves into the morning of January 17, 1994.

Nedra woke first, feeling something stir—was it inside her or outside? At first she couldn't tell. The feeling that the room was trembling and that the ground beneath her was giving way was not that unfamiliar. She remembered having nightmares like this in Denmark, when she was a child. But why were they returning now? Then the room jolted and Nedra knew this was not a nightmare. She called her husband's name. He stirred in response, but miraculously Aaron remained deep in slumber. When Nedra tried to rise and dress she found she could not. The room was in constant motion.

Nedra began to tremble as much as the room. She looked at Fred, but his calm demeanor did not calm her. She felt very alone. "Shouldn't we wake Aaron?" she whispered to her husband, but he nodded no. Nedra put her head in her hands. The shattering of mirrors and lamps all around her made her cry, but she tried to muffle her sounds so she whimpered like a beaten dog. Even when the room stopped shaking, Nedra did not. When, at last, dawn came, Nedra was amazed that they were all alive. She woke Aaron whose eyes grew wider as he looked around in awe. "Wow," he said, "what happened?"

"We had an earthquake," his father replied, "but everything is alright. Let's get ready to go."

"Do you really think the plane will take off?" Nedra managed to spit out, furious at her husband's cavalier attitude.

"Of course," Fred answered.

When they got to the airport, despite the chaos all around, they found that indeed the plane could leave without a problem. They boarded and found their seats and the plane took off on time. But Nedra was still shaken, and she remained that way, unable to find any stability within herself, her feeling of loneliness building in intensity until she secretly feared for her sanity.

It wasn't until they were comfortably situated in their condo on Kauai that Nedra felt she could take account of her plight. Aaron and Fred had raced right off to the beach and Nedra stayed back, saying she had a headache. She still could not stop herself from shaking, though the tremors were now thoroughly internalized and undetectable. It was then that she called me.

"I was thinking about you," I said, "when I saw the news about the earthquake. How are you?"

Nedra started to shake again in earnest as she heard the genuine concern in my voice. I heard her sobs and her trembling and knew that was her answer.

"I know something that can help you," I said, "just cradle the phone on your shoulder or, if you can, put it on speaker, and hold the areas on your body that I tell you about and your shaking will stop. Put your right hand on the outside of your left armpit and put your left hand on the top of your right foot, near the space between your little toe and the toe right next to it. Just hold there and see if you can feel a pulse in your fingertips and wait for the pulse to balance. If you don't feel a pulse, don't worry about it. Just notice what is happening to your body." (See Flow Out of Panic on pages 120–121.)

Nedra was able to put the phone on speaker and follow my suggestions. She could feel herself calming down a little.

"How's it going?" I asked.

"A little better," Nedra replied, tentatively.

"Okay. Now just switch sides, holding the same points, only on the opposite sides."

Nedra followed my directions. When she switched sides, she could identify that something was changing inside her. She involuntarily took a deep breath and I heard it.

"Great," I said. "Now switch sides again and just keep doing that, back and forth, until you have held both sides three times."

When Nedra was done, the shaking had stopped.

"Thank you," she said out loud, as much to herself and to the space around her as to me.

"I'm so glad you and your family made it safely to Hawaii where you can recover and feel the value and beauty of who you are and your life. You have survived all the ordeals of your life for a reason, Nedra, and I for one celebrate you for this."

"Yes," Nedra answered, not quite sure if she could accept all this positive talk. "Thank you."

"Listen," I went on, "do you have a fax there, or e-mail?"

"I have both," Nedra replied.

"Great. I am going to send you something I put together. It's a collection of energy medicine treatment you can do when things like this happen. It's called 'Shock Is in the Moment, Healing is Forever.' You will likely have more coming up for you in response to this devastating encounter, and you may need and want to do more self-treatment until you find your way back to yourself. Give me the information and I'll get it out to you right away."

Nedra gave me the numbers, and when the document arrived, she spent a lot of time on the beach practicing the treatments. The following is what Nedra received from me.

Shock Is in the Moment, Healing Is Forever

Guides to the quick reversal of immediate shock. Self-care and treatment options for everyone.

We have at our fingertips the means to come out of shock as quickly as it strikes. The quicker we come out of shock, the more empowered we are, the more rational and wise our choices will be. When we come out of shock, we rise to the occasion and act with purpose and clear intent.

Our bodies are designed to move through shock rapidly. The quantity and quality of our previous exposure to shock and the resolution of those prior experiences, however, can dramatically alter this capacity. Healing from past shock, when the time and space is available to do so, will make you much less vulnerable to being trapped in shock when it reoccurs.

No matter what your previous history with shock, there are some simple steps anyone can take to come out of shock when it strikes. These steps involve the application of a subtle and forgiving touch on certain areas of the body. All that is needed is that this touch be applied as soon as possible after, or even during, the shock. Precision is not important. The contact of your hands on these areas is all that is needed. The entire process of coming out of shock should take a maximum of three minutes, sometimes five. Less than one minute is necessary to initiate the process. There is a general internal state that will foster the resolution process. This includes:

1. Saying, inside yourself, "I am in shock and I will come out of shock now."

2. A willingness to bring your hands to certain areas of your body or the body of someone in need.

3. An ongoing awareness of your own sensation.

All of these suggestions can be used for you or for others. Some applications are more easily done on oneself; others are easier as treatment for others. However, it is the versatility of this system of regeneration and its applicability to one and all that makes it perfectly suited for the treatment of shock.

Coming Out of Shock Through Gentle Touch: The Healing Practices

Releasing fear and centering

- Hold your index finger: Wrap the fingers of one hand around the opposite index finger so that it rests securely in the palm of the other hand and hold. Continue holding until your breath deepens and you feel calm. You may also feel a deep, constant pulse in your palm. Hold the index finger of one hand, and then the other if you have the time. Let your instinct guide you as to whether you hold the right or left index finger.

- Hold the top of your head with the palm of your right hand and the center of your forehead with the palm of your left hand.

- Bring the palms of your hands together, the palms of all fingers touching, as if in prayer. Your hands can be held in this position anywhere it is comfortable: in your lap, in front of your heart, or to your side.

- Rest one hand in the center of your chest and the other hand at the base of your cranium, at the top of your neck.

Shaking, quivering panic

When you or someone else is in this vulnerable condition, you can come out of it very quickly by placing the fingertips of your right hand just behind the armpit, on your back. The left hand simultaneously holds the front of the right foot, on the top, between the little toe and the toe next to it. Your hands are almost making a big Z on the front of your body. Now, switch sides so that the Z is going the other way and your left hand is crossing your chest to find the outside of your right armpit, while your right hand comes down to hold the top of your left foot. Then switch again. Do this three times on each side of your body and you will no longer be shaking. You will take a deep breath and know what to do.

Breathing difficulties

Breathing reflects shock. In addition, in situations such as New York after the September 11 attack, smoke inhalation and the inhalation of toxins produces secondary shock for the body. Simple touch can relieve this pressure and open the lungs, while encouraging your body to move away from the toxic environment. There are many approaches to opening and protecting the lungs. The ones listed here are just a few. You can do them all. Let the circumstances direct which application to use.

♦ Hold the ring finger, right and left sides, one at a time. Wrap the ring finger with the fingers of the opposite hand. Hold until breathing deepens.

♦ Palm the calves: Place the palms of your hands on the calves of the legs of the person having breathing difficulties. Breath will deepen in both practitioner and recipient.

♦ Release the shoulders: Stand behind the person in need. Rest your hands on their shoulders so that your palms are on the top of the shoulders and your thumbs hold a point 2–3 inches below the top of the shoulders, on the back. If you are doing this for yourself, release one shoulder at a time, bringing the arm of one hand to the top of the opposite shoulder so that the fingers touch the point 2–3 inches below.

Fatigue

Fatigue can be a parasympathetic response to shock. It prevents proactive behavior and clear perception. It avoids confrontation and retreats to safety. It is dangerous, especially in times of aggression. But there are simple ways to reverse fatigue and transform it into clear, present, and wise action from the heart. If your fatigue is beyond an immediate response to shock, a more consistent application of these simple practices will be necessary.

♦ With your right hand, touch the coccyx, the base of your spine, and with the fingers of your left hand hold the center of your chest, between your breasts. You may also do this for another person or suggest they do this for themselves.

♦ Hold the base of your thumb, in the fleshy mound. Hold the right and then the left thumb area.

♦ Hold underneath the collarbone, in the area closest to the neck where the collarbone begins with a knobby insert, on both the right and left sides of the body.

Anger

Anger is a healthy reaction to stress and shock, but unless it is transformed into positive action, it can add to the shock. To transform anger into useful behavior:

- Hold the middle finger of either the left hand or the right hand, or both, one at a time. Wrap the middle finger with the fingers of the opposite hand, letting it rest in the palm of the opposite hand until the energy of anger has sequenced through your body and given rise to creative, positive thinking. Before this you may feel a resonant and deep pulsation in the palm of your hand.

- Hold the base of your sternum, placing the palms of your hands softly under the long rib line there. Hold until your breath deepens. You may feel a calming pulsation in the palms of your hands.

- Hold the base of your cranium, placing your fingertips at the outside of the right and left occipital ridges.

Helping Yourself and Helping Others

In many regards, it is easier to help someone else than to help yourself. In helping others, we usually help ourselves simultaneously. However, in order to be of ongoing service, we have to help ourselves or we will be destroyed by our overextension. This said, let me shout from the rooftops that every single one of us can be profoundly helpful to other human beings. Using simple touch and awareness we can be instrumental in bringing others and ourselves out of shock.

You do not have to be a psychologist, a neurologist, a pharmacologist, or a psychiatrist to bring someone out of shock. All the interventions suggested here are completely noninvasive, nonchemical, and harmless. They are also profoundly effective and have been used with great success by people who have experienced many different kinds of shock.

Do not be afraid to use these suggestions. It is your birthright and your instinct to come out of shock quickly and to be alert and prepared to make the necessary ensuing decisions.

If you practice these applications on yourself consistently, whenever you are disturbed, even by minor things, your recovery process will increase in speed and eventually will be instantaneous.

Being an intelligent woman Nedra found herself reviewing her history in light of the earthquake she had just experienced. She felt enormous gratitude for her life and her family, more than she had ever known before. For her husband and her son, the earthquake was not a threatening experience. They felt confident about their successful survival. In fact, her son even regretted that he had slept through it. Nedra, on the other hand, had seen the earthquake as a horror that took no notice of her or her life. Yet the evidence was unquestionable. She had been spared. She entered a period of deep reflection that would take many months to complete. In it, she let go of her feeling of being strange and weak because of her trembling and her resentment towards her family for not noticing her needs. Instead, she was glad they were unscathed. Nedra returned from Hawaii no longer trembling but shaken up in a very positive way.

Gabriel Restrova: The Best America Has to Offer

If you want to know what your experiences were like in your past, examine your body now. If you want to know what your body will be like in the future, look at your experiences now.

—Ancient Buddhist Wisdom

Some survivors of shock lose what most other people take for granted. Healing in these cases is not about "getting back to normal." It is a paradigm shift, an awakening, a rebirth, and a spiritual transformation. Gabriel Restrova, a remarkable cyclist and athlete, demonstrated this to me in a way I never could have anticipated.

Gabriel remembered his first bicycle very well. It was yellow. Later, when he grew up to be a professional athlete, he could trace his choice of career back to the first time he rode that yellow bike by himself. The moment was clear in his mind. His uncle Vasel was helping him. Each day, he would go out with Gabriel and hold him from behind, supporting the little boy as he gained strength and balance. "Training wheels are for sissies," Gabriel told his uncle, so they took them off.

Then, one glorious autumn, it happened. Gabriel was pedaling and he suddenly felt lighter. He gained speed quickly and glanced back in surprise to see his uncle waving at him from down the block. Gabriel was on his own. The freedom was unforgettably exhilarating. It felt like flying and he committed himself, there and then, to the joy and glory of this take-off.

That autumn day returned to Gabriel often now. The cascading leaves tumbling in flurries of gold got stuck in the spokes of his wheels, slowing him down until he plucked them out, frustrated with their interference. On his yellow bike, he toured the neighborhood through the swirls of wind and leaves, over and over. The thrill of active, vital embodiment was so ecstatic, Gabriel knew then that he could never live without it.

Life was good. Gabriel was able to follow his dream of becoming a cyclist. His loving family was generous and supportive. His grandparents on both his mother's and his father's side had immigrated to the United States from Eastern Europe. In the process of becoming Americans, they had become deeply unified with one another, and they transmitted this unity to their children. They were a strong family. Gabriel loved his younger brother, Yuri, and the two boys loved athletics almost as much as they loved each other.

Gabriel and Yuri were not really competitive, though Gabriel always felt he had to work harder than his younger brother did. Yuri grew taller and stronger and things just came more easily to him. But nothing undermined their fun together. Even now, Gabriel remembered that and smiled. They always had fun, no matter what.

The morning of the accident, paradoxically, was very much like the day he rode that yellow bike on his own for the first time. He woke unusually early with an irresistible need to be out on his bike right away. He burst out the door before his wife was even awake and hopped on his bike, heading for his favorite mountain trail. Yes, this was the good life; the best America had to offer.

As he pedaled uphill, he felt the power of his muscular legs, and he rested in the confidence that they could take him wherever he wanted to go no matter how steep the incline or how far the distance. It all felt so good that he could cry. After this ride, he'd go home to his wonderful wife, and they would share this awesome autumn day together. The leaves on the ground were churned by the early morning wind while the rising sun gave them a nimbus of gold. Everything appeared magical, even numinous.

A voice inside spoke suddenly then, a part of himself that he recognized as trustworthy, but this time it told him something very confusing. "Go another way!" it insisted. "Go somewhere different. Change your path. This isn't the way. Stay out longer. Don't hurry home."

"No way," Gabriel thought. But then the voice repeated its command and Gabriel, distraught, wobbled on his bike. This was weird. He felt spooked. Frustrated, he swerved off the dirt road and steered his bike onto the paved highway that would lead him more quickly to his wife and his breakfast. It wasn't more than a minute later that the car hit him.

There was nothing he could have done. The car hit him head-on, and he was ejected from his bike. Gabriel was thrown through the car's windshield. The impact shattered his spine. He remained in a coma for three days. When he awoke he was told that he had a 1 percent chance of ever walking again.

In the hospital room, alone after everyone had gone, Gabriel went through the list of what he had lost on that exquisite autumn morning when he had rebelled against his internal voice. His sexuality, his bladder and bowel control, the use of his legs, his bicycle, skiing, rock climbing, hiking, wrestling with his brother, and independence. The list went on and on, into his dreams, and continued in the morning when he awoke.

"This was never supposed to happen," Gabriel told me after his wife introduced me to him for the first time. "This just isn't me," he declared with force, slapping himself smartly on his muscular thighs that rested, helpless, in his wheelchair.

There were two things that I could offer Gabriel. One was pain relief. Jin Shin almost always can be relied upon to lessen pain, if not relieve it entirely. The other thing I could offer him was a path to the discovery of who he truly was and who he could become in the face of this accident. Gabriel wanted the first thing I had to offer, but he wasn't sure that he wanted the second. A year and a half after the accident, Gabriel still hoped to regain all he had lost. He had no interest in becoming someone new. While we worked together and he and his wife studied with me, he slowly began to focus more on what he had gained than on what he had lost. It is precisely this shift that let me know that Gabriel was going to experience the human miracle that survivors of shock are blessed to know. He was on his way to finding the gift that he would emerge from this accident with, a gift impossible to lose.

We started with pain relief. This demanded a focus on Gabriel's head injuries. Even prior to the accident, Gabriel had fallen on his head many times. All those previous falls were reactivated by the massive impact to his head that he had sustained in the collision. In a pattern similar to Rebecca Loveland's treatment, I used Points 4, 20, 21, and 22. This relaxed Gabriel so deeply he sighed in relief as soon as these areas were touched, particularly when I, or his wife Ilana, held both the right and left Point 4 simultaneously.

Gabriel Restrova had lived his life by exertion, and by doing his best and trying his hardest in everything. This was how he had found success and satisfaction. Touching these points instantaneously allowed him to let go, something he was not prepared to do on his own. In addition to the enormous tension he felt in his head, Gabriel had pain along his spine where metal plates had been inserted, and down the sides of his legs. As I held both the right and left Point 4, or the right 4 and the left 20, followed by the reverse, Gabriel slipped into a twilight-zone state. He would tell me later that this was the only time he felt true relief from "all of it." He was referring not only to his physical discomfort, but also to the daily pressure of what it meant to have a spinal cord injury. The complications that now accompanied every physical function in his life, including bathing or going to the bathroom, and the humiliation he felt because of how dependent he had become on the support of others, including his wife, disappeared in this treatment.

Gabriel's legs moved involuntarily during treatment, and he tried to apologize for these spasms. I told him they were important demonstrations of the healthy release of action that was incomplete from the time of the accident when he could not protect or defend himself from harm. This seemed to relax him enough to return to the twilight state where he could restore himself from shock. It was easy to teach Ilana how to provide her husband with these same treatments so that he could have even more opportunities for this critical regeneration.

The more challenging task was to get Gabriel to treat himself and to embrace this new and unexpected phase of his life. Gabriel was mad at God and everyone and everything. No matter what anyone tried to do or say, he felt isolated without the use of his legs. Worst of all, he was resentful of everyone who was walking around doing just what they wanted to do, while he stayed inside struggling with the effort to do what he needed to do just to live. No theory or promise could change this reality.

I knew we had to start with acceptance; the word Gabriel hated the most. Acceptance was not a destination. It was a foundation, a beginning, and a runway for Gabriel's new take-off.

"What am I going to do?" Gabriel asked me as he pulled himself up from my treatment table one day and organized himself for the move from the table back to his wheelchair.

"I can't just keep throwing money at this thing," he declared, looking down at his legs.

"I am going to ask you to meditate on the word acceptance," I ventured, very tentatively, not sure how he would respond.

Gabriel looked at me from under the shock of dark hair that hung over his furrowed brow and I could see through his defiance to his pain. "Alright," he answered.

At our next meeting, Gabriel told me that he had tried holding Point 1 with Point 2 (see body map on pages 46–47), as I had once suggested. Holding these points, I had told him, would begin to energize his pelvis and send a message of engagement to his legs. While holding the points did not result in being able to stand up and walk, which was what Gabriel, of course, wanted to do, they did lessen the pain he felt constantly along the sides of his thighs. This was encouraging. He wanted to learn more.

Then Gabriel handed me a compact disc. "What's this?" I asked.

"It's my music," he answered, sheepishly, rather like a little boy who confesses that he likes to paint or color.

"I didn't know you were a musician," I countered, truly amazed that he had kept such an important secret.

"I don't know if I am, but I've played the guitar most of my life. I don't like to write words much, but sometimes I do, or sometimes I find a poem or something and put that into the music," was his response.

"I'll listen to this today," I told him, and I did. The music was incredibly lyrical, almost hypnotic, and it truly made my heart soar. I was stunned and delighted to experience this aspect of Gabriel. His music was a blessing in many ways. I honestly did not know if he would ever overcome his physical paralysis. But clearly, in this music, he had already overcome his spiritual paralysis.

Each time I saw Gabriel I asked him if he was making more music. He'd nod his head vigorously until the hair on his forehead bobbed up and down.

"You know your music speaks for you. It's amazing. I would even call it brilliant. I'm surprised you ever doubted your musicianship," I told him. "I honestly think your music is your new path, a new direction in your life."

"Maybe," Gabriel answered. "Maybe."

Both Gabriel and Ilana are continuing to study not only with me but also with others who can nourish Gabriel's essential energy. As he develops his musicianship, primarily for the peace, comfort, and fulfillment that making music brings him, he is able to acknowledge how grateful he is that he can play the guitar and use his voice. He has met others with spinal cord injuries that have lost these capacities as well as the use of their legs and other functions.

Gabriel titled one of his guitar instrumentals "Icarus." It was a recollection of his first bicycle ride. He has written songs dedicated to his brother, his uncle, his wife and other family members when he soars with the love he feels for those around him. Life has begun to feel rich for Gabriel Restrova, and that is why I know he has taken off from the runway of acceptance.

Your Right to Regenerate: How These Treatments Work

We have the capacity to fully regenerate from overwhelming experiences. In order to do this, we need the tools of energy medicine and a basic understanding of three major aspects of human functioning: physiology, neurology, and human energy fields. The fourth component for optimum regeneration is the one this book repeatedly underscores—self-knowledge and its twin, self-love. This last factor is the most critical ingredient in the regeneration recipe. Without it, the other parts are insufficient to produce the needed result of complete and lasting regeneration. Self-love leads inevitably to another essential ingredient in the resolution process. This is adequate time to integrate and reorganize yourself, on all levels, as you are made new by the healing process. This time is usually spent in restful reflection or in meditation, and often includes energy medicine treatment. In our busy, materialistic world, there is little value placed on integration, but to resolve shock, integration has a very high priority.

The process of resolving shock, from the TARA Approach perspective, first requires that shock be acknowledged and identified. Acknowledge-ment itself, because of the shift in consciousness and the differentiation between the past and the present it implies, encourages both reptilian and limbic neurological reorganization. The accompanying energy medicine treatment then restores the adrenal system directly, thereby healing the depletion that shock engenders. As one of my students said, "The TARA Approach gives me everything I need—a new perspective and the strength to embody it."

The combined shift in awareness and energy medicine treatment impacts the etheric body—the subtle body closest to the physical body. The etheric body, frequently referred to as the bridge between consciousness and physical manifestation, must release shock completely in order for a thorough resolution to take place. Everything in TARA Approach treatments works to meet all these objectives. In each case study in this chapter, the acknowledgement of shock is fundamental, as is the differentiation between the past and the present. The energy medicine treatments, which bring with them the practice of self-love and integration, communicate strongly to the etheric body that change is underway and old messages are being replaced with new ones.

An excellent demonstration of this process is Estrella Muñoz's story. For Estrella, the focus was on the fourth chakra and its energy medicine treatment corollary, Point 13, The Mother. (See the chart on page 107.) Another way to describe Point 13, which we have already called the Emotional Center and the Expressive Center, is as the Love Center. Estrella had been unconsciously trained to express her love through suffering. By touching her heart center with self-love and compassion, she reeducated this area of her body both physically and energetically. Her new message of respect and honoring overrode the previous message that was stored in her reptilian and limbic memory. The etheric body holds both intellectual and emotional memory. Shock speaks very convincingly to the etheric body, and the etheric body, in turn, translates its held messages into physical symptoms. Once the old message was completely gone from Estrella's heart and mind, her etheric body released the old belief.

Estrella, therefore, was speaking to her physical, neurological, and energy body self, all at once, when she held Point 13. "Can it be this easy?" you may be asking. The answer is yes. The p.s. to this answer is that you will likely have to repeat the steps in the healing process many times, including the energy medicine treatments, but the treatments will always work and their cumulative effect will always be transformative.

In the TARA Approach, there is a wonderful rule of healing that never fails to be useful: Always attend to the most dramatic and dominant need first. In Estrella's case, this was the pain in her chest. In Lonnie Delaney's case, it was his skin. Lonnie's treatment involved palming the calves of his legs. You may wonder how such a singular act can heal acutely irritated rashes and a lifetime of loneliness. The answer lies in several factors, all of which are silently condensed into the quality of touch used in Jin Shin Tara and the information about the vibrational field where the touch is applied.

The calves of the legs are an important meeting ground for several energy vortices, including the Bladder Meridian that, from an alternative perspective, is a pathway that rules memory. The Bladder Meridian's energy pathway goes directly to the basal ganglia and the reptilian brain. From there it travels to the frontal lobes. This route creates a channel of release, washing away obstacles to fluid presence. The combination of Diana's unconditional commitment to Lonnie and the energy field she touched while feeling this loving focus was the perfect formula to free Lonnie's skin to finally push out its long held expression of grief.

The polar opposite of loneliness is joy in relationships. Diana's touch, guided by my awareness of energy fields, opened Lonnie to a new experience and ultimately allowed him to replace the message of loss with a receptivity to joy. It is true that learning the meaning of the energy pathways, energy bodies, vibrational fields, and areas of the body so that you can use them to design similarly effective treatments will take some time. Virtually all of the fundamental information you need is in this book. It is also important to know that you can begin designing treatments from whatever level of awareness you have, and those treatments will always be potent and helpful.

The rule of dominant need also led to the treatment design for Rebecca Loveland. Rebecca's dominant need was to sustain positive self-contact and rebuild a healthy sense of self from the ashes of torture. Therefore, it makes sense that her treatment would involve Point 26, the point of self-love and self-acceptance. Point 26 fuels Fire Energy (see Chapter 7 to learn more about the elements), and that is exactly what Rebecca needed—to recreate her Spirit Fire. Rebecca also had to heal from the physical damage inflicted on her by her torturers. Her treatment was therefore also designed for this purpose. (See the following information about Gabriel Restrova's treatment to understand why I chose the points I did for this aspect of Rebecca's recovery.) Finally, Rebecca's femininity had been attacked and, holding Points 15 and 6 together sent a message of restoration to her pelvis and reproductive system.

Nedra's treatment for panic is, like the other treatments described in the "Shock is in the Moment" compendium, earmarked for the common responses to immediate and overwhelming events such as earthquakes, terrorism, sudden loss, etc. These treatments will work for any crisis and they will always be effective and useful. When you don't have a great deal of time to discover historical precursors to shock, and when the shock is in-your-face in its immediacy, these are the energy medicine treatments you want to use.

In the case of Gabriel Restrova, I had to prove to him that energy medicine could give him something he desperately needed—immediate pain relief. Gabriel had to have some hope that he could be pain-free long enough to find his way back to himself after his shattering accident. Fortunately, this was not difficult. Gabriel had already tried many things before I met him, and none of them worked as well as Jin Shin to relax him and lower his levels of pain. Thus Jin Shin Tara became a profound source of hope and empowerment for Gabriel. But the creativity that emerged from this hopefulness was purely a reflection of Gabriel himself. It is this kind of experience of emergent creativity that makes the challenges of working with shock and trauma more than worthwhile. Those of us who partake in the miracles of energy medicine are just midwives to the magnificence of the heroic human spirit.

Why are Points 4, 20, 21, and 22 so effective in the treatment of head injuries? One simple answer is that these points energetically relax all intercranial structures while stimulating the healing velocity of cranial sacral fluid. Several meridians and elements are put to work when these points are touched, including the Liver Meridian, the Stomach Meridian, and the Gallbladder Meridian. Both Gabriel and Rebecca, who received this treatment, were vigilant "doers." By surrendering these survival functions, they allowed their natural healing responses to take over. Their cranial sacral fluid washed over their internal wounds, and harmonizing energy calmed the intercranial structures that had been rattled.

In addition, for Gabriel, the treatment I used was designed to send supportive energy to his legs (Points 1 and 2). Gabriel's legs would need, as you might suspect, ongoing and consistent energetic support. Gabriel eventually became devoted to treating himself whenever he could. He had nothing to lose and everything to gain by doing so. His determination to walk was replaced with a determination to be healthy and to be all that he could be. This did not mean that Gabriel gave up the hope of walking. He just gave up thinking of himself as a failure if he did not walk.

In all of these cases, overwhelming, shattering experiences came close to making Estrella, Lonnie, Rebecca, Nedra, and Gabriel into victims. But by virtue of the powers of energy medicine, consciousness, awareness, spirit, and will, these individuals were not diminished by shock. Rather, they used their experiences to become more of who they really were and to shine as beacons in the world.

Section II

How to Heal

4 How to Use Energy Medicine to Resolve Shock

*Work out your own salvation. Do not
rely on others.*

—The Buddha

Now that you understand more about shock and can identify it, here are some of the energy medicine tools you can use to resolve it. These simple routines will stimulate neurochemical change, awakening neurotransmitters to help to free you from the residual tensions of shock. These basic treatments will regenerate tired adrenals and, most rewarding of all, you will find yourself experiencing unexpected new levels of creativity and enthusiasm.

Resolving shock with energy medicine is like weaving with energy or orchestrating inaudible, yet exquisite, music. Think of your hands as the instruments that link your mind and body, your past and present, your personality and spirit, and your heart and soul. Your hands already have intelligence. This practice will educate them further. They will readily become masterful communicators of unconditional love. When you become your own healer and know that healing yourself is your highest priority, you have already taken a giant step towards resolving shock. This step is one you can never turn back from. Now, whenever shock occurs, your brilliant hands will be ready to help.

Resolving shock means developing new neurological and physiological resources to replace the coping mechanisms that allowed you to survive shock, but of necessity, repressed essential aspects of your true self. These mechanisms, such as rigidity, resistance, defensiveness, aggression, resentment, workaholism, isolation, over-efforting, caretaking, withdrawal, and passivity, to name just a few, are no longer appropriate. Nevertheless, we continue to use them out of habit and conditioning, and because not using them feels too risky. In order to replace these worn-out responses with spontaneity and resilience, we need to clear the neurological channels that control our movements, voice, and action. Nothing does this more comprehensively than energy medicine.

When we follow the suggestions for self-care treatment contained in this chapter, we educate body and mind about the freedom to act and speak naturally and uniquely. This is how we let the genie of ourselves out of the bottle of past shock. The process of resolving shock is like self-mentoring. We teach ourselves that we can be anything we want to be. We teach ourselves what it means to be fully human, fully alive, and in the center of life. We do this by awakening the sensations and feelings of empowerment, inspiration, faith, and vitality that have been dormant in us as a result of shock. These sensations and feelings are stimulated and sustained by the practice of holding designated areas of the body while maintaining a focus on internal experience and pulse. This chapter will help you identify energy pulses and energy centers in your body.

The process described in this book has its source in traditional Asian healing arts. In ancient China, Japan, and India, physicians were able to locate areas on the body where energy is most easily awakened and balanced. The correlation of these areas with the symptoms associated with shock is one of the unique contributions of this book. In using these tools, we join Eastern and Western wisdom for conditions specific to this time.

Mary Iino Burmeister, the master of Jin Shin Jyutsu, was the first person to introduce me to the concept that the body is actually a map of potent energy points. Mary learned this life-changing information directly from Jiro Murai in Japan. He discovered this map when he was suffering from leukemia. He actually experienced the map in his own body as a highly charged personal awakening. He discovered that the map was part of a long-buried comprehensive healing system. After his own health was restored, Jiro Murai dedicated himself to unearthing everything he could find in relation to this system and revealing it to others.

Mary's mission was to bring this wisdom to America from Japan. For my part, I saw the map as a doorway to recovery from shock, and I have interpreted it for that purpose with extraordinary results. In sharing this system and its origins with you, I honor the lineage of transformation that I have adapted in the TARA Approach for the Resolution of Shock and Trauma.

Jin Shin is also part of a broader spectrum of healing intervention used in both the East and the West that fall under the umbrella of energy medicine. Energy medicine means treatment that is subtle, noninvasive, and attuned to the recipient's natural healing responses. Energy medicine encourages human evolution and maximizes the development of human potential, including our innate self-healing capacities. No matter what form it takes, energy medicine is based on our organic capacity to align ourselves physically, emotionally, and spiritually for the highest good and, thereby, to create our own personal definition and experience of health.

As a form of energy medicine, Jin Shin Tara has the specific attribute of being quintessentially a self-care system. No other form of energy medicine emphasizes self-care so adamantly. Always fundamentally empowering, Jin Shin Tara directs everyone to discover the healer within. Through knowing that we can address virtually all of our own health needs, Jin Shin Tara provides interventions for every conceivable disease condition. In designing Jin Shin approaches for shock, I have expanded the use of this remarkable tool for today's world. The TARA Approach, the integration of the hands-on subtle touch of Jin Shin Tara with a therapeutic use of language and the understanding that resolves shock and trauma, adds to our universal wealth of healing resources.

The Art of Self-care

The treatment routines suggested in this chapter call for a focused environment, especially at the outset while you are learning. Honor and support the process by creating time alone in the morning, evening, or whenever it is possible, to hold the recommended points. By giving yourself this gift, you can more easily attend to your sensations and feelings, and then to writing in your journal. This latter suggestion is one I would like to underscore.

The combination of self-care treatment with writing has been essential for me. Writing substantiates, memorializes, and validates internal experience. Writing also helps me follow my process, keep track of my responses, and learn from them. It is deeply therapeutic and self-honoring.

You can benefit the most from the extraordinary information in this chapter if you isolate private time for daily practice. An hour is best, but 15–30 minutes is good too. When more time presents itself, use it. Seize those moments and use them for your own healing. As you become more familiar with the material, privacy will not be as mandatory; but even then, it will be treasured and enjoyed.

The results of self-care treatment with energy medicine are cumulative. The more you treat yourself now, the less you will have to treat yourself later. After consistent practice, you will experience greater resiliency quickly, even after very brief self-care. Still, long periods of self-care treatment in solitude will always be deeply regenerating no matter how many years you have invested in this practice.

Look at the body map on pages 46–47 and familiarize yourself with the points/areas. You will learn how to treat specific conditions related to shock by using these areas in flows. A "flow" is a combination or series of points that you hold, focusing on balancing the pulse in two points at a time. You've already been introduced to some flows in the preceding chapters and you will find them referenced throughout this book. Do not be afraid to use any of these flows. You can even create your own flows by combining points however you like.

Whenever you are practicing self-care, sit comfortably and direct your awareness within. This is your time to be with yourself. If images arise while you are holding the points, notice them. If feelings and sensations dominate, be aware of them. Never disregard or judge your internal experience. All the while, you are paying attention to pulse—the rhythm and tone of your energy that you feel in your fingertips. Learn to be present for yourself, your wisdom, your vitality, your uniqueness, and your beauty. Remarkable healing will arise from this time of cultivation.

Pulse: The Rhythm of Life

Holding the points or areas designated for treatment with the fingertips or the palms of your hands feels like meditation. It's like listening for the sound of life with your sense of touch. Gradually, you may recognize a pulse in your hands, a rhythm that varies in tone, speed, or texture. It is important to differentiate energy pulse from blood pulse. Energy pulse is highly changeable. It responds very rapidly to temperature, contact, stimulation, and intention. Blood pulse has the unchanging quality of a throbbing and constant bass line. Energy pulse, on the other hand, is more like the guitar melody.

Reading energy pulse is called "listening to the secrets." It is an art in many traditional healing systems. In the treatments explored in this book, we learn when pulse is balanced and when it is unbalanced. We focus on the energy pulse we feel in the points and areas of the body. We will not learn to identify the meridian pulses here, though—that is part of this system and you may pursue it in further study.

Energy pulse that is balanced has a depth, tone, and rhythm that is resonant and full. When you feel this balanced pulse, you may spontaneously take a deep breath or sigh. Energy pulse that is not balanced may be pounding, thrusting, thin, erratic, electric, tingling, or almost impossible to detect. There is an endless variety of pulses. The study of all these different possibilities and the information they provide is fascinating. Pulse that is not balanced does not stimulate the relaxation response. Finding the difference between balanced and unbalanced pulse is central to learning how to read energy.

It takes most people some time to feel confident that they can perceive anything at all in their fingertips. In my own experience, there was a moment when I just knew that my perception was accurate. That moment was preceded by a period of confusion. However, despite my own hesitation, I got many confirmations from others and my own body and mind that my understanding of energy and pulse was correct. I want to share that encouragement with you. No matter what your age or history, something profound is initiated in your life when you touch yourself with subtlety, hear your own pulse, and understand its message to you.

As you begin to use your hands to experience the pulse of energy, focus on what you do know rather than what you do not. Some people can assess balance or disharmony without relating to pulse. You can feel temperature changes or even see colors when you hold the points or areas of the body. Don't hesitate to validate these other ways of perceiving energy. Give credence to your sensation and your intuition, and do not let yourself be discouraged by internal critical messages. In this way, you build your confidence in what you experience as sensation (body experience) and feeling (emotional experience).

Touch

To touch is to give life.

—Michelangelo

Let's clarify the meaning of touch in the resolution of shock and trauma. The touch that resolves shock is infused with the intention to do so. It is touch that listens to the voice speaking through the skin or connective tissue. Everyone has the capacity to listen with his or her fingertips to the whispering of the skin. Our fingertips are replete with nerve cells designed for this listening.

The skin responds to this caring attention and, by using the language of sensation, sends its messages directly to the brain through the spinal column. The spinal column is the highway on which sensation travels to signal neurological instructions for the body. Skin remembers all the ways it has been touched. Its reports are filed in the amygdala, an almond-shaped file box in the mammalian brain. When skin is touched with love, it reports that to the brain. When it is touched with unconsciousness or violence, it reports that too. In this way, the skin contributes to memory. Honoring the wisdom and consciousness of the skin with touch is like sending love letters to the brain.

Touch is transmission. The skin is an organ of learning, and touch is its teacher. The skin's education is instantaneous neural feedback. When we touch with unconsciousness, the skin goes into either sympathetic or parasympathetic shock. The former will produce rigidity, hypertonicity, and heat; the latter will make the skin flaccid, hypotonic, and cold. These qualities, in combination with pulsation or even on their own, give us very useful somatic information about resolving shock when we touch the sacred sites of the body. The touch that listens with love and respect, when practiced repeatedly, creates a memory of safety and acceptance that will eventually erase the sensations of shock.

The Sacred Sites of the Body

In this chapter, we will learn how holding two different areas on the body together helps us to resolve shock. I refer to these areas as sacred sites of the body because they are energetically potent. We hold these areas until the pulses in both of them feel balanced (resonant, full, and deep).

Some of these sacred sites or points on the body map are ascending and some are descending. All the descending points are on the front of the body and draw energy downwards. They pull energy from the head and chest into and through the pelvis, legs, and feet. These points are embodying or grounding. They awaken physical presence. Ascending points are all on the back and send energy upward. Ascending points stimulate motivation and inspiration. They generate ideas, enhance creative problem-solving, provide a vision of what we truly want to do with our lives, and illuminate how to proceed. We must feel both descending and ascending energy to know vitality. Descending energy and ascending energy are not separate from one another. They are one fluid movement, forming a constantly circulating oval of energy. In Chapter 2, I asked Leticia to experience this

The Chakras and Sacred Sites

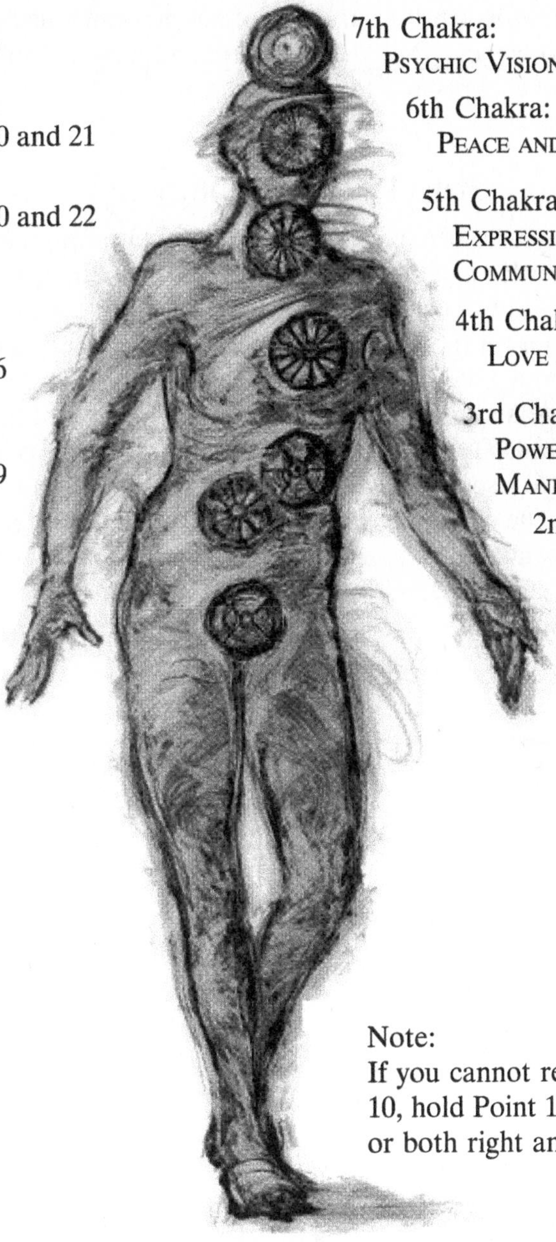

Point: 20

Points: 20 and 21

Points: 10 and 22

Points:
13 and 26

Points:
14 and 19

Points:
2 and 15

Points:
1 and 5

7th Chakra:
PSYCHIC VISION

6th Chakra:
PEACE AND CLARITY

5th Chakra:
EXPRESSION AND
COMMUNICATION

4th Chakra:
LOVE AND CREATIVITY

3rd Chakra:
POWER AND
MANIFESTATION

2nd Chakra:
SEXUALITY

1st Chakra:
SURVIVAL

Note:
If you cannot reach Point
10, hold Point 19 on either
or both right and left sides.

oval of energy so that she could feel embodied. I invite you to do this same visualization as a self-care practice. It will give you four things that are pearls of great worth for survivors of shock: containment, safety, integration, and wholeness. (See the illustration on page 107 for the connection between the chakras and the body map.)

Step Into Self-healing

The best way to learn about energy is to touch it, tap into it, experience it, and use it for healing. Place your fingertips gently, without applying any pressure, just beneath your collarbone. Put one hand on the right side and the other on the left side. These are both Point 22 (see below). Don't worry about holding the exact place. Nor do you have to worry about which fingers to use. You can use one finger, several fingers, or the palm of your hand. Try all the possibilities and find what is best for you. You may want to use different kinds of touch for different points and different flows. The most important thing is to feel at ease. Rest comfortably with your hands in the general area of Point 22 on the right and left sides, breathe, and notice your sensations.

POINT 22
WHOLENESS IN THE MOMENT
"BE HERE NOW"

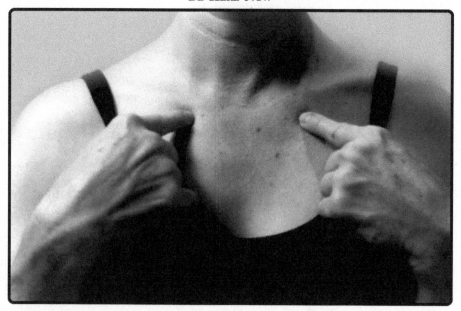

If you notice pulse, pulsation, or a rhythm in your hands, be aware of how it changes. When you feel that the right and left Point 22 have the same pulse or the same rhythm, release your hands and notice what you feel. This quiet time of noticing is important, so do not skip over it or rush through it. Remember that this practice is subtle. At first you may not notice anything, but the gift is what arises from this empty space. Writing in your journal is especially valuable at this time because it will support integration, particularly if you write freely.

Point 22 is called Adaptation or Wholeness in the Moment (see page 47 for the names of all the points). This area of the body has the capacity to awaken the feeling that everything is okay right now, no matter what is happening. Shock destroys that feeling. People who have experienced shock, especially multiple shocks, rarely feel like everything is alright in the moment. On the contrary, they are often looking for what is not right; vigilant about where the next shock might come from. Certain environments might increase this vigilance. If you have experienced shock, for instance, in a dark room, all dark rooms might increase this tension or they might hold the threat of shock happening again. The human body is conditioned by its original experience of shock to generate certain hormonal responses. Holding Point 22 in a moment of activation allows you to come out of that conditioned response into the present, and to feel and understand the shift in your system.

What happens to create this shift is that your adrenal glands behave differently in response to your touch. If you continue to treat yourself, your endocrine system gets the message that the original shock is over and that you can take care of yourself should shock happen again. You stop over-protecting yourself and protect yourself appropriately. Your muscles come out of their hypertonicty (tension) or hypotonicity (collapse). You feel the safety you create.

All the points on the map have a right and a left side position, and some have a central position, such as Point 13. Point 22 is descending, meaning it brings energy down the front of the body so that you can feel grounded and stable wherever you are. I hold this point whenever I travel long distances, particularly on planes. It is the "be here now" point and thoroughly prevents jet lag. When you hold these points, you may feel yourself letting go of distractions. You may discover a new alertness that includes seeing the purity and brightness of the colors around you, or seeing objects or people more clearly.

As a descending point that emphasizes coming into the present, Point 22 gives the power of focus. It reduces confusion to the simple knowledge of being present in the body. It helps us learn how to simply do one thing at a time, or to do nothing at all beyond being present. Along with this, Point 22 helps us to breathe more deeply, to drop our shoulders, to relax our jaws, and to feel our hearts.

Each of the points has its own function and purpose designed to allow us to recover our innate energy, strength, and inspiration for life. The easiest and most productive way to become familiar with the sacred sites of the body is to use the same procedure we have just employed for Point 22 for each of the points. Hold the right and left sides of each point, read the name of the point, notice whether the point is ascending or descending, and feel the effects in your body.

After you have done this with all the sacred sites of the body, you will feel rejuvenated, as if you have just had a complete "tune-up."

Experiments with energy medicine are all experiments with belief, self-validation, and credibility. Initially, there may be skepticism: Am I feeling sensation at all? Maybe that pulse would change anyway. Maybe that pulse is just the blood in my hands. How can my sensations help me remember who I am or empower me in any way? Awareness of sensation increases the more energy medicine is practiced. Pretend that you are a great artist and your feelings could lead to composing a brilliant sonata, painting a masterpiece, or writing a great poem. While you may have to pretend at first, this is truly the case. You are a great artist, and your work of art is your life. Do you notice that your feelings take on value when you allow them to be important?

Bring this confidence into your private treatment time. Believe in what you feel.

Palm Inju

Let's try another experiment with energy medicine. Bring the palms of your hands together as in prayer. (See illustration on page 111.) The palms are potent conduits of energy and can be used instead of the fingertips for any treatment. For this particular flow, the palms and the fingers must all be in contact and you may find that you need a slight pressure to strengthen this contact. Your hands can rest in this position wherever it is comfortable. Observe your breath. It may deepen. Notice your chest. It may expand. What else do you notice?

Simply letting the palms of your hands meet brings you into the center of your experience. This means you feel as though you are in charge. You make your own choices. I use the prayer position or Palm Inju whenever I speak to groups of people because I tend to be very influenced by their stories and their needs. One of the ways I survived shock was by losing myself in other people. I have shed this outworn and ultimately destructive coping mechanism through this practice. Whenever the old behavior resurfaces, I simply place my hands together and I am back in the center of my own life. The prayer position, or Palm Inju, helps me become a better listener without giving myself away. I can take my time answering questions when my hands are like this. It is a great way to listen to your children, especially when they become teenagers!

PALM INJU

PALM INJU

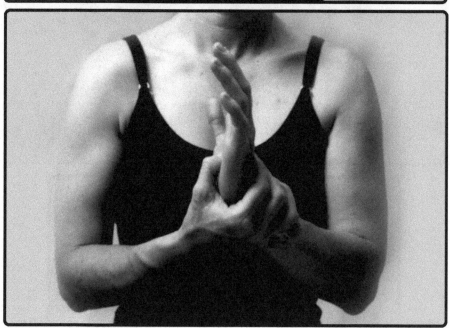

HOLD THE CENTER OF THE PALM OF THE HAND AND THE CENTER OF THE BACK OF
THE HAND TO COME OUT OF CONFUSION, DISCONNECTION, AND DISASSOCIATION

Flow

These treatments create the opposite of stagnation or stasis, which is flow. Stasis is a breeding ground for disease of all kinds. When energy is repeatedly stagnant in certain areas of the body, illness is the result. For example, the stagnation of energy in Point 22 can result in chronic shoulder tension, inflammation of the rotator cuff that allows the shoulder to move, constriction in the heart and chest, breathing difficulties, insomnia, hypertension, intense anxiety, and confusion. Flow dislodges obstructions, washing them away in a wave of energetic movement similar to the way a river frees rocks and pebbles from where they are trapped. That is why we call Jin Shin Tara treatment routines "flows."

Right or Left Side?

Flows can be done for either the right side or the left side, and some flows encompass both sides. How do you know which side to treat? There are many ways and all of them are valid. One is to close your eyes and focus your attention inward. Notice if one side of your body is darker or denser. That side needs to flow. Do you repeatedly injure one side? It is asking you for help, so give it a treat! It is also extremely effective to treat both sides of your body, and I recommend you do this whenever you have time. You will learn more ways to make this determination as you continue to study energy medicine.

Treating the right side addresses more immediate concerns such as those that have to do with our present living conditions and our present relationships. Treating the left side of the body focuses on past events and experiences. This difference between the treatment of the right or left sides applies to all the points and all the flows.

Flow Into Embodiment

Practice this flow whenever you feel unstable, numb, inattentive, dreamy, spaced-out, or tired. These states reflect both dissociation and parasympathetic shock. Remember the parasympathetic triumvirate from Chapter 2? They were the folks who became isolated and unresponsive in relationships. The Flow Into Embodiment is designed to dispel that trance like state and invite the present moment. The treatment described here is for the left side, but it can easily be reversed, point for point, to treat the right side.

FLOW INTO EMBODIMENT

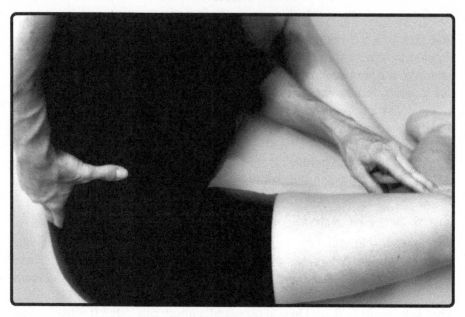

HOLDING POINT 2 AND POINT 1

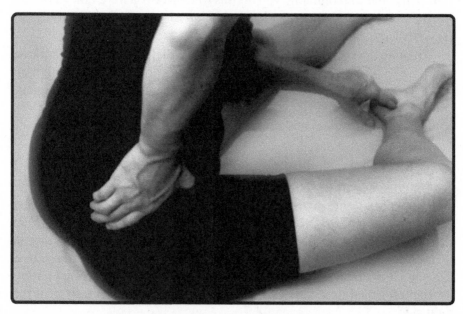

HOLDING POINT 2 AND POINT 5

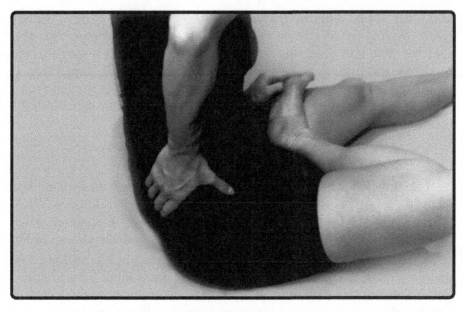

HOLDING POINT 2 AND POINT 7

Place one hand on the left lower back, just on top of the iliac crest and below the waist (see FLOW INTO EMBODIMENT illustration). Place the other hand on the inside of the left knee. Feel the pulse in these two places. You are holding Point 2 with Point 1. Hold these points until you have the experience of pulse balance—the relaxing sensation that accompanies feeling deep, resonating pulses in your fingertips. Now, move the hand that was on the inside of your knee (Point 1), to the inside of your left ankle (Point 5). Wait comfortably until these pulses become resonant and harmonious. Perhaps your eyes are closed. You are focused inside—on the pulses in your fingertips, your breath, and yourself. When you experience balance in these two points, move the hand that is on Point 5 on the ankle to the left Point 7 on the base of the big toe, on the sole side of the foot. Now, wait for these pulses to balance. Congratulations! You have completed the basic energy medicine treatment for embodiment. Embodiment is the antidote to dissociation.

Frieda's story illustrates an example of shock leading to dissociation. Her father committed suicide by shooting himself in the room next to hers, when she was a child. Despite years of very effective therapy, Frieda still dissociated whenever she heard a sound like a gunshot, such as a car backfiring. By holding the points in the Flow Into Embodiment, Frieda could stop the process of dissociation each time it happened. This also gave her time and space to use tools such as self-talk to distinguish the past from the present. Eventually, the activation ceased completely. If Frieda was extremely tired and stressed, she was more vulnerable to reactivation. But by holding the points again, she could quickly come into the present and take care of herself.

Flow Into Integration

Use this flow whenever too much is happening in your life and you feel like you are being pulled in many different directions at once. When shock occurs, we lose the capacity to sort things out. We cannot make choices for our own best interests. In fact, we cannot make choices at all!

The feeling of being overwhelmed is like being in a crowded room where everyone is talking at the same time and you want to have a conversation with just one person. It seems impossible to hear anything clearly. Use this flow to come out of the noisy room and hear yourself.

The Flow Into Integration treats the right and the left sides of the body simultaneously. Place your right hand on the center of your chest, on your breastbone. Place your left hand in the center of the base of your skull. (See illustration on page 117.) These are central points, rather than bilateral points. You are holding Central 13 (on the chest) and Central 4 (at the base of the cranium). Wait for the pulses in these points to balance, as we have previously discussed. You will feel deep, resonating pulses in your fingertips, and you may find yourself sighing or spontaneously breathing more deeply. If these experiences do not occur, just wait and they will. When this happens, remove both your hands and cross them in front of your chest. Your thumbs will rest on the inside of your upper arms, and your other fingers will rest on the outside of your upper arms. These are the right and left High 19.

You are now waiting for these four areas to come into energetic balance, which will be revealed to you through the experience of pulse in your fingertips. When this happens, release your hands. Now, hold your ring finger and then your index finger on your left hand. Next, hold your ring finger and then your index finger on your right hand. Just hold the entire finger, letting it rest in the other hand easily. When you hold fingers, the energy pulse is felt in the palm of the hand where the finger rests. This completes the Flow Into Integration. Take note of the shifts in your sensations and your feelings.

FLOW INTO INTEGRATION

STEP ONE: HOLDING CENTRAL 13 AND CENTRAL 4

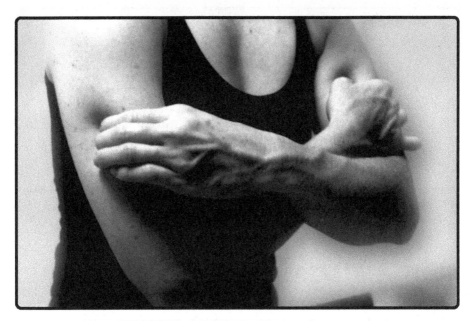

STEP TWO: HOLDING BOTH HIGH 19S

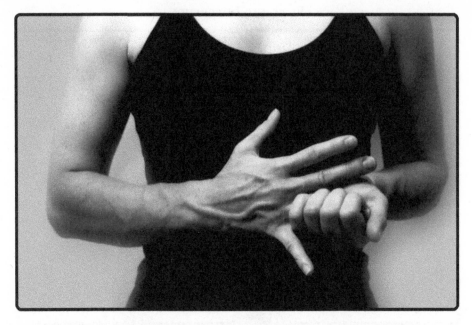

STEP THREE: HOLDING INDEX AND RING FINGER, RIGHT HAND

STEP FOUR: HOLDING INDEX AND RING FINGER, LEFT HAND

Flow Out of Panic

Survivors of shock feel panic quite readily, like Nedra who experienced the Northridge Earthquake. Remember how different her reaction was from her son's and her husband's? This difference was shaped by their different histories. The more unresolved shock in one's background, the stronger the reactivation by a new shock.

Driving on the freeway, being too close or too far away from someone, certain times of day, or seasons of the year can all evoke panic for someone who has not resolved the shock in their lives. Panic is very physical. It frequently includes agitation in the stomach and chest, tightness in the throat, sweating or feeling very cold, constriction anywhere in the body, rapid blood pulse, tensing of the jaw, shaking, and crying. Imagine the joy of knowing that you can come out of a panic response into a calm, steady feeling in your body. The following treatment does exactly that. This is the treatment Nedra learned to do over the telephone. It is repeated in several places in this book because of its potency and usefulness.

This flow is designed to provide treatment for both the right and the left sides simultaneously. It involves the use of only two points: Point 24 and Point 26. Consult the pages 46–47 to locate these points. Point 24 is on the top of the foot, between the fourth toe and the pinky toe. This flow will feel better if your shoes are off when you do it. If for some reason that is not possible, the flow will still be effective.

Point 26 is on the back at the outer edge of the armpit near the bottom of the shoulder area. You begin by holding Point 26 with the opposite Point 24. (See the illustration on page 120.) It does not matter if you begin with the right or the left Point 26 or Point 24. Once you feel the definite sensation of balanced energy pulse, you reverse sides. Repeat this until you have completed the flow by holding both sides three times.

Whether the shock you have experienced is immediate or it has been held in your body for a long time, this flow will change the physical experience of panic into calm. This flow should be taught at all crisis centers and to all emergency workers, along with the other information in the compendium "Shock Is in the Moment, Healing is Forever" in Chapter 3. These are miracle interventions! They alleviate trembling and shaking, and instantly erase the feeling of terror that overtakes the mind in the midst of panic. The powerlessness that is associated with the experience of shock is displaced by a natural flow of smooth energy that leads to clear functioning once the compressed energy of the shock response is released. This is something that animals do naturally by shaking until they

FLOW OUT OF PANIC

HOLDING OPPOSITE POINTS 24 AND 26, BOTH SIDES

come out of shock, but human beings often need more than that because we hold accumulated unreleased shock responses in our bodies unconsciously. Just knowing that there is a way to release held shock and immediate shock, changes forever the dread of being thrown helplessly into panic.

Flow Into Intimacy

Shock will manifest dramatically in relationships. You will know that you have healed a great deal of suffering when you are able to have completely intimate, truly nourishing, and mutually satisfying relationships that are committed and enduring.

Holding two points, 22 and 14, on the same side, not only heals relational shock, it simultaneously strengthens lung capacity. Asthmatics or anyone with breathing difficulties will benefit from this flow. Several people in this book illustrate the healing of relational shock, such as Lonnie Delaney in Chapter 3.

FLOW INTO INTIMACY

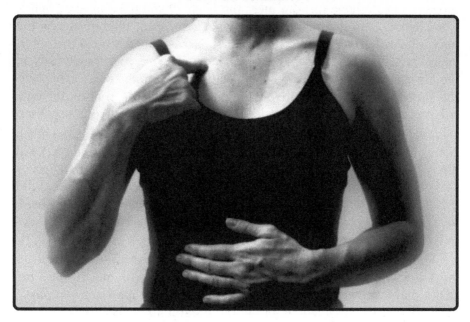

HOLDING POINTS 22 AND 14 ON THE SAME SIDE

The Flow Into Speaking Up and Out

When you can finally verbalize what you have always longed to say but have held back, a refreshing, almost magical feeling of vitality results. You will find the energetic encouragement you need to express yourself fully in the Flow Into Speaking Up and Out.

The simple expression of personal truth is silenced in shock. Neurological overload caused by the complete absence of resources in shock, in combination with fear and panic, makes verbal articulation virtually impossible. In this book, I frequently use the phrase "conditioned shock responses." This refers to the reactivation of the neurology and physiology of shock because an environment, a season, a time of day or tone of voice, or someone's appearance stimulates the body's memory of shock. If we want to be free of shock's shackles, it is our job to educate our neurology (and thereby our physiology) that this memory belongs in the past. The present is a new reality full of infinite possibilities. This flow supports neurological education and its manifestation through articulation that marks the moment as new.

The Flow Into Speaking Up and Out involves only two points, though actually your hands are contacting four areas, and each one of them is significant. Locate them on your map: the High 19 and the opposite High 1. The High 19 is in the middle of the upper arm. Your thumb rests on the inside, medial area and your other fingers are wrapped around the outer, lateral area. The High 1 is on the thigh. Similarly here, your thumb rests on the inner area and your other fingers fall naturally on the outer area. (See the illustration on page 123.) Hold the points on one side, wait for them to balance, and then treat the other side. Take the time to notice your responses.

My favorite healing memories are stories of speaking up. I see so much power and maturity brought into focus by clear, honest articulation. I will always remember the time when I was working as a therapist for an agency that served people with physical challenges. I conducted groups and did private individual sessions for people who were paraplegic, head-injured, deaf, and blind. I taught them a variety of tools to enable them to live independently, including Jin Shin.

One day, after a group session in which I taught the Flow Into Speaking Up and Out, a participant asked to talk alone with me. He told me that a staff member, the person who was actually my supervisor, was physically abusing the disabled people in the program. He also knew that she was using drugs at work. She had threatened to take away the privileges of anyone who told about her violations.

I held the points in the flow as I talked to the director of the agency. The hearings, meetings, group therapy sessions, and confrontations that followed demanded that I, as well as the agency's clients, maintain the capacity to speak up. We had to keep telling the truth and answering questions, over and over. My supervisor denied the charges. She was a charismatic and convincing person, and she vehemently resisted admitting her violations.

In the end, truth prevailed. In the group therapy conducted after my supervisor was dismissed, the clients at the center revealed that because of practicing the Flow Into Speaking Up and Out, they saw that this entire process made them examine their self-worth. Being physically challenged, they realized, did not mean they were less than whole. They discovered that they had the right to protest and that they would be heard. The use of this flow helped us all.

The Flow Into Speaking Up and Out also clears the throat, eases tightness in the chest and in the pelvis, and lets nervous butterflies take flight from the stomach.

FLOW INTO SPEAKING UP AND OUT

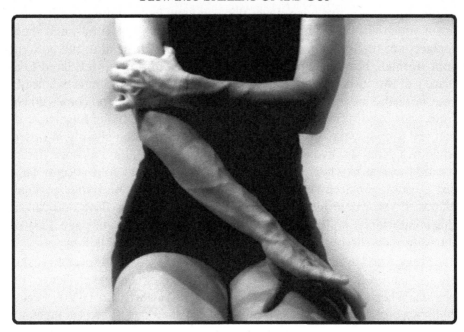

HOLDING HIGH 19 AND OPPOSITE HIGH 1

Flow Into Rest

In Chapter 2, we discussed sympathetic and parasympathetic shock in detail. When sympathetic shock dominates, and adrenaline is rapidly and frequently discharged, rest is elusive. Insomnia, agitation, anxiety, hypertension, hypervigilance, and apprehension are common, even regular, states. The Flow Into Rest changes these reactive, habitual patterns by balancing adrenal gland functions. Longer than most of the other treatments given here, the Flow Into Rest is best done in the morning and in the evening when you are lying down in bed. It is a central, comprehensive flow, addressing many conditions at once. It has provided many restless adults and children with peaceful sleep, and it has allowed many in distress to face the day calmly.

Begin the treatment by placing the palm or the fingertips of your right hand on the very top of your head. Place the fingertips or the palm of your left hand in the middle of your forehead. Wait for the sensation of balanced pulse, and then move your left fingertips to the tip of your nose. After pulse is balanced here, move your left hand to the "v" of your collarbone, at the base of your throat. When there is resonant pulse here, move your left hand to the breastplate. Your right hand has been resting on the top of your head this entire time and will remain there until almost the end of the flow. If you are lying down this can actually be quite comfortable, but if your right hand feels cramped, move it and shake it out, and then replace it at the top of your head. Now move the left hand to the base of your sternum, between your lowest ribs. Finally, move your left hand to a place just two inches above your bellybutton. When this point is balanced, your left hand moves to your pubic bone and your right hand comes down from your head to touch the base of your coccyx with your fingertips. If you are lying down, you may have to shift your position slightly in order to do this. You may even choose to turn on your side. Find a comfortable position to rest in while you hold your pubic bone and your coccyx. This last position is extremely important for the tonification of your adrenal glands. If you would like to increase the potency of this flow, and can do this comfortably, hold Points 15 and 6 (see illustration on page 128) on the same side (first one side and then the other) for completion.

Peggy, who has been a student of the TARA Approach for over 10 years, attests that this flow has made it possible for her to accept the challenges of her life. When she discovered that her youngest daughter was HIV+, Peggy entered a prolonged period of shock. This flow allowed her to rest at night, to face the pain of her child's diagnosis, and to gather the strength and the fortitude to be present for her daughter, her family, and herself.

FLOW INTO REST

STEP ONE: RIGHT HAND ON TOP OF HEAD, LEFT FINGERTIP ON FOREHEAD

STEP TWO: MOVE LEFT FINGERTIP TO TIP OF NOSE

STEP THREE: MOVE LEFT FINGERTIP TO "V" OF NECK

STEP FOUR: MOVE LEFT FINGERTIP TO CENTER OF CHEST

STEP FIVE: MOVE LEFT FINGERTIP BELOW STERNUM

STEP SIX: MOVE LEFT FINGERTIP ABOVE UMBILICUS

STEP SEVEN: MOVE RIGHT HAND TO PUBIC BONE; MOVE LEFT HAND TO COCCYX

Flow Out of Sweet Cravings

The desire for sugar can be an outcome of the physiological sequence of events involved in sympathetic shock. When the adrenals have been forced to fire, or repeatedly secrete adrenaline due to ongoing threat, this behavior becomes habitual. The feeling of being highly alert and primed for action becomes a lifestyle rather than a physiological strategy reserved for necessary defense. Survival seems to always depend upon maintaining an aggressive, excessively vigilant state. Sugar sustains this pattern. Shock survivors develop hypervigilance as part of their choice to live. The art of resolution means restoring a balanced capacity to respond to threat and that may mean eating much less sugar.

There is a supportive interaction between the Flow Out of Sweet Cravings and the Flow Out of Addictions (see page 129). Use them together. The Flow Out of Sweet Cravings traces the beginning route of the Stomach Meridian, just as the Flow Into Intimacy traces the beginning route of the Lung Meridian. Hold Point 21 and Point 22 on the same side to Flow Out of Sweet Cravings. Choose the left or the right side, or treat both sides. Notice what happens to your jaw as you hold these points. Your forehead may soften, shedding worry furrows. Be aware of how your eating impulses change.

FLOW OUT OF SWEET CRAVINGS

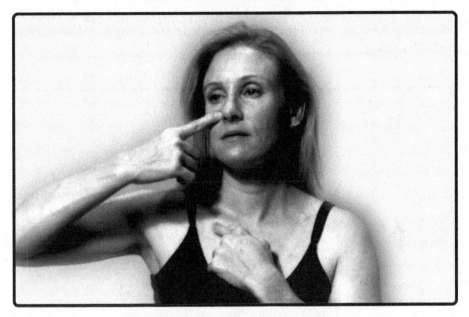

HOLDING POINT 21 AND POINT 22 ON THE SAME SIDE

Flow Out of Addictions

Like sweet cravings, all addictions can be the result of shock. Addictions are acts of anger against oneself. No one suffers more profoundly from addictions than the addict. I consider addictions to be virtual acts of suicide, despairing anger, and helpless self-violation, all as results of shock.

The Flow Out of Addictions consists of holding Point 14 with the opposite Point 19. Look at the illustration to see that this flow creates a protective field for the center of your body. This area is also known as your Third Chakra, or your Power Chakra. (See The Chakra and Sacred Sites chart on page 107.) Addictions steal our power, just as shock does. Coming into and holding your power or energy for yourself, and using your power to grow stronger, as we do in self-care, is the antidote to the self-hatred evidenced by addicts. This flow can be done on either side or both. It is easily accomplished in a variety of public situations, and so it can be used whenever it is needed. Like all the flows, you can practice this one as frequently as you like.

I do not mean to imply that this flow alone will work to stop a serious addictive pattern. But it is both a great place to start and a great flow to maintain when you are employing all the help you can find to stop using and start living.

FLOW OUT OF ADDICTIONS

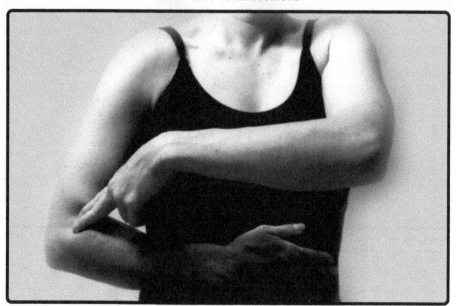

HOLDING POINT 14 AND OPPOSITE POINT 19

Flow Into Self-acceptance

How can you embrace and accept yourself when you are disconnected from yourself? How can you hug someone who is not energetically there, who is disembodied? We literally lose a sense of self in shock and become accustomed to being lost. The longer we are separated from ourselves, the harder it is to find our way back to wholeness. The sooner we begin the quest for integration, the sooner we find our way back home. No matter what your age or the amount of shock you have experienced, a profound reorganization is initiated when you begin to touch yourself with the intention described in this book.

The Flow Into Self-Acceptance is the one that turned things around for both Rebecca Loveland and Estrella Muñoz in Chapter 3. You reclaim yourself in the experience of this flow that awakens the energetic sensation of being fully accepted, in the moment, exactly as you are.

FLOW INTO SELF-ACCEPTANCE

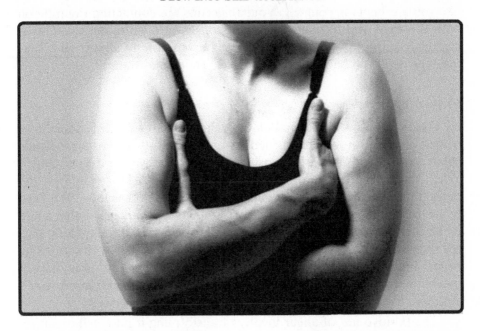

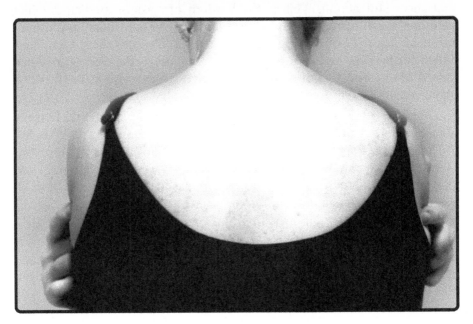

HOLDING RIGHT AND LEFT POINT 26

As the illustration on page 131 clearly demonstrates, this flow looks like you are hugging yourself. Your fingertips are contacting Point 26 on both the right and left sides, simultaneously, in a self-embrace. This is clearly a central flow. Self-acceptance is the antidote to almost all suffering. This flow will benefit all survivors of shock and trauma.

Flow Out of Anger

Anger is a much-maligned emotion. In the Flow Out of Addictions, we talked about how anger turned inward can result in substance abuse. What we lack, culturally, is a positive and creative way to express anger. When shock occurs, and anger arises, we frequently have to suppress the natural outrage and protective impulses that course through us. We have to use incredible discipline to prevent outbursts from emerging that could make the situation worse. However, we prolong this strategy, long past the time when shock is a real threat. We become identified with supressing anger, and push the remarkable force of anger's energy into some part of our body where we hold it unconsciously. These pockets of unexpressed emotion, in turn, block the smooth flow of healthy energy.

The positive use of anger involves transforming it into well-organized and successful action. This is the wisdom of astern medicine, which identifies the Liver and Gallbladder Meridians as the rulers and harmonizers of anger. Thus, the Flow Out of Anger references these meridians. When we harness and reframe anger, we repattern the energy of shock stored in our bodies and empower ourselves to act with strength when shock occurs in the present.

The two points for the Flow Out of Anger are Point 16 and Point 6. These points balance and strengthen the expression of anger in our muscles. By holding these points, we make it possible for our bodies to move forward or away, to stop violation, and to shout No! when appropriate. Hold these points together on the same foot, releasing either the left side, the right side, or both (see illustration on page 133).

It is important to note here that this flow is not the only Flow Out of Anger. I have chosen this one because it is the most effective in the most generalized way. Similarly, for the other flows, there is always more than one flow for each situation, and if you choose to continue to investigate this system, you will learn the many options available for treatment.

FLOW OUT OF ANGER

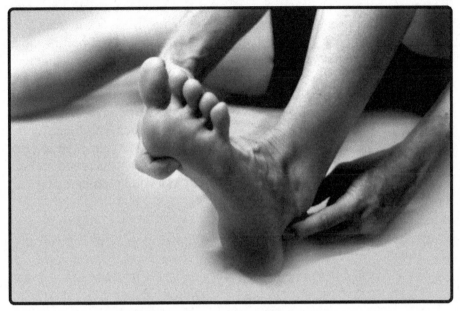

HOLDING POINT 6 AND POINT 16

Flow Out of Headaches: Fingers, Toes, Hands, and Feet

There are at least as many reasons for headaches as we have fingers and toes. Certainly, headaches are not unique to survivors of shock. I include a comprehensive treatment for headaches here because they are common responses to shock. Headaches are strong messages of distress. For people who experience migraines, headaches mean it is time to stop and go inward. If shock has occurred, a migraine allows you to retreat. In this regard, they are an unconscious survival strategy.

Headaches can also signal shock from environmental pollutants. If you think this is the source of your headaches, investigate what and where that pollutant might be, and protect yourself.

Headaches can also signal emotional overload. Very few people can ignore a headache. The treatment that is suggested here is comprehensive and can address virtually every conceivable reason for a headache. By holding the fingers and toes one at a time, you provide yourself with an extraordinarily thorough treatment. You energetically stimulate, release, and tonify all the meridians.

The treatments shown here are simple and practical, but they also invite you into a world where you have the power, through your own hands and your own awareness, to completely resolve shock in your body and to prevent shock from doing extensive damage when it occurs. Obviously there are many more treatment possibilities. This book is intended to provide help for the most common manifestations of shock. You can receive further training in The TARA Approach, if you choose, to tap into the vast number of possibilities energy medicine offers for healing from shock and trauma. Through your own experience with touching the points, you can also create your own flows to expand your repertoire of treatment possibilities. Feel free to share what you have learned and developed with others, and encourage them to join you in self-care and self-healing.

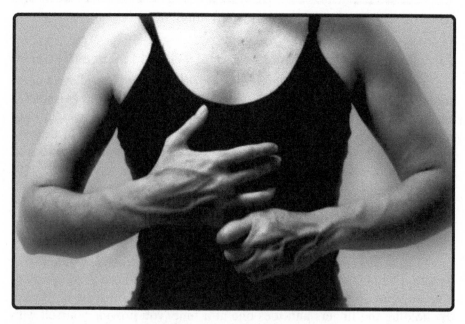

HOLDING RING FINGER OR LITTLE FINGER OPENS CHEST, ALLOWS EXPRESSION, FREES GRIEF, AND RELIEVES HEADACHE

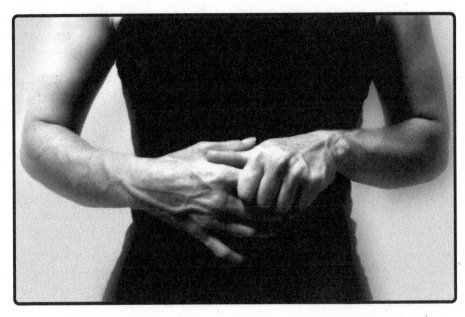

HOLDING INDEX FINGER RELIEVES HEADACHE CAUSED BY FEAR

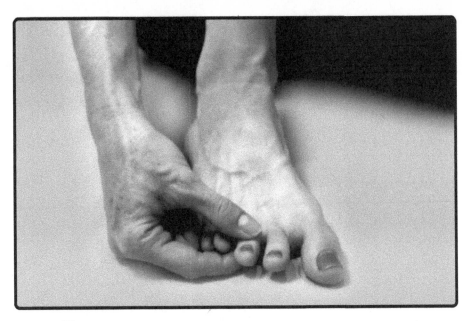

HOLDING MIDDLE TOE RELIEVES HEADACHES CAUSED BY ANGER

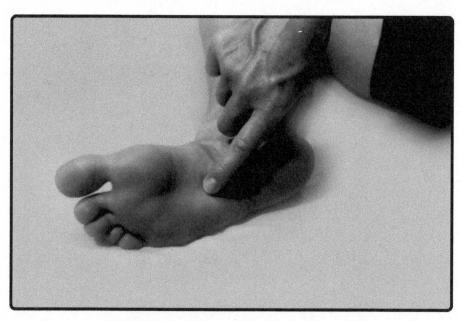

HOLDING CENTER OF PALM OR SOLE OF FOOT
RELIEVES HEADACHES AND NAUSEA

Treating Others

You may be surprised to discover that it is easier to treat other people than it is to treat yourself. In the many years that I have been sharing energy medicine and teaching people how they can heal themselves, I have consistently heard reports about this. Compassion, respect, safety, and presence heal shock. Sometimes these are more readily available to others. However, using the information provided in Chapter 2, be aware of sympathetic and parasympathetic activation when treating others. Notice skin tone, expression, body movements, and language. Be sensitive to the needs of the person in shock, and be attentive to how you are responding to them. Notice if you are being activated yourself. Shock tends to be contagious. Stay out of shock yourself. Do your best to create sacred space for yourself as well as the person you are assisting. The Palm Inju, previously described, is an effective tool for doing this and can be used at the beginning and ending of treatments.

Always ask permission before you touch anyone and make sure they are comfortable. If you are invited to touch, hold the same points on someone else that you would hold on yourself. The flows that you have learned in this chapter can be applied either as self-care or as treatment for someone else. Trust what you feel when you work with others just as you attune to and trust what you feel in your own body.

The pulses you feel with your fingertips can direct you to specifically address either sympathetic or parasympathetic shock. If pulse is erratic, quick, thrusting, and hard, it suggests sympathetic shock. If pulse is barely discernible, reluctant, or slow, it indicates parasympathetic shock. Sympathetic shock calls for calming contact and descending, grounding flows. The Flow Into Embodiment, for instance, would be an excellent choice. Parasympathetic shock calls for ascending flows and the encouragement to express feeling. The Flow Into Speaking Up and Out can be used for the treatment of parasympathetic shock. See the guidelines for reversing sympathetic or parasympathetic dominance on page 60.

Particularly, in circumstances of immediate shock, you will find yourself treating in many diverse situations. I have treated people on buses, street corners, in hospitals, on the ground, and even on a trampoline and in an ice-skating rink. If someone is lying down for treatment, be sure that you do not stand above him or her. Seat yourself at the same level as they are so that you can have eye contact and feel equal. There is real intimacy in treatment, and this can either be soothing or it can be threatening.

Make sure you feel safe being close to someone when they are looking directly at you. You also need to be sensitive to how much distance is necessary for the other person to feel comfortable. The more you respect the other person's needs, the safer they will feel. Do not only intuit their needs, but also inquire into their experience with genuine interest and believe what is said.

Treating children has some special requirements. Be prepared to become a storyteller when you treat children. I encourage my students to cultivate stories for this purpose. They can be traditional fables and myths and/or stories developed from life events. Practice telling these stories to children expressively and see how it captivates them. Storytelling is what makes it possible for children to hold still longer for treatments.

Never force children to lie still for long periods of time for treatments. It is unnatural for them. It is wiser to follow them around and treat them as they move about. Similarly, do not make children endure the holding of points that feel uncomfortable for them. Keep your touch light. Be playful. If you are treating your own children, treat them as you tell bedtime stories, snuggle, or after they fall asleep.

See Chapter 5 for more detailed guidelines on what to say when treating children. My book, *The Dreaming Child: How Children Can Help Themselves Recover from Illness and Injury,* provides specific treatments for children's needs as well as story examples. The bibliography also cites excellent books to help develop storytelling skills like *Once Upon A Story* by Jean Grasso Fitzpatrick and *It Doesn't Have To Be This Way* by Luis Rodríguez.

All human beings have the capacity to serve one another. The closeness and love we feel when we come together in this way is our birthright. It is shock that makes us withhold our capacity to be helpful to one another. Be generous and conscious in your offering of service and feel confident that your touch, combined with your wisdom, will always be healing.

5 Language and the Voice of Healing

> *The knowledge of word meaning is not stored in the brain as a separate, compact module. Different aspects of word meaning are distributed in close relationship to those aspects of physical reality which they denote.*
>
> —Elkhonon Goldberg

Recent neurological studies indicate that language is understood throughout the brain, and cognition is an aspect of the physical experience and personal history we have with words. The neural blueprinting that shows us how language is processed also tells us that speech awakens the memories associated with the words we use. When we use language in the healing process, our intention is to be sensitive to neural responses and, when necessary, to open new possibilities with the voice of healing.[1]

Think of words as seeds going into the soil of the brain, replacing the ruts of old thinking with new root structures. As shock resolves, a harvest of new mind-food feeds unique, inventive possibilities for problem-solving. Shock resolution, through insight and action, awakens dormant or sluggish neurochemicals that foster creativity. A neurological description of this process would say that state-dependent or "conditioned" dissociations stop when the memories attached to words change.[2] When creative and knowledgeable self-talk is combined with hands-on treatment (an integration that you will soon find you can accomplish), deeply destructive patterns shift markedly and eventually are completely eliminated. This is evidenced in all the real-life studies in Chapter 3, as well as those in this chapter, especially Karen's.

There are two ways of using language that we will focus on in this chapter. One is self-talk. The other is the use of language in helping others resolve shock. The latter includes what you need to know in an immediate crisis or when shock occurs for those around you or those who seek your counsel.

Resolving shock with your own self-talk is the most potent medicine there is! The more you resolve your own shock, the more effective you will be in helping others. But healing self-talk demands that you carefully observe yourself and notice how you are replicating and repeating patterns formed by shock.

Negative self-talk is one of the ways we use language to perpetuate shock and trauma. It cuts deeply into the tender geography of the brain. It is nourished in the isolation of rejection and abandonment, or it reflects what is or was directed toward you by others. It must, and certainly can be, dismantled and discarded. This chapter shows you how to use language as medicine to stimulate neurotransmitter support to first mute and then permanently end the self-sabotage that perpetuates shock conditioning.

The marvelous neurochemicals that stimulate feelings of being comfortable in our bodies (primarily dopamine and serotonin) are initiated at crucial developmental periods early in life. Any circumstance that robs us of the loving contact we need dampens our neurochemistry.[3] To awaken it, we must give ourselves concentrated doses of self-love through language and touch.

Self-deprecation limits our social interactions, interferes in our most intimate relationships, and blocks professional development and intellectual acuity. It fills the pool of shock that will overflow unless it is consciously and carefully drained. Self-sabotage is the dull background static we must clear to calm our frightened basal neurology and make way for our neocortical awakening. Because self-criticism is such a primary response to shock, we have to be persistent to uproot it.

Loving self-talk is not only the repetition of affirmation, it arises out of a sincere relationship with yourself. It counteracts patterns of self-blame by bringing them into the light of consciousness. The process is as simple as, for instance, noticing that you are berating yourself for not doing everything you said you would do on a day when you are very tired, and then changing your inner commentary accordingly. For instance, you could see the humor in your long lists, or you could give yourself permission to cut your lists in half or even be "listless." This is the practice of being your own best friend. It will clear your brain of the neurological backfiring that separates you from your essence and from the world.

Language can either enforce conditioned shock patterns or change them. You need to make the choice about how you use language in your relationship with yourself and others. Otherwise, shock and trauma will make the choice for you. Authentically positive self-talk is your most important ally in the healing process. You cannot heal completely without it. No matter how well you may communicate with others, you must make transformation happen inside to reap the lasting rewards of resolving shock.

Develop the Compassionate Inner Witness

The first step is to develop an inner witness. An inner witness is an aspect of you that neutrally watches, listens, and pays attention. Cultivating an inner witness is the preface to life-changing self-talk and using the voice of healing. It is a necessary development for your own healing, and it is also a crucial ally in your work with others. The witness provides the alternative to obsessive reaction by identifying the behaviors that resulted from shock and developing new and healthier forms of protection. Once you can do this for yourself, you and your inner witness become gifted in assisting others to do the same.

It is through the capacity to witness that the lineage of self-inflicted hostility ends. It ends with loving awareness. The witness establishes a bond with the truth rather than to the lies shock forces upon us. The cycle of violence stops with each one of us, in our own bodies, when we end our personal violence against ourselves. Mindfulness is the lifestyle of the compassionate witness who presents us with this startling paradigm shift: You do not have to believe your thoughts![4]

The inner witness is devoted to awareness and self-reflection, and is thoroughly compassionate. In fact, the key to finding the voice of healing is compassion. Compassion is not knee-jerk sympathy or feeling sorry for anyone, especially yourself. It does not interpret or analyze. It does not strategize or plan, though it is the seedbed of inspiration. Compassion is seeing with consciousness. The compassionate witness can and will see the true origins of behavior and invoke the power to change.

What is compassion? "Compassion practice is daring," says Buddhist nun Pema Chodron. "It involves learning to relax and allow ourselves to move gently towards what scares us. The trick to doing this is to stay with emotional distress without tightening into aversion, to let fear soften us rather than harden into resistance."[5]

An example of compassionate, witness-driven self-talk comes from my experience writing this book. I was working on a chapter and I kept feeling that I wasn't writing well at all. Then, after putting the writing aside for a while in disappointment with myself, I picked it up again and read what I had written. Suddenly, I saw clearly that because my words were infused with strong intention and purpose, most of the writing was good. My witness showed up to reflect on the entire process. I saw that what had made me feel discouraged was an old habit of not feeling like I could ever do anything well enough. This habit originated with my father's constant dissatisfaction with me. I had long ago learned that his punitive attacks were not about me, but about his own pain. Yet, the habit of beating myself up had continued. My witness awakened compassion and acknowledged my work, and I soon found myself writing with gusto, faith, and enthusiasm. In this very consistent practice of witnessing and compassionate self-talk, we first mute and then dissolve inappropriate and inaccurate self-criticism until it no longer arises. This weeding process assures that the self-evaluation that is compassionate and that stimulates evolution and development continues to serve you because it is not self-destructive.

The compassionate witness is neither the victim nor the rebel. The witness arises from the frontal lobe, the higher brain, and is nursed by the nourishing neurobiology of love, which I spoke of in Chapter 2. The wise witness silences the desperation of the reptilian brain and thereby reorganizes and reframes memories of shock stored in the midbrain. The more self-care you do, particularly to regenerate adrenal function, the stronger the witness becomes, until you merge completely with it, integrating higher (neocortical) awareness into all your actions and speech, at every level of your life. Then, even if shock occurs, it can be sustained and integrated by your nervous system and your neurology because your higher brain is in charge.

Following are some examples of the voice of healing used in a variety of circumstances, modeling both self-talk and language for others. They reveal how natural it can be to end the lineage of shock.

Parents and the Voice of Healing

Monica was born with a severe cranial deformity. After repeated surgeries on her head and her face, she was declared cured. However, the impact of seven surgeries in the first seven years of her life took a heavy toll. At eight and a half years old, she was very shy. She rarely made eye contact or engaged directly with others. Her favorite play activity was hiding.

Monica could really scare her parents by hiding from them for long periods of time. Her mother became frantic each time she couldn't find Monica. Once, when the family was travelling, Monica managed to hide so well that her parents called the local police in the small town they were visiting. Monica was under a table draped with a long cloth in a bookstore the whole time, watching the drama and waiting for the outcome.

At school, Monica spent most of her time hiding behind something or someone. Once the principal of the school had to be called because all the other children had gone home and Monica could not be found. She had fallen asleep while hiding in an alcove-like structure in the library, behind a large stuffed bear. Monica's mom was anxious whenever she went anywhere with her daughter. She was concerned that her hiding would result in some kind of catastrophe. Maybe a stranger would find her and kidnap her. Monica's behavior was arousing her mother's deepest fears. She was almost ready to put her child on a leash when she came to talk to me about her frustration.

Interestingly, when Monica was conceived, her parents were not planning to become pregnant. It took a long time for Monica's mom to acknowledge that she was pregnant and not just missing her menstrual cycle because of stress. Then, Monica's parents argued over whether they should abort her. Though they did not consider themselves ready to parent, they finally decided to continue the pregnancy.

When Monica was born, her cranial deformity was apparent. Her misshapen head influenced everyone's first response to her. For years, Monica had been seen over and over again by medical staff. They sedated her, prepared her for surgeries, and wheeled her down hallways as passersby cast worried looks her way. She was brought to meetings of doctors and interns as a sample of cranial anomaly. Therefore, she was always being seen for what was wrong with her, but she was not seen when she needed to be. Often, when Monica would emerge from surgeries, she would find herself alone. Though her parents rushed to her side as soon as they were given permission, they did not insist on breaking the rules and seeing Monica immediately after surgery. She was, therefore, frequently abandoned at crucial moments, and her drugged state added to her terror.

Monica's dominant response to the shock she had experienced was parasympathetic, evident in her hiding. Her mother, conversely, responded with her sympathetic nervous system, and became so agitated that she disabled her higher vision. Parasympathetic and sympathetic nervous system responses are survival strategies. To understand how shock works it is necessary to understand these two dominant responses. (See Chapter 2 for a thorough discussion of sympathetic and parasympathetic shock).

In therapy, I asked Monica's mom to focus on the joy of discovery rather than her frustration. I encouraged her to say, each time she found Monica (and while hugging her), "There you are! I am so happy to find you. It is wonderful to see you." I asked Monica's mom to feel as if she were seeing her daughter for the first time each time she found her again.

The words "I am so happy to see you" were focused on reversing Monica's entire history of shock. Simultaneously, through the contact between mother and child, neurochemicals and endorphins were stimulated that would allow Monica to feel, in her body, the joy and comfort of being here and being wanted. Probably the most charged word in the phrase I suggested was the word "see." Through repetition and contact, we were neurologically repatterning Monica's "state dependent" or shock-conditioned relationship to that word.

The phrase "I am so happy to see you" worked miracles for both mother and daughter. The words were Mom's deepest truth. Repeating them opened her heart to the joy she felt that Monica had made it, having survived abortion ideation and horrific surgeries. For Monica, the same words were empowering. She had, albeit unconsciously, been waiting to hear them. By the time she was 12, Monica did not hide in any way. Quite the contrary, she was ready to come fearlessly into the world and be seen.

The Voice of Healing Essentials

This story reveals some of the basic elements in the voice of healing, with a special emphasis on the role parents can play.

1. Know the difference between sympathetic (aggressive and actively defensive) and parasympathetic (withdrawn and passive) activation and use the tools specific to each (see Chapter 2).

2. Use physical contact appropriately while speaking.

3. See the whole picture. Feel and read the messages behind behavior and respond to those messages.

4. Parenting brings with it the challenge of self-reflection so that we do not project our own problems and needs onto our children, but rather see them as separate individuals. The poet Kahlil Gibran said this exquisitely: "Our children are not our children. They are life's longing for itself."

As a reader, you may wonder how you can find the exact words to resolve shock. I know that everyone has the capacity to do this. Intention and practice will ultimately make you masterful at finding your own voice of healing. Until then, it is helpful to just sit quietly and ask your inner witness, your higher self, or your guides, guardians, or ancestors for help in finding the most beneficial words.

Helping Others Resolve Shock

The most valuable thing you can convey to someone reeling from the impact of shock is that they have the resources to recover. What are resources? Resources are what you do and feel to come into direct contact with who you really are, such as meditation, writing, prayer, communing with nature, or talking with a trusted friend. Resources awaken your sense of self when it is asleep or missing. While primarily internal, resources include the external world.

Resources stimulate a feeling of grounded presence. They encourage the natural mind-body-environment connection. Resources are worth *more* than gold. They are the manifestation of your unique life force. They are your sanctuaries. Each time you connect with your resources, you come out of shock. My resources include energy medicine, dancing, writing, reading, meditating, hiking, my friends, and my family. Everyone can have a long list of resources. If you don't, it's time to build such a list, and use it.

Karen's story demonstrates that even when you think you have nothing left, you cannot lose your internal resources. Ultimately, your resources become your guides, gifting you with problem-solving skills and the inspiration and motivation to move out of entrapment and into your uncharted, exciting future. Obsessive shock-driven patterns have a known dependable quality. Living free of shock and using your resources to shape your direction means living freely.

The events in Karen's life forced her to separate from her assumed resources: her neighborhood, her friends, and her family. To survive emotionally and physically, she would have to change both her residential location and her career, thereby redefining virtually *all* her resources.

She was the one person in her community willing to stand up and tell the truth when a priest abused her. She had to become herself or she would be sentenced to a life of disabling illness.

Karen's parents had struggled with alcoholism, so her childhood had not been happy. After leaving home she turned to the church and religion for comfort. The church, and spiritual practice, brought her great joy. Her connection with a particular priest was a special source of delight because Karen felt she could really confide in him. When he abused her, her whole world fell apart. All the pain of her childhood returned. What made it worse was that no one in the church community believed her. Everyone chose to avoid her. She not only lost her special confidante, who completely denied her accusations, she also lost her friends. Within a year following this, Karen became ill. Her health deteriorated so rapidly she had to stop working and live on her savings.

Karen's life history seemed to reveal almost a complete lack of resources. Her parents were not a resource because of their alcoholism. Her siblings had inherited their parents' patterns so they were not resources. Karen was alone. The real question to ask was what had helped Karen become the strong, outspoken, persevering, courageous, and fun-loving person she was?

Karen's illness was a response to not only one incident, but to compounded shocks. One shock after another had cumulatively assaulted her nervous and immune systems. The experience of abuse in the church was not the causative factor behind her collapse; it was the final factor that completely undermined her.

Karen's physician recommended antidepressants, but they made no difference except that they slowed her down even more, and she gained 15 pounds! This further lessened her self-esteem, and added to her deteriorating health.

As has been emphasized many times in this book, the adrenal glands are the first part of our endocrine system to respond to shock. Simultaneously, their health is the key to immune system strength. When stresses are added to already overburdened adrenals, the immune system is undermined. (See Chapter 2 for more information on the role of the adrenals in shock.) Karen's path to recovery had to include the strengthening of her immune system through a variety of interventions (nutrition, subtle energy medicine, and exercise), as well as crucial changes in her relationship to herself. Her task was daunting. To recover, she would have to not only reform her lifestyle and eating habits, but she would have to uproot herself from her toxic environment.

I asked Karen what had allowed her to cope with her erratic and unpredictable early home life. Immediately her eyes lit up and an adorable smile spread across her face. "My grandma," she said, without a moment's hesitation. The light that came into Karen's face was the signal that we had found a core resource that had to be cultivated to end the pattern of shock repetition in Karen's life.

Karen's grandmother, who had been dead for almost 10 years, had sensed her early suffering. She had also believed in her granddaughter's uniqueness and her ability to transcend what she felt powerless over. She had encouraged Karen, both directly and indirectly, to follow her heart and her truth. Grandma's eye contact spoke volumes of support to the sensitive, receptive little girl. Grandma wrote Karen notes on paper into which she had pressed dried flowers, and she gave her gifts, all of which were scented with Grandma's special floral aromas. Karen kept all these notes and gifts in a beautiful box. This relationship was stored so deeply inside Karen that it was overshadowed by the more recent overwhelming betrayal.

What I said to Karen was less important than what I encouraged her to say to herself. The keywords Karen needed to hear from herself was "believe" or "I believe in you." She had been invalidated as a child and as an adult. Now, through her own self-talk, she had to validate herself. By saying to herself, "I believe you," she invited her survival instincts (her reptilian brain) and her adrenal glands (the first shock absorbers) to relax their overworked, defensive postures. It is amazing how much safer and less desperate we are when we know that we are believed and supported. I suggested to Karen that she consider her grandmother an ally and call on her for help during this difficult life transition.

When Karen thought about invoking her grandmother's presence, she felt embarrassed. She thought it was really odd that the only person she could find to rely on for support was dead. She did not know that calling on an ancestor who really knows who you are, at the core, is traditional in many cultures.

"You have the right to remember your ancestor and invoke her," I assured her. "It is an ancient way of recovering from loss and finding the guidance to move ahead in life.

"Think of the Tibetans whose prayers always include a lineage chant, or the Dagara people in Africa who ritualize their recognition of those who came before, or the Mexicans who celebrate the Day of the Dead.

They have an ongoing awareness that our ancestors are always with us, guiding and supporting us. Ancestors are an essential resource and they want to be used as such."

I encouraged Karen to reexperience in her own way the loving energy her grandmother had directed toward her. I asked her to do this daily, for a minimum of 15 minutes a day. This meditation on the resource of her loving ancestor helped build a foundation for Karen. Having been so enmeshed with the shock of being an outcast, she had lost track of the wonderful feeling of acceptance that she always felt with her grandma. Karen came out of shock slowly and surely. It took almost a year, but Karen was able to physically leave behind those who did not believe her and create a new life elsewhere that was based on her commitment to herself.

Later, I asked Karen if she would share some of her meditation experiences with me. She said that during her communion she would ask Grandma to say what she loved about her. Grandma had replied, over and over, that the most precious things about Karen were her spirit, her will, and her humor. The genuine truth of these observations allowed Karen's heart to relax. Her dangerously high blood pressure lowered to a normal rate. She changed her eating habits and lost weight, thereby reversing the onset of adult diabetes. She gained the strength to turn away from what was hurting her and to take the risk of moving towards the unknown.

Of course, Karen also learned how to give herself energy medicine treatments, but these alone would have been insufficient to fuel her metamorphosis. It was not surprising that as Karen changed internally, she eventually brought into her life people who saw her for who she really was and gladly included her rather than cast her out. Her own voice of healing, even when it reached into the past for resources, summoned her future.

Use the Voice of Healing to Build Resources

How can you know what to say to help others build their resources? Here are some clues:

1. Inquire into the experience of survival from shock and trauma. How was it made possible? Ask what actions immediately followed a shocking or traumatic experience. Frequently, the responses to these questions will provide clues about resources. Reinforce these resources verbally.

2. Notice how facial expression or movement change as people talk. Whenever someone brightens or becomes enlivened, a core resource has been touched that can be cultivated and nourished. Mirror this back with words.

3. Suggest the use of resources whenever shock is activated. Shock is so thoroughly overwhelming that resources can be forgotten completely in the face of shock.

4. Make a list of resources and post them where they can be accessed easily at any time.

5. Tell your resources to your trusted friends and ask them to remind you of them, especially when you need them the most.

6. Make resource-building an ongoing part of life. Never stop building your resources and encouraging others to do the same. Remember to add your new resources to the list you keep posted.

Laughter Is the Sound of Love

What place does laughter have in the resolution of shock and trauma? Laughter is both a healing response in itself and a healing resource physiologically. The movement of laughter through your body stimulates the secretion of those neurotransmitters that will wash shock from your nervous system. Think of a baby laughing in response to the joy she sees in color, light, and in the eyes of her loving admirers. This gurgling laughter is the antidote to shock. How can you bring laughter into your own healing from shock or use it respectfully with others?

First of all, laughter has to be authentic. The brain responds to authenticity. The thalamus and the corpus callosum thrive on experiences of comfort and genuine connection. The shock of being lied to by those we thought we could trust early in life, or even later on, is erased by repeated experiences with your own honesty. The person you can trust the most is yourself. When you really smile into your own heart, then you become your best-humored companion! When you laugh at your own failings, you gain the capacity to laugh away the manipulations of others.

Humor is not always an appropriate response, but it is the safest catharsis and a loving release. It takes true compassion to bring humor to an experience of shock. An authentic healing process will inevitably lead to both humor and forgiveness. As we resolve pain, it is easy and natural to find humor and joy in life.

The most articulate testimony to the way humor and laughter can heal is in Norman Cousins' beautiful book, *Anatomy of an Illness.* The dramatic recovery that Cousins experienced from a disease described as "progressive and incurable" he attributed to "the chemistry of the will to live." One of Cousins' self-directed treatments was laughter. He holed up in a motel room (so as not to "disturb" the other patients in the hospital) and watched one comedy after the other. He healed completely. The only additional intervention was large doses of vitamin C.[6]

Mr. Cousins concludes: "I have learned never to underestimate the capacity of the human mind and body to regenerate—even when the prospects seem most wretched. The life force may be the least understood force on earth. Protecting and cherishing that natural drive may well represent the finest exercise of human freedom."[7]

The Voice of Healing Laughs

Pay attention to laughter. It is like water—fluid and cleansing. Each time you hear laughter, each time you laugh, let the energy of laughter come into your body. Let it in like a massage from a trusted masseuse. Let laughter into your tissues and your joints. Don't turn away from it. Make space for it. Prolong your laughter. See how it makes your whole body move, like dancing. Laughter has the ability to disperse congested muscular tension and to aerate compressed, dense thinking. Look at the faces of laughing people. Smiles make everyone incredibly beautiful.

Let your laughter meet your self-criticism. Can you find the humor in what you dislike most about yourself? When you laugh at your most detested characteristics, you will have found a remarkable, regenerating key to the resolution of shock. In even the most frightening and threatening moments, this key will open a door to freedom.

I do not talk about laughter as a resource for shock resolution casually. I know that it can feel offensive to suggest laughter in the context of horrific suffering. Sensitivity and timing are essential. My appreciation of the role of laughter is hard won. Remember that the laughter I am talking about is never belittling or minimizing. The laughter that heals resonates with wisdom and joy. It opens the backdoor to the heart and invites your resentment to dance itself out.

Listen to Rick's story to see the truth of this. From his earliest years Rick had wanted to be an actor, or some kind of performer. His favorite childhood activity was dressing up and doing comedy and song and dance routines for the imaginary audience in his mirror.

His mother had a nervous breakdown when her son was 11 years old. By the time his family admitted the severity of her condition, Rick's mother had brutalized him. His face was permanently scarred from the burning and beating she had inflicted on him. What is this story doing in a section on laughter? Believe it or not, it was Rick who taught me about the power of laughter to heal.

The lower part of Rick's face was marked with scars and his jaw was permanently rotated to the left. It wasn't until he told me about his mother, though, that I actually noticed this. What I was always drawn to when I was with Rick were his eyes. They sparkled with laughter.

Rick attended one of my workshops in Mexico. Because these programs were residential, the students and I had evening time together. In April, when Rick participated, the heat was pervasive during the day. We were all thrilled by the coolness of the evening and came together over pungent meals, eaten outdoors on the patio.

The Mexican people are famous for their sobremesas, or after-dinner talk. They sit together for hours after the meal to share stories, sing songs, enjoy each other's company, and laugh. On one of these nights, Rick showed us how he used to trick his mother when she was on a rampage by impersonating different people. He would become first one person and then another, hiding and emerging from different parts of the house until she was thoroughly confused and would retreat to her room, unable to catch him, unable to identify or find him. Thus, on some occasions, he was able to avoid being hurt. Rick played the characters he performed as a child and he imitated his mother's responses as well, doing a one-man show that was hilarious. We laughed so hard, the tears ran down our cheeks.

Rick's ability to be so lighthearted about his suffering was the reward of his many years of healing. He lightened all of our hearts that night in Mexico, under the bright moon, with mariachi accompaniment in the distance. Rick taught me that profound resolution of shock is possible through the power of love and laughter.

How to Incorporate Joy, Humor, and Laughter Into the Voice of Healing

Wit is the only wall between us and the dark.
—Mark Van Doren

1. Say something surprising, with a twinkle in your eye.

2. Watch comedies, or listen to recordings of funny stories to learn the rhythms of humor.

3. See the people you dislike or who hurt you wearing funny costumes.

4. Laugh at your own mistakes, such as spilling things or losing your keys.

5. Tell a funny story about something that happened to you to others and enjoy *their* laughter.

6. Do a puppet show or read a story to a child. Be as expressive as possible.

7. Make a list of whatever makes you smile or laugh. Do whatever is on the list as often as you can.

The Marriage of Voice and Touch

When the voice of healing joins forces with educated touch, the result is the resolution of shock. This remarkable combination, which is available to everyone, is all that is needed for healing.

The best demonstrations of this combination happen in the treatment of children. Whenever I treat a young child, I include storytelling. These are "healing stories" because they are designed to completely relax the child and awaken a natural healing response. The stories I tell are usually spontaneous and reflect my intuitive sense of what will relax each child the most. Relaxing a child often means delighting them!

To develop your own fluidity in storytelling, you can read great stories, such as myths, and practice telling them aloud to whomever will listen. Or, you can find books of stories in your own religious, regional, or ethnic tradition. There are many wonderful collections of folk tales from virtually all the countries of the world. These stories will acquaint you with the rhythms of storytelling and will stimulate your own creativity.

You can also practice by writing or telling stories from your own life. Pay attention to what holds the interest of your listeners and what makes them become more and more receptive. Use this almost hypnotic state in a positive and respectful manner to introduce healing concepts and possibilities, and your listener will do the rest.

An excerpt from "Tumors are All the Colors of the Rainbow," a chapter in my children's book, *The Dreaming Child: How Children Can Help Themselves Recover from Illness and Injury*, illustrates the potent formula of healing voice plus touch perfectly:

A few days after his first operation, James was resting in his hospital room. His favorite nurse, Ginger, came in. Ginger always had a big smile on her face, but this morning she stood by James' bed with a furrowed brow and a frown.

"What's the matter, Ginger?" James asked.

"Your face is covered with hives. It must be a reaction to the medications," Ginger said. "Will you let me hold the calves of your legs?"

James and Ginger always had fun together. Ginger knew a lot of special games, like the war between the good germs and the bad germs, so James trusted her even though she said things that nobody else did. James believed Ginger, sometimes even more than he believed his mom, his dad, or his doctor.

James was 10, and Ginger was a lot older than that, but somehow when they were together, James never felt like he was with an adult. He felt like he was with a friend who had really good ideas. Her red hair and sparkly bright eyes made him feel like he was with a very special person. Most important to James, Ginger listened to EVERYTHING James said.

Ginger dragged a chair over to the foot of the hospital bed, pulled up the sheet from the bottom and put her arms through the bars of the bed. She placed the palms of her hands on the calves of James' legs and asked him how the war between the good germs and the bad germs was going.

Her hands felt cool and James took a deep breath as soon as Ginger touched him. He hadn't realized how lonely he had felt since he came out of surgery until Ginger's angel eyes and tender touch were present.

"The good germs are definitely winning," James answered, "but one bad germ just went back into my body a little while ago. I couldn't seem to keep it out."

"What shall we do about that?" Ginger asked.

"Let's go get it!" James answered, a warrior's electricity raising his voice.

"Get the submarines out!" Ginger countered, thrilling to the battle.

"Find that bad germ!" James gave the command.

"Have they found it?" Ginger asked after an interlude suitable for search, find, and attack.

"Mission successful," James responded. "And it's a greenie."

"Well, what are you going to do with it?" Ginger asked, forcefully and pointedly.

"Destroy it," James replied, without hesitation. "Torpedoes ready."

As the torpedoes blasted off, shattering that green germ to smithereens, James noticed that he felt cooler all over, not just on the calves of his legs which had been burning hot. Little trickles of sweat dripped from his armpits, and he heaved a sigh of relief.

"Good work," Ginger said, withdrawing her hands slowly, and standing up to look at James' face. An entire half an hour had gone by, but it seemed like just a few minutes. James was tired.

"Good work," Ginger repeated, her face softening as her eyes scanned James' body. The hives were slowly losing their puffy quality, and the color in James' face was changing from flushed to rosy.

"What color is your tumor now?" Ginger inquired. She was the one who had started the process of examining the color of James' tumor from James' point of view. Ginger had noted James' report on the color of his tumor matched the results from the tests. The darker colors always reflected a worsening of the tumor; the light and brighter colors indicated improvement.

"Dark purple," James reported, "but getting lighter and lighter all the time."[8]

In this story, the interactive relationship between the courageous and attentive nurse and her creative and insightful young patient, combined with educated language and touch, lessens substantially the shock of hospitalization and invasive treatment, including surgery, radiation, and chemotherapy. The willingness to bring play and storytelling into this life-threatening intensity comes from a deep commitment to healing potential.

How, you might wonder, can the average person cultivate such a perspective? Isn't it extremely difficult to focus on both touch and language at the same time? Don't you have to be a masterful healer to be able to do this? The answer is no to both questions, but there is some training you can do on your own to easily integrate voice and touch.

How to Make the Magic Mix: The Voice of Healing Plus the Touch of Love

1. If you want to add storytelling to your treatments, you can, as mentioned earlier, find transformative, healing stories and read them, taking in the theme, focus, and intention of the stories until you get the idea yourself and can make up your own. You will find some resources in the bibliography.

2. Practice your original healing stories on any willing listeners, notice their responses, and adjust your stories accordingly until you become a natural. Children are the best audience for honest feedback.

3. If you are shy to enter the role of storyteller or to just be expressive and dramatic, notice how much healing happens when you are. People love it! Of course, storytelling is not required for the integration of touch and language, but consciousness of the healing function of words is. Awaken this consciousness by paying careful attention to how people respond to the language you use.

4. The more easily your language flows, and the more the voice of healing becomes *your very own* voice, the simpler it will be to orchestrate the combination of touch and language. You will not have to think about what you say, and that will free you to know what areas of the body to contact to promote energetic change.

5. Familiarity with the map of the body will educate your hands, freeing your healing voice.

6. Language flows from intention, as does touch. When your intention is clarified, this integrative healing approach will be dynamic, fluid, unique to every situation, tailored to the needs of the recipient, and completely natural.

Treating Immediate Shock and Treating Shock From the Past: Using Language for Differentiation

Shock from the past is restimulated when a new shock happens, so the more you have resolved your own residual shock, the more valuable you are to others when shock occurs in the present moment. If your compassionate witness and higher brain are directing your life, you are far less likely to be disarmed by immediate shock. The speed of immediate shock demands that your skills be innate, such as differentiating past from present.

Language is an essential way to differentiate past from present. When you are successful in communicating this difference, you make it much easier to come out of shock quickly. Naming resources is a sure way to do this. For instance, you can remind yourself or others of a resource they did not have when the original shock occurred, such as the capacity to physically move away from a toxic influence, whether human or environmental. You can also mirror someone's resources back to them by noting how expression or skin color changes when contact with a resource is made. Or you can recall the resources that allowed them to survive and express gratitude for them. Karen's story demonstrates this and additional examples follow.

Discerning sympathetic from parasympathetic shock should be virtually instantaneous, and interventions must be employed without a moment's hesitation when immediate shock occurs. This includes the voice of healing. This story demonstrates these crucial aspects of treating immediate shock.

My husband came home much later than expected one afternoon, his face looking unusually pale and distracted. "What happened?" I asked, with concern. He told me that he had just been in a car accident and that he could hardly move his head or his neck.

His white coloring revealed that he was in parasympathetic shock. I knew that when he was younger he had been in a severe motorcycle accident that almost cost him his life. I sensed that the shock from that experience had been reactivated.

I asked him to lie down on the bed on his back. I was able to help him release the tension in his neck and at the base of his cranium by first touching the right and left Point 12, holding the two together, and then the right and left Point 4. (See illustration.) As I gently made this contact with him, I asked him questions about how the accident happened. When he answered, I carefully pointed out the differences between his earlier near-death experience, and this less severe accident at every appropriate opportunity. One difference was the availability of subtle energy medicine as a resource to help him immediately after the accident. I encouraged him to express gratitude for his minor injuries, along with reminding him of the gratitude he had felt for surviving the previous accident. This juxtaposition of past and present helped him to differentiate the two accidents.

But what Bob really felt was rage at the other driver who had caused the accident. He wasn't ready for the gratitude yet. "What do you want to tell her?" I asked.

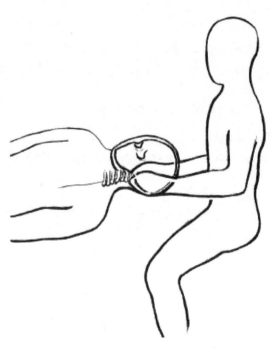

HOLDING RIGHT AND LEFT POINT 4

"I want to tell her she was stupid and unconscious. What she did made no sense, and then she just drove away, completely unaware of what she caused."

It made perfect sense that Bob was angry about this and I encouraged him to say it aloud and let it go, so that he did not have to carry this anger in his body. After all, he was here now, and he was going to be okay.

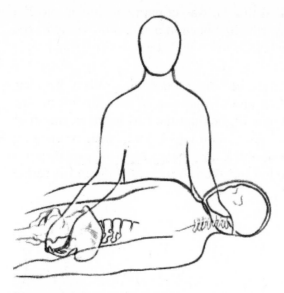

HOLDING HEAD AND TAILBONE

That was a blessing. As we had this conversation, I felt the tight rigid knots unwinding in his neck. I moved to hold the middle of the base of his cranium and his tailbone. The pulse in my hands told me that energy was restored to his spine.

Later, when Bob went to see his chiropractor, she remarked on the lack of trauma in his vertebrae. She said she had never seen anyone who had regained resiliency so quickly after an accident. Addressing his injuries so close to the event made an enormous difference in his recovery. When Bob happily reported his chiropractor's comments to me, I reminded him again of how different this accident was from his earlier one that had required years of rehabilitation.

Drugs are not always necessary.
Belief in healing always is.
—Norman Cousins

Jeanette and Jay had a promising new relationship. They were excited about their upcoming holiday in the mountains. They would have a few days to themselves and then friends and family would join them for a relaxing week of hiking and sharing. It was early summer. The warm sunny days were inviting and romantic. They started packing Jay's camper late in the afternoon, and it took much longer than they expected. Nevertheless, they were eager for their getaway and left very early the following morning, despite getting little sleep. Jeanette snoozed as Jay drove in the exquisite light of sunrise. The highway was free and clear and a CD of happy road trip songs put a broad smile on Jay's face. Every once in a while he would glance to his side to see his sweetheart. The world was innocent and open, and the best was yet to come.

Jay kept smiling as he slowed down for the stalled truck in front of him. His smile left only when he was rammed from behind by another vehicle, pushing him into the stalled truck. It all seemed to come out of nowhere, suddenly changing this summer of love into a summer of shock.

Because none of the emergency personnel could detect the subtle differences in Jay and Jeanette's responses to this tragedy, they were treated in ways that increased rather than decreased their escalating shock levels. For instance, they were unnecessarily sedated. Jeanette almost died as a result of their failure to perform a blood transfusion in a timely manner. No one had encouraged them to express their feelings about the accident. When I saw them 10 days later, they were functional, but they were functional in shock. Highly competent people can mask shock, but it continues to damage them.

It was clear that Jeanette was in sympathetic shock and Jay was in parasympathetic shock. I encouraged Jeanette to focus thoroughly on her own needs rather than assuring everyone else that she would be alright. On the other hand, Jay repressed his anxiety and withdrew. Deeply introverted, he concluded that no one could bear the complexity of his feelings. I drew him out and asked him questions about his feelings until he felt safe enough to tell his truth.

The use of subtle energy medicine in the treatment of accident shock is remarkably helpful. Physically, it stimulates immune and anti-inflammatory responses. Spiritually, it brings a sense of internal organization and centrality to someone who has been invaded and scattered by powerful outside forces. Most importantly, it lifts the mind-fog that is the hallmark of shock.

The language that accompanied the energy medicine that I used for Jay was focused on freeing him from the guilt he felt as the driver. Jeanette, on the other hand, was intent on taking charge, organizing everything around her to compensate for her fear about the magnitude of her injuries. I used eye contact to empower her to slow down and feel her true physical state and honor it. This was a much more realistic way for her to regain her strength. Both of them learned to treat themselves with subtle energy medicine and self-talk.

One year after the accident, Jeanette and Jay were pain-free and reclaiming their romance and their careers. Neither of them had used antidepressants. This is in dramatic contrast to the statistics on the frequency of post-traumatic stress disorder and severe depression for survivors of auto accidents such as the one Jay and Jeanette experienced.[9]

This story is not meant to disregard the life-saving interventions of the emergency crews that help people after accidents. It is only meant to suggest additional interventions that can be included to add even greater value to their services.

Checkpoints for the Treatment of Shock in the Moment and the Appropriate Use of Language

1. Provide treatment as soon as possible after the shock occurs. Talk to survivors to bring them out of shock.

2. Differentiate sympathetic from parasympathetic shock and use the appropriate interventions and language for each.

3. Whenever possible, separate current shock from past shock through the use of language. For instance, refer to present resources that weren't available in the past.

4. When you are the care-provider, allow your inner witness to assess not only the needs of those around you, but your own responses as well. If you notice you are in shock, use self-talk to bring yourself out as quickly as possible.

5. Avoid burnout—the most common by-product of crisis—by listening to the reports of your inner witness.

For a compilation of subtle energy medicine treatment for immediate shock, see "Shock Is in the Moment, Healing is Forever," in Chapter 3.

Section III

The Bigger Picture

6 Birth, Prenatal Experience, and Shock

Lucidity begins at conception.
—Thrangu Rinpoche

The hearty cry of a newborn fills the room. Life emerges from the cave of time—the womb of the mother. But life does not begin with this emergence. It continues. What transpires before life speaks audibly is as significant as what happens after that first utterance—the declaration of arrival.

"We are nine months old at birth," says pediatrician, Tony Lipson. We are born with memory, though that memory is not cognitive or verbal until much later. Prenatal experience is a chapter of unacknowledged personal history for most of us. It is an epic tale of challenge and survival that includes struggle and loss, as well as constant learning and discovery. Once we gain access to these archives, we understand much more about ourselves. We can completely free ourselves of the fears that shaped our primitive responses, allowing us to see ourselves, our families, and the world with new eyes. Of equal importance, we can help the children of the future by, first of all, clearly acknowledging this early time and, secondly, educating parents-to-be and all those involved in the birthing process about the prevention of prenatal and birth shock.

Awareness of what happens during the miraculous incubation period, attention to the specifics of development, and protecting the growing fetus from whatever is threatening ensures potent shock prevention. When I was pregnant with my first child, I was struck by how little was relayed to me about this process or birth. My mother said the same thing. Her mother and five sisters had never shared their pregnancy and birth experiences with her. The information that is in this chapter is designed to remove this strange, unnecessary, and harmful veil.

In the last 25 years, research about prenatal and immediate postnatal human development has validated the potent force of relationship and environment. A large portion of this literature, though, is for a clinical audience. It is the purpose of this chapter to provide more people with this vital information in understandable language and with practical tools to prevent early shock.[1]

In these pages, you will find useful and completely safe resources that support the entire family in making pregnancy and birth as shock-free as possible. Subtle touch and healing language, recommended throughout this book for adults, are just as strongly recommended for prenatal health. Open and honest communication that recognizes the sensitivity of the fetus nourishes the well-being and neurological development of our most important resource—the children of the future, to whom this book is dedicated.

How to Support the Developing Child

Learning starts in the womb. Each phase of this experiential schooling contributes decisively to personal evolution. The story of Lonnie Delaney in Chapter 3 is one example of prenatal learning that shaped decades of relational choices that shifted only when healing occurred. Remember baby Amelia's struggle to communicate and Jeremy's battle with cancer in Chapter 2? These were driven by prenatal experiences. Imagine the difference if there had been someone in Jeremy's life who advocated for him when he was in utero? Imagine if Amelia's parents had been attuned to her sensitivity earlier? These possibilities represent what education about shock prevention could do.

The chart on page 165 reviews the hallmarks of prenatal development, and throughout this chapter, I will provide energy medicine we can use to encourage optimum health and stimulate growth. This offers new ways for parents, family members, and healthcare providers to care for and express love to the beings who will be our future leaders, teachers, artists, politicians, healers, mothers, fathers, scientists, and great creative thinkers. The illustrations throughout this chapter demonstrate how pregnant mothers can treat themselves to support their babies along with their own health. Fathers, or other family members, can also apply these same treatments on the mother's body, creating an even wider circle of welcome and stimulation.

You can also use this information in conjunction with the following summary of life's turning points to heal your own incomplete developmental

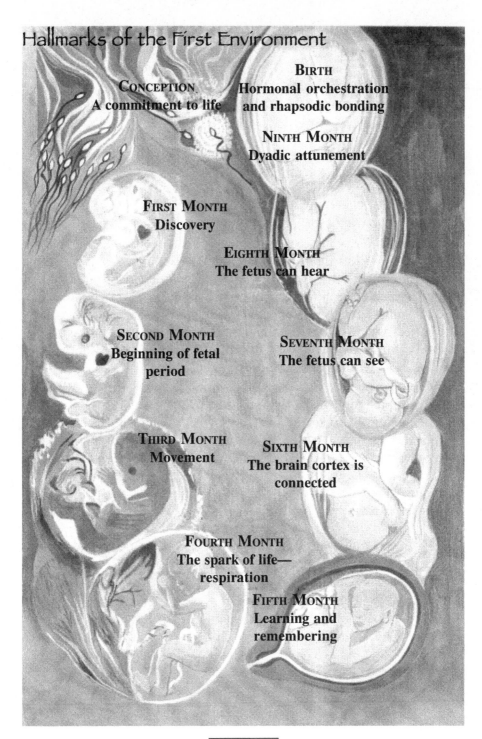

Hallmarks of the First Environment

CONCEPTION
A commitment to life

BIRTH
Hormonal orchestration
and rhapsodic bonding

NINTH MONTH
Dyadic attunement

FIRST MONTH
Discovery

EIGHTH MONTH
The fetus can hear

SECOND MONTH
Beginning of fetal
period

SEVENTH MONTH
The fetus can see

THIRD MONTH
Movement

SIXTH MONTH
The brain cortex is
connected

FOURTH MONTH
The spark of life—
respiration

FIFTH MONTH
Learning and
remembering

sequences. This will stimulate self-understanding. Memories and insight from your early life may arise and will help you to link with your own history and differentiate it from the present. Virtually every person I know who has found a way to identify and repattern early shock has become more conscious and more grateful for their life and their unique, essential self.

Life's Turning Points in the First Environment

Discovery and Welcoming

It is usually within the first two months of pregnancy that a mother discovers or confirms that she is pregnant. This is a critical moment in the child's life as well as that of the parents. Welcoming can and should be articulated clearly, either verbally or silently, with conscious intention at discovery. Sometimes, however, the moment of discovery can be very complex. I do not want to perpetuate the myth that discovery always has to be a delirious cascade of ecstasy. Biologist Sandra Steingraber's moment of discovery, for instance, in the bathroom of the university where she is teaching, is sweet, humorous, and delightfully honest.

"Am I pregnant? At this particular moment I'm not sure what answer I'm hoping for. Mostly I'm unnerved by the ease of the experiment I'm conducting. I reread the instruction sheet. I notice it refers to the plastic stick as 'the wand.' The faucet drips. The radiator hisses and bangs into action. I guess that another minute has passed. I wonder what time it is. Down in the parking lot, the last of my students are negotiating their way through rows of cars. But I am not ready yet to consult the plastic oracle on the stick. I look at my watch. Five minutes! I look down at the stick. Two lavender lines. Unmistakable. Now there are two of us. And I am late for class."[2] The recognition and contact that Sandra articulates marks the moment of discovery clearly. It is precisely this consciousness that matters.

I believe that what prevents shock is an honest and communicative discovery. It is genuine, heartfelt communication that always builds the strongest bond, even under the most difficult of circumstances. Leona's story reveals that the welcoming of a child can come at any point. If necessary, it could even happen in adulthood! A teenager, for instance, who feels unwanted by a social group, or one who feels swept away by superficial values in school, would benefit enormously from being reminded of what their authentic presence means to their family and to the world. Welcoming can be repeated often and at any time.

Leona thought she would never be able to conceive. Years of anorexia and bulimia had made her periods highly irregular, and frequently months and months would go by without any menses at all. She had resigned herself to childlessness. Nevertheless, when she fell in love and married, her desire to parent was rekindled. She had explored the history and motivation behind her eating disorder and she felt thoroughly resolved about it. Her marriage was deeply satisfying, and she was finally truly happy with herself, her body, and her life.

Leona was a long-time practitioner of the energy medicine system described in this book. I had taught her self-care treatment to strengthen her reproductive system and awaken fertility. She was skeptical, though, that the energy flows could overcome the damage she had done to her organs. Because the likelihood of pregnancy was so remote, her menstrual cycle so infrequent, and because of that hibernating hope, Leona and her husband, John, did not use birth control. While taking medical precautions for a trip to a remote location in Asia, Leona learned she was entering the third month of pregnancy. It was the week after her 40th birthday.

Discovery, in our modern Western world, has been interfered with by amniocentesis, which cannot be done until the 14th week in utero. This creates a double discovery. Reserving acceptance on the basis of the amnio's results has to impact the fetus and this needs to be acknowledged. Because of her history and her age, Leona and her husband were quite concerned about their baby's health, and so they requested amniocentesis. What if they had conceived a compromised child? Would they abort if this were the case? These are heartrending questions. Of course, they were delighted when they learned that their baby was perfectly healthy and that they could stop agonizing.

When the time for delivery came, Leona labored for over 48 hours. Her baby's progress down the birth canal was slow, and then, in the end, he had to be suctioned out. Was he unsure of his welcome? Ultimately, only he will be able to answer this question.

For Leona and John there were two discovery points. Because they were not consciously intending to conceive, their awareness of the baby was delayed. This means the baby was there without recognition, waiting to be seen. Their first response to their pregnancy was amazement, even some dismay that their travel adventure would likely have to be cancelled. The second discovery came after they got the results of the amniocentesis. All of this is part of their child's history as well as theirs.

Their decision to cancel their trip to Asia and stay home for the journey of life was easier to express than the hesitancy they felt while waiting for the results of the amniocentesis. But they persevered in their honesty and were introduced to how parenting is a confrontation with your deepest self, even before the baby is born.

If you have never said it before, or even if you have, tell your children now, no matter what their age, that you treasure their existence. Even if they roll their eyes, tell them sincerely how deeply you value them. And if no one has ever said that to you, say the same thing to yourself right now or whenever you can with the same level of authentic commitment. This is how John and Leona transformed the delays in welcoming their baby into a genuine ritual of family-making that they created in their hearts and expressed repeatedly.

The First Trimester: Organogenesis

The first month of pregnancy is a time of astounding growth. Implantation at seven to 14 days is when we, in our cell form, find a home in the uterine wall. Virtually all the organs that we will use during our lifetime begin formation within the critical third week after fertilization, including the tissues destined to become the brain and the spinal cord. This is the incredible phenomenon of organogenesis that marks the first trimester.

It is also within the first month that the placenta is created, allowing the fetus to be fed inside the uterus. The placenta and the umbilical cord are marvelous constructions designed to support new life. They are the channels by which nutrients from the outside world enter the complex, rapidly evolving structure of the new being. But along with these precious nutrients also come the pervasive poisons of the modern world that shock and confuse the developing child. To protect the vulnerable fetus, parents can practice energy medicine to diffuse toxins and actively educate themselves to avoid them.[3]

Sandra Steingraber, the respected biologist, author, and mother (whose discovery story I quoted earlier), in writing about her own first pregnancy, articulates a poetic call to awareness of the placenta and the umbilical cord. She describes the placenta as "an intertwining of mother and child in the closest embrace that is biologically possible." Dr. Steingraber's litany continues, defining the placenta as "an evolutionary shapeshifter," "the flat cake that feeds us all," "a blood-drenched forest," and "the sapwood of pregnancy." The placenta will continue to grow throughout pregnancy, ultimately weighing more than a pound, with an attached umbilical cord—the feeding tube and the carrier of potential toxins of all kinds.[4]

In the first month, we evolve from an embryonic cellular disc to a fetus with a human shape and a heart that beats. These remarkable accomplishments invite celebration. While these beginnings of organogenesis are awe-inspiring, if the prenate experiences them without the awareness of his or her parents, it is a lonely pilgrimage. Acknowledged and appreciated, the mission has deeper purpose and, most importantly, includes human connection. I recommend that all family members participate in the joy of emergent life in an expressive and tactile way. This is the simple and natural approach to preventing the shock of loneliness and isolation.

"Bonding, it turns out, is not limited to one specific time when all benefits are gained or lost, but should be considered a continuum of opportunity from preconception onward." This is the conclusion of David Chamberlain, Ph.D., one of the founders of the American Association for Pre- and Perinatal Psychology and Health, and author of *The Mind of Your Newborn Baby*.[5]

First month: Points 22/13

The possibility of twins is also made evident very early, within that whirlwind of change in the first 14 days after conception. Recent evidence, according to my correspondence with Dr. Chamberlain, indicates that twin pregnancies are actually quite frequent. "In a study of 6,000 early pregnancies," David reports, "188 twins were identified, but only 86 were delivered as twins." Drs. Landy, Weiner, and Corson report the vanishing twin phenomenon in "21.9 percent of 1,000 pregnancies" tracked by sonogram. They agree that multiple gestations are "higher than previously believed."[6] Slight bleeding or the loss of a small amount of fibrous material might identify loss of a twin by the mother. However, the embryo is usually reabsorbed into the body. The death or disappearance of one twin must be included as a disquieting and likely early shock for the remaining fetus.

This shock is mitigated the way shock of loss is always mitigated by contact and companionship in the grieving process. What is true for adults is simultaneously, perhaps doubly, true for the prenate. When it was assumed that twin conception was much less frequent, such as one in every 80 pregnancies, parents were not educated to be sensitive to the possibility of twin loss. Now, however, this awareness and attention can lessen the shock of twin loss considerably.

Second month: Point 17

The second month of pregnancy is the time when the nervous system develops. At six weeks, the brain's activity is measurable. The baby's sensitivity is aroused and the body becomes expressive, relaying this sensitivity and demonstrating that the link between body and brain is established.

Within the first two months after conception we move, and we all move differently because we are unique, expressive beings. While the link between baby and mother is profound and the baby develops its sense of internal balance as a result of its interaction with the mother's system, nevertheless, babies find their own movement patterns. These patterns hold the keys to who we are. Alessandra Piontelli's observational study of fetuses began at the mother's first exam. She then tracked movement for the fetus through pregnancy, birth, and into the fourth and fifth years of the child's life. She found that prenatal movements are harbingers of later movement patterns. One child, for instance, expressed her fear of her father by hiding in utero. Observed later, as a toddler, she continued to hide from her father. Her father's gruff style and dark sense of humor made him appear as an ogre. He simply did not reveal his other dimensions. If the father had been willing to be softer for his daughter, her response might have been less avoidant. He had been quite skeptical about the consciousness of the fetus. In fact, this was the subject of many of his jokes while his wife was pregnant. The fascinating point here, however, is how attunement to movement can help us see the baby's feelings about life outside the womb.[7]

Touch communicates even more clearly than words, and attuned touch even more so, as I emphasize in Chapter

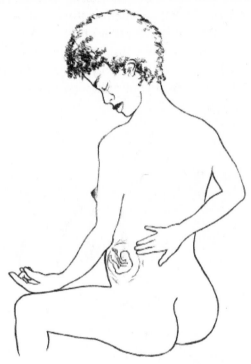

Third month: Points 23/middle finger

4. How, you may well ask, does a fetus experience touch from inside the womb? The answer to this lies within the incredible link between mother and child. What the mother feels is immediately and essentially conveyed to the fetus within her. By touching the mother with gentle healing, the growing child, the preborn, is also touched. The research and work of Frans Veldman, the founder of Haptonomy, supports this hypothesis.[8]

The simple treatments that are illustrated in this chapter create opportunities for the child's movement development to be energetically nourished by the clear and loving communication of touch. Combine these treatments with those you learned in Chapter 4 for an even more comprehensive use of touch to support pregnancy and fetal health. This is one easy and important way to prevent shock. In addition, you can treat residual early shock held in the body with these gentle applications.

The fetus' sense of community and confidence is enormously enhanced when its movement is supported. Pregnancy is a time of passion, even adoration, and playfulness. The baby learns through play in utero. You can share that fun. The relationship between the parents and their child is an enduring and exquisite love story, and pregnancy is the honeymoon. This is not a time to be shy, or to hold back expression! The baby bathed in the nectar of love will unquestionably flourish.

Try this. Lie down on your back. Let your knees rise up and then your legs, and look at your ankles and toes. Do the same thing with your arms. Let your elbows drift up, then your forearms and your fingers. Feel the natural excitement of discovery as your limbs rock and sway from a gentle internal impetus. Experience the pleasure and ease of these simple organic gestures of being alive, with a body. This is the extraordinary innocence and sensuality of prenatal life. (See illustration.) It may seem silly at first, but imagine that you are seeing your limbs for the first time. This will remind you of the tender and innocent pleasures of new life.

Baby Exercise

The Second Trimester: The Breath of Life

The hallmark of the fourth month is breathing. The prenate is now almost six inches long. The mouth and lips are fully formed and so everything is in place to breathe amniotic fluid. This liquid breathing is absolutely necessary, not only for survival at this juncture and for the rest of incubation, but in order to develop the capacity to breathe air after birth.

In fact, the respiratory capacity initiated in the fourth month will need ongoing support and protection to reach its full capacity at about eight years old.

Exposure to pollutants is always an extreme danger for prenates and for newborns, but in the fourth month, this danger is substantially increased because of the significance of this developmental window that emphasizes respiration. Toxins of any kind, internal or environmental, will have a dramatic impact on the prenate's breathing rhythms that will be encoded now for life. Whatever prohibits steady and calm respiratory rhythms will strain the emergent capacities of this remarkable being. Parents need to be alerted to the impact of environmental toxins in their locale. The references at the end of this chapter will assist you in uncovering them.[9]

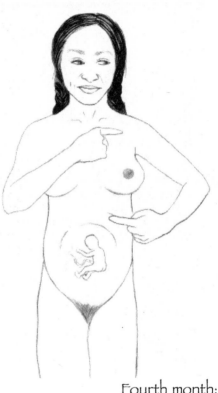

Fourth month:
Points 22/same side 14

The wonderful master of healing, Mary Iino Burmeister, who taught me the remarkable art of Jin Shin upon which Jin Shin Tara is based, called the fourth month of prenatal life the time when the "spark of life" is lit. What she was referring to is rephrased this way by Dr. Tony Lipson: "The fetus at 18–20 weeks is finally connected. The brain is connected to the spinal cord and the fetus is a person, with a spirit." Anxiety, hyperactivity, pervasive tension, rejection, abortion ideation, and both chemical and substantive toxins, such as cigarette smoke, can wound this blooming spirit with its newly evolved direct line to the brain. By protecting prenates and children from pollutants, we demonstrate our love. If instead we permit exposure, we communicate something else.[10]

Fifth month: Points 11/3

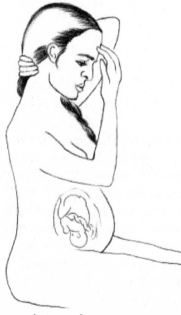

Sixth month: Points 20/4

The Halfway Point

In the intrauterine environment of the fifth month, the fetus hears. Perhaps the fetus is only an eavesdropper, but he or she is aware not only of who is speaking, but of the emotional implications of dialogue through intonation, particularly in voices heard regularly. The fetus is using sound to learn how and who to orient toward after birth. If we know this, then the sounds we make respect the presence of the listening fetus, who then feels included.

To match the hallmark of hearing in the fifth month, the sixth month is marked by the capacity to see. The light shining through the belly of the mother highlights the images the baby perceives. By the end of the second trimester, the fetus has completed the secondary school level of preparation for meeting his or her family and the world. By this time, the fetus is very familiar with the rhythms and behaviors, and the stressors and the relaxants in the family environment. Songs, television programs, arguments, eating, and drinking patterns—these are instructions to the fetus about what is to come after emergence from the protective covering of the mother's belly.

Movement and brain activity interact consistently, memory is thoroughly engaged, and feelings about warmth, light, sound, discomfort, pleasure, need, and response are being shaped into meaning for the five-month-old fetus.

The Final Trimester: Blooming Intelligence

*In general, nerve cells cannot regenerate in the way
that a cut on the skin can heal, so that if injury or
disease occurs, the cells will not reform and grow as
with a skin wound. Adaptation can however result
in a meaningful and apparently complete recovery
in function, as some functions can be taken over by
other parts of the brain.*

—Tony Lipson, M.D.

In the final trimester and in the period including and immediately following birth, the impact of whatever shock may have occurred has already made its developmental impact. Yet with acknowledgement, communication, care, and attention, compensatory enrichment and recovery can facilitate alternate routes of neurological growth.

After birth, agitated movement patterns, erratic sleep, digestive stress, and excessive crying with sharp high-pitched plaintive tones suggest that shock has occurred prenatally. Treatment with subtle energy medicine and recognition of the causative factors, along with communication with the baby, will significantly counteract early shock. This is especially true if treatment occurs soon after birth.

The seventh, eighth, and ninth months are critical for the integration of the learning processes that come to fruition in the second trimester. The third trimester is a condensed "human brain growth spurt" that continues into the second year of life. During this growth spurt period, says psychiatrist Allan Schore, "the genetic specification of neuronal structure is not sufficient for an optimally functional nervous system—the environment also powerfully affects the structure of the brain."[11] This environment is created in utero and is regulated by maternal hormones.

Seventh month:
Points 12/4

Eighth month: Hold center of palm or Palm Inju

Acute hormonal shifts, such as those that occur under stress, shape brain development. "Environmental experience is now recognized to be critical to the differentiation of brain tissue itself," Schore continues. Because memory is well-established by the third trimester, environmental experiences are constantly being stored, and they are thoroughly shaping the behavior of the limbic brain. This earliest, most primitive brain, is the storehouse of survival responses. Early experiences of threat, or any shock, create a prototype of lifesaving behaviors that are programmed for use over and over again.[12] Engaging in conscious repatterning, as this book recommends, frees us of these stored shock conditioned responses. Imagine the gift to individuals and humanity, however, if these never become entrenched.

The nonverbal right hemisphere, which is known as the "emotional mind," is also dominant in the growth spurt of these final months of incubation. The primary circuits that will establish the capacity to respond to stress are erected now. The communications between parents and child are essential training for the birth and postnatal time. Birth relies primarily on the teamwork of mother and child, and the entire prenatal period has been the training course for this marathon.

Prolonged negative states are brutally toxic in the final trimester. The prenate does not have the capacity to regulate the pain of disregard, neglect, rejection, or aggression. A family environment that acknowledges the delicate bridgework of synaptic construction erected in the third trimester is essential. This includes stimulating learning-oriented interaction, such as singing, listening to music, storytelling, and gentle movement as well as nutritional support.[13]

Dyadic attunement is a phrase that refers to the resonance between mother and child. It is this attunement, built from internal awareness, communication, physical contact, and acknowledging the baby's presence, that builds the baby's capacity to manage stress later. When this dyadic attunement is continued after birth with consistent eye contact, physical contact, touch (energy medicine and infant massage, for instance), stimulation, and mirroring, then the baby grows increasingly more self-regulating.[14]

Families that have the greatest difficulties with cultivating this are those with no history of dyadic attunement. Mothers and fathers who never received this kind of attention from their own primary caregivers can educate themselves and learn how to develop this connection with their children. Using subtle energy medicine will do this naturally. A simple way to awaken your attuning instincts if they have not arisen is to talk to parents who you see uniting with their children. Let them mentor you. Spend time with them and their children. A good prenatal program should provide this mentoring. This is essential at the psychobiological level. Vital hormonal, endocrine, and nervous system development hinges on this symbiosis.

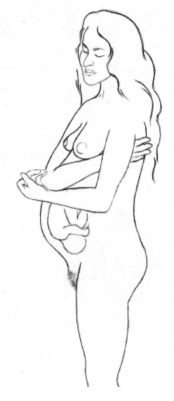

Ninth month:
Point 26/index finger

Birth

Just as the fetus has been practicing for birth, so have the mother and father. While the baby is moving, listening, watching, and remembering, the mother and father are educating themselves about the birth process. Mom is empowering herself to be in the center of the experience and dad is learning how he can support her and their child. At least this is the optimum, shock-free situation that I have been propagating in this book. By presenting suggestions for how to create a shock-free pregnancy and birth, I hope to stimulate my readership, especially those who are considering parenthood, to create this. In addition, I am hoping to initiate family birthing unit enhancements to support the care and delivery of babies who can fulfill their highest human potential.

The fetus initiates birth as an organic outgrowth of its expansion. This initiation originates in the hypothalamus, which produces sufficient cortisone to stimulate labor. Labor is not initiated if there is any malfunction in the glands associated with this cortisone production, including the pituitary and the adrenal glands. Labor is also shaped by the challenges and obstacles the baby encounters navigating the voyage through the mother's body. Everything that has been said earlier about prenatal stress hormones is relevant to birth. If the mother is tense or restricted, labor will unquestionably be affected. This is why a laboring woman needs an advocate, such as a midwife or a partner, who can speak for her. (See Joan Borysenko's story that follows as an illustration of what happens without an advocate in the hospital.) There are numerous gentle interventions, such as water birth, that can help move labor along without robbing the baby of initiative.[15]

Birth: Points 9/10 and opposite 2 on baby

Once labor has been stimulated, there is an ongoing relationship between the production of progesterone from the placenta and the production of relaxin from the ovaries to create the contractual rhythms of the muscles of the womb. The interplay of many hormones (prostaglandins, estrogen, ACTH, CRH, cortisone) participate in a complex score to orchestrate the various activities and necessities of labor. The conductor, however, is the fetus.

The management of the birth process has become standard procedure, but it unfortunately contributes to an environment of shock. In fact, the term "active management" is used to describe the control of the birth process so that women in labor dilate according to the clock, resulting in a 40 percent oxytocin use rate, and delivery within twelve hours. This, according to Suzanne Arms, author of *Immaculate Deception I and II* "has meant the aggressive use of intervention to keep labor to a schedule but, unfortunately, without the one-to-one attention from a nurse or midwife. This has been routine in most U. S. hospitals for years. It fits neatly into cultural attitudes that view labor as without value and sees the best labor as the shortest with the least pain." Suzanne goes on to ask some central questions for those who dare to look at the way many have been robbed of one of the most profound initiations of existence. "We must ask ourselves, is the best labor really the shortest or the most painless? What is the real value of labor and birth? Are they not important rites of passage for the woman and the baby? Don't women in early as well as active labor need and deserve the attention of one-to-one care, support, and encouragement? Who should be in charge of managing this important time?"[16]

The memories of noted writer Joan Borysenko reveal the pattern I point to when I say, "we are all in shock." While all of us may not have been born the way Joan describes the delivery of her son, many have. This creates a lineage of shock.

Even though labor had not technically begun, my cervix was dilated to about five centimeters, an excellent start. But rather than let things proceed naturally, the doctor gave me a shot of pitocin (a pituitary hormone that initiates labor), to speed things along, estimating that the baby might come in 10 to 12 hours. I went right into heavy labor and the amniotic membranes were ruptured to expedite the process further. Within two hours I felt the urge to push. The nurse, who didn't bother to check on the degree of dilation, just assumed that it was too early. But the body cannot be denied. I pushed secretly, simply because the pain disappeared and a wonderful sense of opening and relief accompanied it. After four or five pushes I became aware of pressure between my legs.

The baby was about to make his debut in the labor room bed! And what would have been wrong with that? I called the nurse, who panicked at the sight of Justin's crowning and rushed me to the delivery room screaming, "Pant, pant! Don't push!" Fear immediately interrupted my labor and I had no further need to push. The natural flow had been interrupted. In the delivery room I was given saddle block anesthesia, an episiotomy, and Justin was pulled out with forceps. His eyes were treated with silver nitrate, a standard practice I couldn't stop, and he was wrapped and taken away to the nursery. It was several hours before I saw him again. At that point he seemed to belong to the nurse and I was an interloper. To this day I wish that I'd kept my mouth shut and birthed him in the bed. We were doing just fine on our own without a painful technological finale to what had been a relatively painless, intimate, and natural birth. Experiences like mine are still the norm in hospitals, where normal births are often complicated even further by the use of fetal monitoring equipment, all in the name of "natural childbirth."[17]

To Be Born Again

We must learn nothing less than how to be born again.

—Alice Walker

There are some other changes in standard birthing room procedures that, if they were enacted, could make a significant contribution to ending the repetition of shock and trauma. It is clear that what fosters all physical development, particularly brain development, is the bonding relationship between the baby and the mother—the centerpiece of what I refer to as "dyadic attunement." This is enacted prenatally through energetic entrainment and postnatally through eye contact. Eye contact stimulates first the neuronal evolution of the right hemisphere of the brain, and later the verbal left hemisphere. Therefore, it is quite obvious that the separation of mother and baby after birth is extremely damaging to the child's brain evolution. If this book did nothing more than forever change in all hospitals the unnecessary and deeply destructive procedure of separating mother from baby at birth, I would be extremely satisfied. I believe this in itself would contribute greatly to ending the lineage of shock.

Generally, the harshness, the bright lights and cold temperatures, along with the sometimes neutral or even cold attitudes of the healthcare providers present, are shocking for the newborn. I do not mean to imply that this is true of all such staff. In fact, in my work with family birthing units I have seen the devotion and love that many nurses bring to their work. One student of mine, who was painfully separated from her mother at birth, recalls with great warmth the nurse who cared for her instead. No one, however, can replicate the bond between mother and child.

I was privileged to be present when a retired military man in his 60s recalled his birth. After attending a talk I gave for the family birthing unit staff at a hospital where he was on the Board of Directors, Lester made some life-changing discoveries. He invited me to join him and his wife in their beautiful home one afternoon a few days after the program so that he could share them with me. He told me that after hearing me speak about the ways in which common hospital procedures evoke both anger and terror for the newborn, he had a stunning realization. All his life he had suffered from a secret anxiety when he entered places that were brightly lit. This had been difficult to manage as a career man in the military who was required to attend staff meetings in rooms inevitably lit by fluorescence. What was even more uncomfortable for him was the way he was driven into a quaking fear at the sight of men in white uniforms. Lester was somewhat embarrassed to share these things with me. He had always thought of this distress as a personal weakness to be masked. Only his wife knew of his struggles.

After hearing my talk it all became crystal clear to him. He spontaneously remembered his own birth and the absolute horror he felt when, after his long struggle (his mother had labored for two days), he was met by an "army" (his words) of people who simply stared at him. They brought him out with forceps into a room that struck him with cold and harsh light. Denied the comfort of his mother who was so heavily anaesthetized she didn't even remember the moment, Lester could now feel how he became cold, to match the frigidity of the world he had entered. The precision of his vision and the strength of his sensation erased all possible doubt of its veracity. If it hadn't happened to him he would have thought it was impossible and that what I had said about remembering one's birth was pure quackery.

He wanted to thank me for unburdening him of a mystery that had haunted him. He said that these discoveries gave him a sense of being reborn. He felt much calmer now, and to test the validity of his experience, he had his hair cut in a shop lit by brilliant lights, and all the hairdressers wore equally brilliant white jackets. He doubted anyone had ever enjoyed a haircut so much.

How would you like to be welcomed into the world? That is the question with which I would like to end this chapter. Every child deserves a warm, respectful beginning. Wouldn't you agree? Is it really so difficult to provide this? Every child deserves the security of a mother's closeness. Every child deserves the time to breathe fully on its own. When we cut the umbilical cord too soon, before it stops pulsing, the baby is shocked.

"What should we do during these critical few minutes of the transition of the blood from the old route through the placenta to the newly working lungs? We must understand that Nature herself doesn't take sudden leaps and has her own pace. She has left this time, these last few minutes, so that this changeover from one world to another can be made with ease." Dr. Frederick Leboyer's preface to the revised edition of his book on non-violent birth, written 25 years after its first publication, is eloquent and pointed. Leboyer still asks if it is "madly ambitious" to envision a world where "human beings are born with this fabulous boon: complete fearlessness. Blessed with a life free from anger and aggressivity, able to tread the path of life with an unthinkable smile and eyes glowing with burning love."[18]

7 Mother Nature, You, and Me—the Seamless Matrix of Life

The elements without and within arise together, from the same source. The warmth of the sun and the warmth of the heart are different in degree, not in kind. The water of the oceans is not different from the water of our bodies. Our flesh is formed from the elements of the earth and it will dissolve back into the earth. The air in our lungs is the same air the hawk rides.

—Tenzin Wangyal Rinpoche

My purpose in this chapter is twofold. First of all, I want to awaken and stimulate your sustained, intimate relationship with the natural world around you. It offers perhaps the greatest reward for being alive. Secondly, I want to be an advocate for that world because it is suffering. Throughout this book I refer to "the children of the future," to whom this book is dedicated. This planet Earth, our home, is where they will live. It is also where we, the survivors of shock, find joy, beauty, and inspiration.

There is an unbreakable link between our environment and us. The environment lives, breathes, and communicates with us just as our bodies do. I come to this not as a hardy outdoorswoman, but as someone who later in life discovered a scintillating body of resources available in the natural world to succor and shelter her. I consider this relationship as ongoing, evolving, and central to who I am. Even though I am a novice as a naturalist, I thoroughly believe that if we find our oneness with Nature, we can resolve shock completely.

Nature Has Resources for Everyone in the Five Elements

Autumn

Color: White*
To awaken this element: Make a real
    connection with someone or
    something.
Finger: Ring
Meridians: Lung, Large intestine
Feeling: Joy in relationships
Helps: Breathing, Assimilation,
    Elimination, Mammalian brain
** Key Point: 13

Air

Winter

Color: Blue Black*
To awaken this element: Rest or do
    gentle fluid movement.
Finger: Index
Meridians: Kidney, Bladder
Feeling: Courage and Endurance
Helps: Back support, Brain stem,
    Kidney, Adrenals
** Key Point: 23

Water

In-Between Seasons

Color: Yellow*
To awaken this element: Sit on the
    earth. Feel your roots going
    into the earth. Feel the earth
    supporting you.
Finger: Thumb
Meridians: Stomach and Spleen
Feeling: Trust, Freedom from worry
Helps: Primitive brain, Jaws, Teeth,
    Gums
** Key Point: 21

Earth

Summer

Color: Red*
To awaken this element: Pray.
    Meditate. Look into the heavens.
Finger: Little
Meridians: Heart, Small intestine,
    Pericardium (Diaphragm), Triple
    burner
Feeling: Love, Individuality
Helps: Chest, Arm, Shoulders,
    Circulation, Digestion
** Key Point: 26

Fire

Spring

Color: Green*
To awaken this element: Push an
    obstacle, like a wall or a hard
    surface.
Finger: Middle
Meridians: Liver, Gallbladder
Feeling: Clear thinking, Planning and
    Decision-making, Balanced anger
Helps: Hips, Pelvis, Eyes, Frontal
    cortex
** Key Point: 4

Wood

* This color may be dominant in skin tones.
**If you can only hold one point, hold this one on either the right or the left side, or both sides.

Relationship is not only about family. Our relationship to the world around us is active whether we attune to it or not. The premise in this chapter is that shock is the only reason why we would *not* be in dynamic, loving relationships with the Nature that surrounds us. Coming out of shock will inevitably awaken our birthright to engage with Nature as a wise elder and source of great counsel. A relationship with Nature can deeply fulfill previously unmet needs, and thus support the resolution of shock. I consider Mother Earth and Father Sky such significant resources for those of us who are here now and those yet to come that I have devoted an entire chapter to them.

Shock causes separation, and feelings of separation reveal that shock has occurred.

Recently my family and I visited the Denver Natural History Museum where they had an exhibit about space travel. All the astronauts commenting on their experiences said the same thing—from the perspective of space (or from a larger perspective), there were no boundaries between countries or continents.

There was no separation. But shock causes us to withdraw from or defend against another. It separates us from our essential selves. These behaviors make it extremely difficult to notice and cultivate deep connections with people, nations, or the natural world, even though that connection is always there, as the astronauts observed.

I grew up in the Bronx, New York, in a concrete tenement building divided into apartments. My family members were basically at war with each other most of the time. The walls were coated with lead paint that seeped into our respiratory systems and skin. Both my mother and I had bronchial conditions, and mine progressed early in life to asthma. The world around us was poisonous and threatening. Except for the starry sky that fascinated me and one or two trips to the countryside that were glorious, the world was grey and consisted of blocks and stoops. Nature was not an identified ally for us in the Bronx. We lived in sad separation from each other and the environment.

Slowly, despite this early training in alienation, I have moved more and more into intimacy with the natural world. My exploration of the five elements of Nature that are discussed in this chapter and their role in the healing process has been instrumental in this movement. My relationship with Nature is becoming the most thrilling new dimension in my life. Resolving shock means reclaiming a birthright to be part of the vitality that is unceasing in the natural world. Nature is ready to participate with us in every instance, to help us solve our dilemmas, and to model health. Nature speaks to us in millions of ways, and, just as we can learn to really listen to our bodies, so too can we learn to hear the messages of the natural world.

The five primary elements of the natural world are within us. When I first read this in my study of astern medicine, I was stumped. What could this possibly mean? What I longed for as a child who stared out her New York window at bits of sky between buildings was a nourishing relationship with the world I lived in. Now, having found my own Earth, Air, Fire, Water, and Wood, I know that I am not separate. Implementing the ideas and practices in this chapter is a way to create your own link with the environment.

As I write these words, my toes sink into the sand on the beach where I sit in Mexico. Overhead, a long line of well-organized gulls fly just above rocks that jut into the churning ocean. They are, without doubt, collectively assured of their destination. In their flight, they demonstrate the power of certainty. A little boy stumbles awkwardly over the pebbles and shells as if learning for the first time about this terrain. I identify with him.

The Sea of Cortez and the children playing in it do not appear to be affected by the way that pollutants have altered the natural world. On the beach words, such as "cancer" and "developmental disability" are not appropriate. People are "on vacation," and the generous environment is healing them. How long, I wonder, can the masquerade that all is well in the natural world go on? What if we all joined forces and faced the truth? What if we could become one international human team to make the world safe for everyone here and for the children of the future? I feel the grandiosity of my idealism swell in my chest like a bellows fanning the fire of my hope. My toes wiggle in the sand and the ocean expands infinitely before me. Earth and water calm my yearning and my fear with their eternal message of continuity. I breathe deeply, imbibing the message of endurance, listening to and sensing all the elements.

This chapter is my attempt to encourage a process whereby we realize that what we do to the earth we also do to ourselves. I believe that contacting the elements within us is a sure route to ending separation from Nature. What follows is intended to open you to the living presence of the five elements within you. I orient my discussion specifically toward the way the elements respond when awakened and balanced in a person healing from shock. The natural outcome of elemental balance is the discovery of personal truth and the will to manifest it.

There are resources in this book that will help you use the information about the elements that follows. These include the map of the body on pages 46–47, the illustration of the fingers on this page, and illustrations of the beginning and ending points of all the meridians throughout this chapter. Meridians are energy fields. Each meridian has a masculine or a feminine quality (yin or yang), a specific pathway, and precise functions to serve the mind-body. The points or areas on the meridians are highly charged energy centers that activate specific meridian functions. Eventually, the locations on your body that these charts direct you to will become second nature, and you will find them when you need them. This will be very liberating for you and for those with whom you share this remarkable treasure of healing that is accessible to all.

The Story of the Fingers

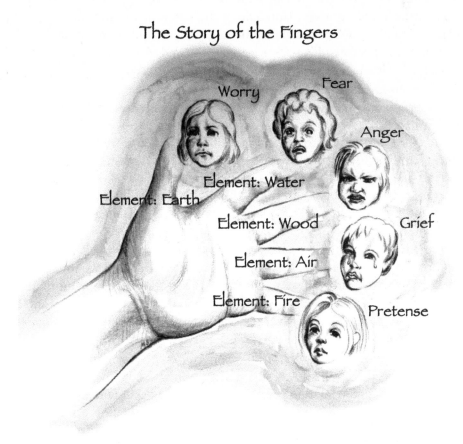

Earth: The Forgiving Mother

For several years I taught in Mexico at a retreat center called Tapalehui, which means "unity," "joining forces," or "cooperation" in Nahuatl, the language of the indigenous people of the region. A very special woman named AnaMaria was an owner and director of the center. She felt an affinity for my work and joined our classes. One year, AnaMaria offered my students something very special—a temescal, which she would lead.

A temescal is primarily intended for renewal through contact with the elements. The temescal is actually the name of the structure where the ceremony of renewal happens. It is made of earth and grasses, and is shaped like a cave with a covered door. The temescal leader is responsible for preparing this structure and arranging the rocks inside that are heated with increasing intensity. AnaMaria, a former nun in her mid-60s, carried the rocks from a nearby river. Conducting the ceremony is strenuous. It includes chants to each of the elements sung with strength, commitment, and feeling as the heat steadily rises. Finally, at the end, AnaMaria would bathe us in fresh, clean water, as we emerged from the temescal to greet the sun.

Of course, I was delighted to include this glorious opportunity as part of my program. AnaMaria instructed us to awaken early for the temescal, which had to conclude precisely at daybreak, and to wear loose-fitting white clothes to symbolize the purification and renewal we would experience. This meant that she would rise much earlier than us to prepare herself and the space. She led us with elegant simplicity, taking charge of every aspect of the complex ritual and also taking responsibility for the care of the participants, all of whom had deep, life-changing experiences.

When I entered the temescal I felt a great deal of fear. I felt alone and unprotected. We sat in a semi-circle around the steaming rocks. I was one of the first to enter. My position opposite the entry meant it would be very difficult to exit should I have to. As I calculated this, I became more and more agitated. When AnaMaria began her soulful chants in Spanish and I found myself chiming in, my fear lessened slightly, only to resume in unexpected waves.

When my fear intensified, it was very difficult to remain in a seated position. I decided to lie down on the dirt floor. As soon as I did, my feelings changed. The cool, hard earth seeped into my skin and soothed me. It deeply reassured me, silencing my fears, and awakening a feeling of comfort. I found myself releasing more and more of my body to this dusty surface until I felt that there was no need to hold myself up. I was held.

Stomach Meridian
  Beginning and Ending
  Points: 21/opposite
  middle toe

Spleen Meridian
  Beginning and Ending
  Points: 5/opposite 22

The earth supported me completely without criticism or ostracism for my slow, difficult surrender. Mother Earth forgave me for my distrust. I was thoroughly cared for by her soil, and I felt completely at home.

The Earth Element, as demonstrated in this story, relieves us of insecurity and anxiety through a felt sense of support. But you don't have to go to Mexico or sit in a temescal to experience the Earth Element. If you tend to worry, and trust, as a way of life, is mystifying, you can awaken the Earth Element in your own body by holding certain points or areas, such as Point 21 on the face, just under the cheekbone; Point 22 under the collarbone; or Point 1 inside the knee. See the map of the body on pages 46–47 to remember where these points are located. You can hold the points separately, one after the other, or in combination (such as holding Point 21 and Point 22 on the same side at the same time).

Another way to feel the energetic power of the Earth Element to provide comfort and relaxation in your body is to consult the illustrations on page 189 that show you the beginning and ending points of the Earth Element Meridians—the Stomach and the Spleen. Hold these. You can use all of these points to awaken yourself to the ways in which this element lives in your flesh and your nervous system. The thumb is the finger of the Earth Element, so just holding it sends waves of sedating, sobering energy down the front of your body. (See page 187 for a chart of the fingers.)

The Earth Element calms the primitive brain. When you contact the Earth inside you, a natural capacity arises to counter the conditioned shock reflexes that have previously organized your primitive brain. The Earth Element soothes your mind with simplicity. It banishes the chaotic thinking and worry that complicate our innate ability to be who we are, right now, with freedom and joy.

You can also awaken the Earth Element inside you by finding a place in Nature and just lying down, allowing its earthy quality to mingle with your body. This is what happened to me in the temescal. A big boulder, a grassy place under a large tree, or a flat rock where you can sit works well. When you find your place, allow yourself to be fed by the contact quietly and deeply. If you have a question that is troubling you, you can try asking the Earth for an answer.

You could say that in the temescal I had asked the Earth what to do about my anxiety, and she replied, "Just lie down on me and I will take care of you." My anxiety was not really about the temescal. It was an expression of the shock-conditioned belief that I was alone and unprotected. The Earth offered me her body for protection and I received her. An old abandonment was resolved, and I greeted a new life that day when I stepped out of the temescal into the sun.

From the standpoint of healing shock, you can see how this option to surrender and feel support can be as refreshing as the water that showered me when I emerged from the temescal. The Earth invites us to do less and feel her more. When you are in dialogue and communication with the Earth, it seems quite natural to do your best to honor and respect the enduring, forgiving, and stable support that holds all of us here through gravity, feeds us through her soil, and welcomes us home.

Air: The Breath of Life

As the Earth Element correlates with the primitive reptilian brain, the Air Element correlates with the limbic or mammalian brain. Air is a carrier, a messenger. In the Five Element system that I study and teach, the Air Element governs interaction, integration, and assimilation. It pushes nutrients through the body with a wave that gently moves things in the right direction, making sure that toxins are eliminated through the lungs and the large intestine. Coming together and separating are relational activities, as we all know. Relationships hinge on our capacity to meet and then move apart fluidly and harmoniously. If you struggle with relationships, the Air Element can help you.

The Air Element within us, like the mammalian brain, remembers what happened in relationships in the past. Just as the gulls I saw on the beach were moving together through the air in a direction they remembered, so do people go towards or away from one another with innate navigation. Shock can shape this orientation with a force as strong and irresistible as a windstorm.

The life-giving Air Element transmits messages, cools what is overheated, and carries seeds to be deposited where they will grow. These are the functions of Father Sky. In intimacy, the Air Element provides responsiveness and spontaneity. When made toxic by shock, however, both the air and relationships can be killers, and the most vulnerable victims of both forms of toxicity are children. When we feel the health of this element, we move readily to protect our children from all forms of poison. We naturally want them to grow up breathing clean air and witnessing and participating in uncontaminated relationships.

Lung Meridian
   Beginning and Ending
   Points: 13/opposite 14

Large Intestine Meridian
   Beginning and Ending
   Points: 11/opposite 22

To awaken the Air Element within you, and simultaneously awaken your innate capacity for vibrant interaction, hold Point 22 and Point 14 on the same side of the body. Hold both the right and left sides to balance both male and female aspects of relationships. Consult the illustrations on page 192 to see where the beginning and ending points are for the Air Element Meridians—Lung and Large Intestine. Hold all these areas and feel yourself breathe from head to toe. Do this often enough, and you will feel a fresh wind blow through your family and your partnerships, whisking away the past and invigorating your present interactions. You can also hold the ring finger to balance Air Element energies.

There is a simple movement that you can do that will also stimulate the relational Air Element energy in your body. Stand with your feet hip-width apart, and extend your arms and your face upwards to the heavens. Rotate from right to left, reaching up into the sky as if to touch the air. Do this as many times as you like and feel the natural joy that flows through your face into your body. Do this outdoors, if at all possible, with your face to the heavens. Breathe in your relationship to everything around you. Receive the breath of life. (See illustration on page 194.)

Fire: The Spirit of Creativity

Nothing reveals the potent human capacity for innovation, creativity, spontaneity, and loving kindness more than the Fire Element. The Fire Element is what arises whenever we fall in love, whether it is with a person, an idea, a way of life, a place, or a work of art. This arousal can (and is intended to) shape our direction in life, so it is vital to not let your fire burn out of control or be extinguished. The Fire Element is what surges in your heart when you feel moved by a great song, a poem, or a prayer. It is the force of intuition that allows you to know without thinking. It infuses you with courage and focus, burning away distraction. It is that glorious single-mindedness that fires you toward your goal, like a rocket aimed precisely at its destination.

The Fire Element's importance is underscored by the fact that there are four meridians associated with it: Heart, Small Intestine, Pericardium (Diaphragm), and Triple Burner (Umbilicus). The first two are the channels for the fire of creative expression and include both unconditional love and spiritual inspiration. The second two direct the energies for personal pathfinding, the passion of purpose, individuality, and uniqueness.

Air Exercise

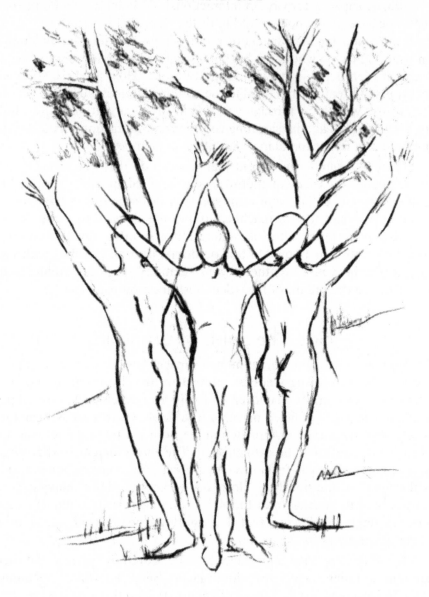

Writing about the Fire Element stirs me to tell you that the beauty of healing with the elements is yours, free of charge. When you yourself understand your elemental balance and imbalance (and you WILL understand this yourself—you don't need an expert to define your condition), you can simply go to Nature and find what you need. The elements are always available to you to bring about perfect balance. No psychotherapist, chemicals, professional can do for you what Nature can do, and no matter what time of day or night, Nature is always available. If your response to this is to say, "Well, maybe for you, but not for me. I'll never get this elemental imbalance thing, and even if I did, I won't be able to change anything," then you probably have a Fire Element imbalance.

When your Fire Element is harmonized, you have enthusiasm and inspiration. At the same time, your passion is well-boundaried, allowing you to organize your commitments. Maggie's story describes depleted fire. Excessive fire is the manic end of manic-depressive mood swings; it is sympathetic shock at its most severe and is tied to obsession and addiction.

But, what happens when the flame of your spirit's fire burns dangerously low? This was the situation for Maggie Lane, who entered her 80th year with a great longing to die. Hiding in her room where the television blared its insistent messages, she thought only of those she had lost: her husband, her favorite daughter, and her best friend. She lit one cigarette after another, as if making offerings to death. Despite chain-smoking, a bad diet, and the fact that she rarely left her apartment to feel the light of day, Maggie's health was stable. She showed no signs of dying soon. She interpreted this as a dirty trick. She had no choice but to wait out the rest of her life.

The repetition of loss had formed a shock so profound that Maggie had lost the spirit to live. Her son Justin, who was studying with me, knew this and asked me if I would meet with his mom, whom he loved dearly. He thought that I might be able to offer some treatment suggestions or insight into her suffering. He was committed to doing everything in his power to assure that his mother's final years were joyful. Even though many people recommended that he put his mother into a nursing home, Justin kept his mother at home and persisted in his search for clues to the mystery of her depression. *His* Fire Element energy was bright! He was unstoppable in his creative quest to help his mother.

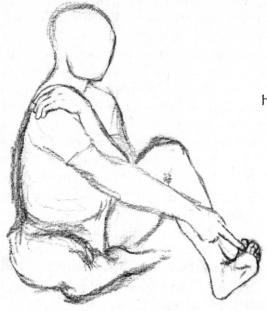

Heart Meridian
Beginning and Ending
Points: 11/opposite 7

Small Intestine Meridian
Beginning and Ending
Points: 11/same side 7

Diaphram Meridian
  Beginning and Ending
  Points: 14/same side ring
  finger

Umbillicus Meridian
  Beginning and Ending
  Points: 20/same side
  ring finger

When I entered Maggie's bedroom, she was lying with her back to me in a fetal position in her bed. She did not stir, even when her son called her name. Finally, at his repeated insistence, she turned around to face us. Though she was pale and disheveled, she was still a beautiful woman. Her snow-white hair was thick and framed her angular, elegant face. Her eyes met mine with an unnerving look of child-like terror and fury. As I faced her, I thought of the powerful mirror of old age. I knew that all of us one day would be old, with our secrets revealed in our faces. She embodied the pain of being trapped in an aging body without a conscious will to continue. Yet her health belied the fact that she was actually *not* ready to die. How could I help her? Her body had closed in around its losses, solidifying them, building a wall to keep life out in case it might bring more pain. Even Maggie's son stood on the other side of her wall.

Justin adored his mother. He offered her his warm home, family dinners, grandchildren, and most importantly, caring connection. How could I invite Maggie to look up and see what was here now for her to receive? Justin suggested that I treat Maggie with energy medicine. At first she agreed, but when I touched her she bolted. We were amazed at how much vigor she displayed in this rejection! I knew I would somehow have to tap that vigor and direct it positively.

I asked Maggie if it would be alright for me to sit next to her and just hold her hand. She nodded yes. I picked up her left hand and placed my thumb in the center of her palm, letting my fingers rest on the top of the center of the back of her hand. I was just holding her hand, but with an emphasis on the center points. Her hand was amazingly soft and responsive. These two points on the hand stimulate the Fire Element. In fact, they stimulate what is known in astern medicine as "essential fire" or the fire of unique, primordial essence. As I held her hand in this way, I asked Maggie to look up into her son's eyes. Justin was a very tall man, and he towered above his mother who sat somewhat crumpled and collapsed on her bed. Justin looked into his mother's eyes with all the love he felt for her.

They gazed at one another as I continued to gently hold Maggie's hand. After a few minutes I heard her sigh, and looking over, I saw a few tears slide down her porcelain white cheek. "Mom, I love you," Justin said. And with her eyes still intent on her son, Maggie replied, quite clearly, "I love you, too. I know you are trying to help me."

Then, glancing at me as she withdrew her hand, she quietly stood up and said, "I'm going to get dressed. I'll meet you downstairs." Justin and I left the room and Maggie appeared a few minutes later, looking quite lovely. She descended the stairs with the grace of the great woman she truly was. Justin's love—his relationship to his mother—blew the air of life onto the flame of her hope, and it rose renewed out of its smoldering retreat. It seems a simple matter to step out of the past and into the present, but it requires will, inspiration, and Fire Element attributes. It can make the difference between life and death.

In addition to the points in the center of the palm and the center of the back of both hands, there are, of course, the points indicated on the charts we have been referencing for all the elements. The little finger, noted on the chart of the fingers, is another route to Fire Element harmony. In addition, key points that you can touch to bring your fire into balance quickly include 26 and 13. Holding both 26s together, or giving yourself a hug as Estrella did in Chapter 3, rekindles the flame of your essence.

You can also awaken your Fire Energy by meditating on a flame, such as candlelight, to absorb its intensity and warmth. Maggie did this when she gazed into the firelight of her son's eyes. This reminded her of her own love of life that he embodied. The four meridians of the Fire Element are all stimulated by looking up—seeing beyond yourself into the divine vastness. In this way, contacting the Fire Element is a surefire treatment for depression!

Use the illustrations on pages 196–197 to help you keep the exquisite fire of your unique and essential spirit burning brightly and steadily throughout your life. Balancing the fire energies is as important as regenerating the adrenal system for the resolution of shock. Shock attacks the spirit on all levels. Overwhelming experience robs us not only of the will to live, but also direction in life. That is why victims of shock often have a lost look in their eyes. In addition to Jin Shin Tara treatment, praying, meditating, and reading inspirational stories such as those in this book will restore sparkle and light both internally and in what we radiate out to the world.

Water: The Incredible Lightness of Being

I conducted my doctoral internship at a center for people with disabilities. The total relief that paraplegics and people with cerebral palsy and spinal cord injuries felt when they swam was striking to me. Once in the pool, they had no limitations. The joy and freedom of movement they experienced was clearly exhilarating. It was a thrill just to see them after their time in the water. The ecstasy of being unbroken, mobile, and strong stayed with them for hours and sometimes even for an entire day. I wanted to find a way for them to be in this state of wholeness all the time.

My research at that time was an inquiry into the very question of wholeness. Was it even possible to feel whole despite extensive physical challenge, such as being unable to walk, see, have sex, or have bladder control? My work with Gabriel Restrova that is described in Chapter 3 reveals my continued inquiry into this question. One thing is clear though: Water and wholeness go together.

From the perspective of many traditions, the Water Element is the key to physical health and longevity. It is also synonymous with adrenal function, the hormonal activity directly connected with shock and trauma, and the Kidney and Bladder Meridians. It is the element that rules our immune functions and reveals our genetic inheritance.

Water Element depletion or weakness is associated with fear in most five-element systems. For the physically challenged population, the fear of being unstable, vulnerable, and of not having all their physical functions available to defend and protect themselves, evoked inhibitions that the water gloriously removed. They were afraid of how others would respond to them when they saw their awkward movements or their wheelchairs, both of which were not present in the water. The freedom of swimming was always over too soon, and my dear wounded friends returned to dry land like fish being taken out of water.

At that time, I did not know what I know now about the elements. If I had, I would have been able to transmit a multitude of methods for bringing the Water Element to life. Exploring a relationship with the Water Element does not mean that you have to live near water or be in it all the time. Even if you live in a desert or in the dry Rocky Mountains where I live, you can connect with the Water Element by using Jin Shin Tara, by doing fluid movement (yoga, hula, t'ai chi, chi kung, to name just a few), and by visualizing water, such as seeing yourself at the ocean or in a lake. Remember that all the elements are always present everywhere.

An awareness of the power of the Water Element to heal is not restricted to astern medicine. Think, for instance, of the great tradition of baptism. Baptism consists of either immersion in water or anointing with water. It brings with it renewal and regeneration. Historical and biblical references to baptism refer to its power to redeem, forgive, illuminate,

Kidney Meridian
    Beginning and Ending
    Points: 12/opposite little
    toe

Bladder Meridian
    Beginning and Ending
    Points: 3/same side 12

and even to rename the one who is baptized. Baptism is the use of water as an experience of rebirth, and that is what I observed with my physically challenged clients. They were reborn to their true vital selves in the water. This is the power of the Water Element for everyone. We have the capacity to restore immune function, to fight disease, and to increase longevity through the strengthening and cultivation of the Water Element. If your immune system is weak, if you avoid risks and make decisions based on fear, if fluid unpredictable change is threatening to you, or if you panic easily, then you can benefit from contact with the Water Element.

It is the disharmony of the Water Element that produces the quaking and shivering that occurs in panic attacks. This refers directly to debilitated adrenal function and reveals extreme and possibly repeated shock. Panic attacks are reactivated by circumstances reminiscent of their original causation. Determining the initial source can pave the way to ultimate resolution.

In the case of panic attacks, however, you have to first calm down enough to identify the source of the conditioning. I have heard amazing stories of panic attacks that stopped completely simply from holding the index finger of either hand. The index finger rules the meridians of this element—the Kidney and Bladder. For a thorough resolution of fear, consistent and deeper treatment is usually necessary. Consult the illustrations on page 201 that show the key points for the Water Element on the Kidney and the Bladder Meridians, and as you hold these areas, your mind will easily and naturally, over time, provide you with all the information you need to stop the recurrence of panic. If you want one point that will immediately harmonize the Water Element in your body, use Point 23, as indicated in the chart of elements on page 184.

Because panic attacks are virtually synonymous with shock, I have provided additional and potent self-care treatment in this book. See Nedra Gordon's story in Chapter 3 for a compilation of dependable methods for coming out of panic. I'll review one tried-and-true approach again here. Consult the map of the body on pages 46–47 and find Points 24 and 26. Hold each of these on opposite sides, and then switch sides. Do this three times on each side. By the time you have completed this process, your panic attack will be completely over and you will feel centered. Your breath will come deeply and fully from the core of your being. You will never again be without a resource in the face of panic. This easy treatment for panic is also essential when shock occurs suddenly for the first time, so become familiar with it and teach it to others.

Wood: The Power of a Clear and Focused Mind

The three elements that relate most directly to the triune brain structure described throughout this book are Earth, Air, and Wood.

The Earth Element's calm ground of acceptance and unconditional love balances the reptilian brain. It liberates the primitive reactions conditioned by shock and replaces them with deep-rooted feelings of confidence and inner security. The Air Element's messages of connection and unity speak directly to the mammalian brain and open neurological pathways constricted by shock. This opening allows joyous community. The Wood Element's clarity and focus transforms rage and resentment, thus empowering the higher neocortical brain. Well-structured planning for the implementation of our dreams and visions is then possible. The Wood Element actualizes intelligence. When the potent energies of anger are harnessed, they stimulate the topmost and newer brain to formulate plans and decisions for action and manifestation.

Shock is disorganizing and disempowering. It ravages the nervous system with chaos and fragmentation. The damage done by shock shapes neurology virulently. It leaves us frustrated and often extremely angry. Gabriel Restrova, for instance, in Chapter 3 was furious at the forces of fate, and this fury held him back much more than his wheelchair. The treatment of the two Wood Element meridians, the Liver and Gallbladder, will restore the definitive functions crucial to the presentation of who we really are in the world. Remember how much relief Gabriel felt when the base of his cranium was held? The head is the physical territory of the Wood Element, and by relaxing the Wood Element within himself, Gabriel was able to see a path of beauty ahead.

In astern medicine, each of the elements is associated with a season. The Air Element is the Autumn, the time of letting go. The Fire Element is the Summer, the season of heat and expression. The Water Element is the Winter, when we conserve energy and go within. The Earth Element is the time between seasons, when we have to find our ground and our trust because things are changing. The Wood Element is dominant in springtime, the time of blooming and coming forth. Nothing impedes our manifestation—our blooming—more than unresolved rage.

What do we do with our anger? Survivors of shock generally respond in one of two ways. Either they turn their anger inward and become depressed or addictive, or they explode with anger that is confused and misdirected. The first response is parasympathetic, and the second

Gallbladder Meridian
   Beginning and Ending
      Points: 12/same side 22

Liver Meridian
   Beginning and Ending
      Points: 4/4

is sympathetic. The balanced option is the way of vision. This is the option to use the powerhouse of anger that is an inevitable by-product of shock, in a positive way. The resolution of shock fuels the intelligence that paves the way to a peaceful future. If you are frustrated because you cannot envision a better future for yourself or your family, if you are unable to focus on projects or tasks, or if you feel unable to push toxic influences out of your body, then the Wood Element is your ally and you will benefit from befriending it.

The Wood Element's sole purpose is to encourage our effectiveness. This book directs you to the healing and nourishment of the Wood Element functions of grounded visionary thinking, planning, and decision-making. It also shows you how to resolve and transform the anger that obscures intelligence.

Use the beginning and ending points for the Gallbladder and the Liver Meridians (see illustrations on page 204) to constantly vitalize these pathways. Hold your middle finger to send messages of awareness and connection to your mind-body, indicating through your action that you want to encourage unification and discourage a mind-body split. You can also hold these areas whenever you feel that anger is overtaking you, robbing you of your centrality or capacity to make good choices. Your contact with yourself sends a very clear message to your higher brain, and you will be amazed to witness the spontaneous transformation of the negative drive of fury into diplomacy and innovation. Also, don't be surprised if you find yourself making different choices in the food you eat without having to use discipline. The health of the Liver and Gallbladder Meridians will speak directly through these choices, and you will not feel like you are giving up anything.

Push-hands is the name of a practice in t'ai chi that suits this element well. In push-hands you are physically setting boundaries gracefully, making sure no one invades your space. Pushing away from a wall or pushing against a hard surface with your hands or your feet is a simple activity that allows you to feel the power of the Wood Element immediately. Virtually all the martial arts, from aikido to karate, teach the movements that embody the Wood Element.

Clarity of mind, demonstrated in choice and action, is one of the great victories in the resolution of shock. Because shock is so much more volatile than trauma, it rips through the entire nervous system, and crucial links between feeling, thinking, and action are destroyed like bridges bombed in a war maneuver. But those bridges can be rebuilt and, as so often happens, the new structures are even more useful and resplendent than the old ones. Survivors of shock who reclaim the full range of ever-expanding intelligence *never* take such a gift for granted!

There is a strong link between intelligence and memory, and the Wood Element, from an astern perspective, rules both. Many survivors of shock suffer from either memory loss, even to the point of amnesia (this is common after an auto accident), or memory distortions. In addition, shock can impact our capacity to retain facts and information and to translate that information to other circumstances, making us feel deficient or inadequate. People often feel very defeated by these apparently irretrievable losses.

The consistent treatment of the Liver and Gallbladder Meridians, as suggested here and, in addition, by holding Points 4, 12, and 20 in any combination and on both right and left sides, will bring sunlight to a foggy mind. These were the points I emphasized for Rebecca Loveland and for Gabriel Restrova, both of whom had suffered head injuries, which damage the Wood Element. The full recovery of coherence is completely within the realm of neurological possibility. Laser-sharp memory function is the natural outcome of cortical reorganization. The capacity of the brain to recover from losses, either directly or indirectly, by developing acuity in other functions, has been proven in the therapeutic treatment of obsessive-compulsive disorder as well as in the treatment of aphasia.[1]

NOTE: Don't be confused if the same points serve more than one element. The sacred sites of the body are all multitaskers! Similarly, I have provided multiple approaches to the awakening of the elements so that you can make choices in different circumstances. None of them are contradictory. You can use all of them or one of them—but please use them!

I cannot end this section on the Wood Element without bowing to Rachel Carson and her book, *Silent Spring*. If springtime is the arena for our brilliant manifestation, what can be said if that springtime is silent? Rachel Carson's answer is clear, as she tells us what has "silenced the voices of spring in countless towns in America"[2]:

> The central problem of our age has become the contamination of our total environment with substances of incredible potential for harm—substances that accumulate in the tissues of plants and animals and even penetrate the germ cells to shatter or alter the very material of heredity upon which the shape of the future depends.

As we heal ourselves and build strength in our bodies and minds, we can, if our vision directs us to, use that strength to protest environmental abuse, just as we need to protest the abuse of children. While this book is about personal health and personal empowerment, it is also about our collective health and the body of the Earth. Rachel Carson died in the spring of 1964, just two years after *Silent Spring* was published. But because she spoke her truth and acted to protect her world, her voice will never be silenced. One book by a single determined woman launched a global movement of environmental advocacy. Each of us has the capacity to make a contribution, in our own way, and each one of us is needed.

> *Tell me, what else should I have done?*
> *Doesn't everything die at last, and too soon?*
> *Tell me, what is it you plan to do*
> *with your one wild and precious life?*
> —Mary Oliver

8 Envisioning a World Without Shock

> *We know that things are getting worse for our children. Overwhelmed, we still wait for top-down solutions—decisions from the president or other elected officials, or the heads of agencies like the surgeon general— which we hope will make a difference. But the problems are getting worse. Top-down solutions will not be forthcoming. Change will come from the bottom up, from everyday people. The hand that rocks the cradle shapes these outcomes.*
>
> —Robin Karr-Morse and Meredith Wiley

There are three warnings we must heed if we are to create a world without shock:

1. We know that when someone has repeated, overwhelming experiences without a sufficient opportunity for resolution and integration, the result will be a debilitating effect on physical, neurological, and psychological functions.[1]

2. We know that shock, trauma, and stress for a pregnant woman negatively impacts the developing fetus as well as the mother, and can inhibit appropriate brain sequencing.[2]

3. We know that the proliferation of shock includes not only the occurrences that are inevitable in life, but also the overwhelming rise in violence worldwide and the massive use of pollutants without adequate restraint or sufficient protective measures.[3]

To counter these three factors, we must do everything in our power to create a shock-free world for the children of the future and for ourselves now. Excellent resources are developing to support this choice, including the following:

1. As our knowledge of the brain and its behavior has increased, so has our awareness of the brain's recuperative powers. The brain has the capacity not only for compensation, but also of restoration and regeneration. What we need are the skills, patience, and attention to nourish these healing capacities. We can make this healing a priority in our families, healthcare systems, hospitals, nursing homes, domestic violence treatment centers, veterans facilities, homeless shelters, prisons, addictions and recovery clinics, and in our communities.[4]

2. Preventing prenatal and birth shock is, I believe, one of the most important actions we can take for the world. The resources *are* available. In Hawaii, for instance, where domestic violence is at its peak in the United States, the Healthy Start Program has successfully reduced abuse in the families it serves by 90 percent. They do this by building a network of support for entire families, not only during pregnancy, but even when conception is being considered. All the evidence points to this early intervention and prevention as the only real way to stop the cycle of violence.[5] Other programs are addressing this issue from this perspective and they need our support and participation. At the end of Chapter 6 you will find resources listed so that you may contact these organizations.

3. We can educate ourselves about the danger of contaminants and take action. This is not as difficult as it seems. For instance, shortly after I read that swordfish contained so much mercury that if pregnant women ate it they would be virtually insuring neurological damage to their unborn child, I saw swordfish on the menu of a restaurant where I was eating. I sent an e-mail to the restaurant owner giving him the facts, and he responded by taking swordfish off the menu. My next step was to send another e-mail to a local store that was selling swordfish. They responded in the same way. It took only an hour or two of my time to make this contribution to protect the children of the future. In these and other simple ways we can become a caring community of advocates for the unborn.

4. In this chapter, I reference recent studies on youth violence, such as the *Safe Start* report from the Office of Juvenile Justice and Delinquency Prevention. These highlight the resiliency of troubled young people. We see them differently if we understand their struggles as the result of a lineage of shock. Care providers can become educated about the neurological and energetic interventions the TARA Approach recommends and mentor youth accordingly, with compassionate awareness.

A component of the activism I point to in this book is the use of subtle energy medicine to stop the replication of shock patterns in your body and your neurology, and to support family members in this same direction. It may seem a long distance between using Jin Shin Tara for yourself and your family to stopping the proliferation of pollutants or protecting the children of the future. You may wonder how the use of subtle energy medicine will help create a shock-free world. There are multitudes of answers to this question. A few of them include:

◈ Subtle energy medicine allows us to safely stimulate and encourage prenatal development so that it flourishes. The general consensus is that early intervention is the key to violence prevention. Government and agency reports reiterate this now, but take few steps to activate their wisdom. We can do that ourselves by intervening with subtle energy medicine as soon as possible.

◈ Through the use of subtle energy medicine and other supportive therapies we can strengthen our immune systems so that we are significantly more resistant to toxins. This immune system strength has many additional benefits. It allows us to pass on immune system health to our children. It helps us push out toxins. It gives us endurance and stamina so that we can make our contributions to the world without suffering from the effort. Burnout is an expression of shock. The more we heal from shock, the less likely we are to experience burnout.

◈ Self-care practice as a lifestyle in personal and family life can free us substantially from reliance on chemical solutions. This, along with the other expense-free advantages of this practice, makes subtle energy medicine the most cost-effective healthcare there is. The current level of healthcare costs is shocking in itself!

◈ As we resolve shock and trauma in our lives and in our bodies, the primitive brain relaxes, allowing higher brain functions to dominate and evolve. When we act from higher brain orientation, we are less likely to perpetuate the lineage of shock, and instead we become embodiments of shock-free existence.

When I speak of a shock-free world, I am actually referring to shock-free *worlds*. These are:

◈ Your own personal world.

◈ The world of your physical body.

◈ The world of your family.

◈ The world of your community.

◈ The world of your country.

◈ The world of the Earth.

We have already envisioned worlds without shock and described them to one another. Poets, artists, neurologists, biologists, environmentalists, birth educators, and healers are building communities to educate, communicate, and share resources to end the epidemic of shock. We must join them.

The Epidemic of Youth Violence

If there is one fact that demonstrates that we are all in shock it is the unprecedented rise in youth violence. Even the Centers for Disease Control and the United States Department of Justice acknowledge that youth violence has reached epidemic proportions and has overwhelmed traditional treatment resources.[6] In addition, sexual assault is one of the fastest-growing violent crimes in the United States. Twenty percent of all rapes and 30–50 percent of child molestations are carried out by youths younger than 18 years of age. This increase in youthful sexual aggression is well-documented by a wide variety of sources, including criminal justice agencies. All use the word "epidemic" when commenting on the rise in sexual crimes that they admit they cannot fathom.[7]

While the data reveals that males are more often the perpetrators of these crimes, in all other regards, the statistics show that the crimes reflect the population in terms of ethnicity and social class. In a national survey of sexually abusive youth, they came from all racial, economic, ethnic, and religious backgrounds.[8] We are all in this together. There is no one to point the finger at and no one to blame. It is a mutual problem and we must solve it together. For the most part, we are not solving it at all and that is because solutions that work have not been articulated and presented by a cohesive forum that can implement them. We are at a loss and feel overwhelmed. This means we cannot successfully use our resources. This translates to: We are all in shock.

It is time to come out of shock. If we do not, how do we expect that our children will? If our youth are killing each other and sexually abusing each other (please bear in mind here that the average age of a victim of sexual assault is 5 years old) can there be any question that we are all in shock?[9] I hang my head in shame that the culture I call my own is degrading so rapidly with so few objecting. I must object, and I must look for solutions. Won't you join me? I pray that we will envision a world without shock together, and find like-minded souls who will support each other in overcoming our personal obstacles so that we can make this a better world, a place of beauty and welcoming for the children of the future.

It is clear that early intervention is required to end the lineage of shock. In 2000, the National Summit on Children Exposed to Violence published its report, *Safe From the Start*. In the very beginning pages of this United States Department of Justice commentary, there is this statement:

> *Recent research on children's brain development shows that what happens very early in a child's life forms the core of his or her capacity for learning, socialization, and success. In fact, for even the youngest child, the feelings of terror, hopelessness, rage, and anxiety are very real.* Beginning earlier means reaching at-risk families even before the child is born. (My emphasis)[10]

Westerners tend to look repeatedly at Western methodologies when they are stumped, but in regard to coming out of shock, we are at a dead end. "Current efforts to prevent violence typically consist of generating lists of effective programs and disseminating information on them in an effort to rally public support program by program, a strategy that has proved to be ineffective."[11] We need a new perspective.

To envision a world without shock is to envision a world that honors birth. This is what early intervention means. "For children, the equivalent of home is the womb. For this reason, it is important for every single couple to go on a healing journey even before they attempt to bring a child to this reality. How can we possibly save the world if we don't save our own children or change the way we deal with them?"[12]

Early intervention means increased education about the meaning of conception and attunement to every stage in utero, as presented in this book. It means addressing the needs of the family before the baby's birth, and it means understanding what it means to be a baby. "Babies want one person close to them all the time. They want to eat around the clock continually. They want us there with them when they wake up, including numerous times in the night. They want to be the center of our lives."[13] It is actually that simple. We must act as individuals and as a community to answer these basic needs for all children, rich and poor. It is the simple solution to the complex epidemic. It all comes down to this: "Our prisons are overflowing with the ghosts of babies lost to unseen and often unintended crimes in their cradles."[14]

Joining Together

There are many ways that we can envision a future without shock, and there are resources available at every level. In addition, at each stage of your commitment you can act powerfully as an independent force, just as I did when I contacted the restaurant selling swordfish. Chapter 6 directs you to who you can contact if you want to join a larger collective for action, but you can also cultivate your internal resources. When you combine internal resources with a larger community, your impact can be substantially increased.

My own particular emphasis is on educating parents, midwives, family birthing unit staff, and physicians to prevent prenatal and birth shock. This is how I feel I can most effectively use my skills to envision a future without shock. I ask you to explore your own potential contributions and to see if you are willing to make them. I make this request not because I think you should or must do this, but to let you know that you can. There is no need to be afraid of taking action, and it can be joyous to join with others for a common and beneficial purpose when it comes from your heart and your inner guidance.

My decision to speak and act on behalf of the children of the future comes directly from my own personal investigations, and always has. However, when I discovered the unquestionable and direct link between my prenatal and birth experience and the most significant choices I was making as an adult, I knew that I had a responsibility to share this information with others. I sought the best outlets for my particular way of communicating and employed them. Writing this book was one of the vehicles of expression I chose.

Beginning with inquiry into your own prenatal life and birth and how these have led to who you are today is, from my perspective, an excellent starting point. Everything unfolds from that orientation. Fortunately, there are people and organizations that have been building over the years to support you in this investigation. In addition to my own program that uniquely focuses on the use of subtle energy medicine, there are trainings offered by a variety of highly qualified mentors.

If you would like to share your commitment to end the lineage of shock and trauma with a larger community, there are excellent opportunities and they are increasing all the time. I would like to especially direct you to the many efforts of Suzanne Arms, who is a crusader and educator in this field. Suzanne and I both spoke out about the importance of baby and mother centered birth at the same time and we have been on parallel paths ever since. Suzanne has seeded several organizations that can provide you with excellent companionship on this journey, such as Birthing the Future and the Alliance for Transforming the Lives of Children.

Another way that you can end the repetition of shock in your family life is to incorporate the consciousness of healing through ritual. This means gathering your family together to honor birth and to celebrate the sanctity of our lives here. Many cultures use ritual to keep alive the bond of love they share despite external circumstances. In my work in Mexico I have always been heartened by the way Mexican families honor their ancestors and their lineage. Rituals that honor conception, the stages of prenatal life, and birth are profoundly healing. Deepening and building bonds of love always resolves shock.

My dear friend and colleague, Melissa Michaels, addresses the need for ritualizing the initiation into young adulthood in summer youth camps that she facilitates called Surfing the Creative. I asked her to tell me what motivated her to create these rites of passage. Here is her response:

> Our young people are desperately seeking connection with themselves, with community, and with something greater than themselves. Due to many factors, including our often fast-paced, media-driven, fear-fueled culture, it is increasingly difficult for our youth to make these life sustaining connections. In order to support their developmental needs, we must gather to dialogue

and share meaningful activities with our teens and young adults. Together we can offer them inspired opportunities to heal their wounds and access their creative potentials.

Surfing the Creative Youth Camp is a way of weaving together generations and cultures. We gather to build the bridge from heredity to destiny. Through the expressive arts, community service, and wilderness experience, inner and outer pathways are cultivated and empower youth to use their power as authentic change agents.

In the end, young people remember that they have creative options, gifts that grow out of their struggles, and people who care deeply about mentoring them into the future. This rite of passage is an invitation to heal, awaken, and co-create a positive future. It is a moving journey of empowerment, connection, and hope.

Out of her personal and committed inquiry into the shock that shaped her own life, Melissa offers a way to end the lineage of shock for youth. She models the generous and confident outreach that is possible when we heal deeply. She knows that community ritual repairs family wounds. She constructs creative launch pads that let young people spring into their manifested essence rather than suppress and distort it through violence and substance abuse.

Shock and Loss

At no time is ritual more important than when loss occurs, particularly the loss of a child. For many families, this is an experience of profound shock. Through the use of ritual, this shock does not have to be borne by any individual alone. Though we have all generally become quite isolated in our nuclear families, the loss of a child is a loss to the entire community. In fact, it is a loss to the world. When we understand and live the truth that shock can be healed by our own hands and by our own communities, then we are actively envisioning and manifesting a world without shock.

One of the hallmarks of shock is powerlessness, and ritual is an antidote to powerlessness. "When ritual delivers us to the other side, to touch the place where spirit lives, it imbues us with an energy that empowers us," says Sukie Miller, founder of the Institute for the Study of Humanistic Medicine. In her research on how people deal with loss, Dr. Miller discovered that many cultures recognize the early loss of a twin. We referred to the frequency of this shock in Chapter 6. In the Yoruba culture, for instance, when it is known that a twin has died, a wooden doll is carved and called "the child who cannot talk." The doll stays in an honored place in the home for as long as the grieving continues. There is not an effort to forget, deny, or cut off the grieving. Thus, the residual shock of the loss is prevented because it is not repressed.[15]

"In societies where individuals are left to figure things out by themselves, some people may choose simply not to deal with their grief because they don't have a context for it, a corpse to mourn over, or the support of their communities. So they don't even allow themselves to acknowledge the loss. Most often, the grieving process is not even considered. The grief will not go away, however, because we hide it somewhere deep within our bodies. On the contrary, it will go deep into our cells. When this repressed grief gets into our very inner being, it leads to physical illness."[16]

One thing that needs to be acknowledged to come out of the shock we are all in now is that we do not have all the answers here in the West. We need to learn from other people, and frequently the people we need to learn from the most are those that materially have much less than we do. We have to admit our vulnerability and our neediness, and receive from those who are rich in heart and spirit. In cultures that have survived with the help of rituals, loss is acknowledged not just by rituals that make a space for healing. There are also rituals that support the journey of the soul that has left this plane so that they can travel onwards and perhaps, if they choose, return here and be welcomed. It may be the people who live in the flow of a ritualized life who can teach us the most about how to envision a world without shock.

Begin Now

It is not too late. Begin now to help bring yourself, your family, your children, and your community out of shock. This book is full of suggestions just for this purpose that are designed for people of all ages, everywhere. Pay special attention to our youth because they are our future. "Of all the problems in child and adolescent psychiatry, violent behavior is the one most suited to prevention because it develops slowly, with risk factors gradually accumulating over many years before overt violent behavior emerges."[17] Be a model of non-shock behavior for the young people around you. Shock is contagious, but so is healing.

Begin now not only to envision a future without shock, but also to manifest it for yourself and your family here and now, and for the children of the future. In particular, use the tools, suggestions, inspirational stories, and resources in this book to cultivate your inner witness, practice subtle energy medicine, feel nature come alive within you, and resolve shock. There is nothing to stop you. You have the book; you just have to begin.

Author's Note

Climate crisis, the reiterative surfacing of racial injustice along with severe immune system threats create a constant sense of looming uncertainty amongst youth. One student, testifying before the American Congress in 2019 called this "a betrayal." Suicide is now the leading cause of death for youth ages 15–24 according to the World Health Organization. Prioritizing adult responsibility to listen deeply to youth and energizing youth leadership are bold steps we can take to end the spiral noted in the statistics above, all of which have risen by several orders of magnitude since then.

◆ Appendix

Super Charged Self-Care

The applications throughout this book ignite and circulate resilience. Super-charged applications are more potent and historically, were taught at an advanced level of learning. Due to the unprecedented demands of our global health crisis and the imperative to empower wellbeing at the grassroots level I created efficient translations of more complex treatment, which can be implemented without extensive study. Timeless wisdom understands that resilient potential can be held in reserve and the methodology for extracting it. That is what manifests through these super-charged flows which I'm presenting in self-care forms.

Breath, Regeneration, and Immunity are emphasized in this section as they are key areas of resilience and the most comprehensive functions that are challenged by epidemics and pandemics.

Breath, of course, refers to respiration;
Regeneration is directed specifically at the consequences of fatigue and exhaustion from physical and emotional challenges; and
Immunity strengthens and expands the activity of the immune system that ancient healing wisdom associates with human destiny.
In order to use these the treatments in this section effectively, please review the following instructions:

1. The quality of touch in each instance is light and steady. There is no pressure, rubbing, or movement. The word "listening" is often used to identify this quality of presence and receptivity. What are you listening for? Some would say "pulsation", but your experience is your own. You may "hear" in any variety of ways. Ultimately what you are listening for is the sensation of balance, flow, or release. This can

occur in varying amounts of time. You can hold the positions for one, two, or three minutes as suits you. Be attentive to how and when balance arrives for you. Perhaps you simply receive a deeper breath of life. As my teacher Mary said, "This is an art and you are the artist."

2. Various words are used to refer to the locations such as Point. Site, Area, or Sacred Site.

   The map in Chapter Two on The Physiology of Shock uses "Points/ Areas." Each one of these has at least a four-inch radius. This means you can be at ease about the placement of your contact with the points. My intent is that everyone feels confident to be creative and intuitive in developing relationships with these bioelectric fields (another way to describe the sites). Similarly, you can use any of your fingertips, the palms of your hand, and even the back of your hand if that is more comfortable.

3. And finally, treatment can be done on both sides of the body for any of the applications in this section.

Breath

Developmentally, the lungs and the heart evolve in intimate collaboration. They have an enduring relationship with each other. By using your touch to help these organs recall their connection you strengthen respiratory capacity including the release of toxins. At the same time these applications amplify your overall adaptive and integrative abilities.

Sacred Sites 22 (under the collarbone) and 14 (at the base of the ribs) frame the respiratory channels. When you place your fingertips or the palm of your hand on these sites you enliven respiratory function. Sacred Site 17 (at the base of the hand) signals the nervous system to integrate this recalibration to a higher frequency.

Guide: Place your fingertips just under the knob of collarbone (22) and under the ribs (14) on the same side. You can also use the palms of your hands in both locations.

For the second step of this application, place a fingertip in the valley between the base of the hand and the knob of the radius or wrist bone (17). Usually the index fingertip fits easily here. The other hand remains under the collarbone on the opposite side (22).

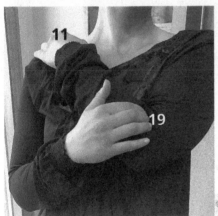

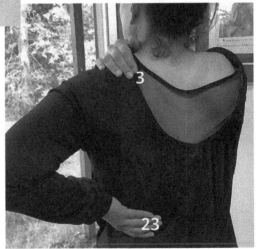

Regeneration

Panic, fear, anxiety, and sleeplessness are natural responses to crisis and become chronic if they are not relieved. Breathe into the ease of this soothing self-care intervention that not only alleviates current fatigue, it lessens the accumulated exhaustion that is often behind it. Feel the sensory experience of your nervous system upgrading and recalibrating as you expand into the relief.

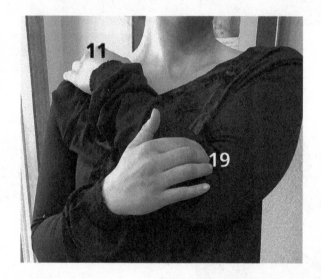

Guide: Rest the palm of the hand on the top of the opposite shoulder (11). The fingertips of the other hand rest in the bend of the opposite side elbow (19).
* NOTE that the index, middle, and ring fingers are lined up close to one another in the bend of the elbow (#19).

Sacred Site 11 is at the top of the shoulder. You can rest your hand there as illustrated so that the palm is on the site. This position releases patterns of over-responsibility and perfectionism that cause depletion. Sacred Site 19, in the bend of the elbow, turns on self-respect and protection. It is known as The Bodyguard. Holding these sites together frees you of resistance so that you are able to create the boundaries that lead to your regeneration.

Immunity

In this era of novel toxins and infections we are called to evolve our immune responses. This application unburdens historic immune depletion while elevating your potential for vibrancy. Imagine a well that is emptied, cleaned out, and then refilled with a fresh, clean supply of living waters.

Sacred Site 3 is located on the back, where the middle finger is positioned in the illustration. It heightens receptivity and also supports respiration and circulation. Sacred Site 23 is positioned on the site of the adrenals. It is sometimes referred to as Destiny. It amplifies the functions of your immune system. Contacting these two sites allows you to receive upgraded or supercharged immune system vitality.

Guide: Bring the palm of one hand to the top of the shoulder with the fingertips pointing downward on the upper back, below the shoulder. The middle finger naturally lands at 3.

The fingertips of the other hand are brought to the middle back area identified with the anatomical positioning of the adrenal gland (23). This is on the same side of the body. Alternatively the back of the hand can rest on 23 if that is more comfortable.

By placing our fingertips on these sites and sensing into our whole body responses we awaken their holistic functions and amplify wellbeing. Breath, Regeneration, and Immunity are nourished and expanded by consciousness and touch. We are responsive to caring attention at every stage of life. We can evolve in relationship to the present moment when we meet it prepared with awareness and love.

Chapter Notes

Chapter 1

[1] William R. Emerson, Ph.D. is a teacher, writer, and lecturer in the field of pre- and perinatal psychology. He has published dozens of articles and seven videos, as well as an excellent audio series on shock. Dr. Emerson is on the board of directors of the American Association of Pre- and Perinatal Psychology and Health (APPPAH). You can find out about Dr. Emerson and his training programs through his Website (*www.emersonbirthrx.com*). Dr. Emerson's extensive clinical research reveals that prenates and babies have their own unique distresses based on their extreme vulnerability to all that happens around them, especially parental distress and cultural disturbance. See his article, "The Vulnerable Prenate," in the *Journal of Pre- and Perinatal Psychology and Health*, 10(3), 1996, pp. 125–142.

[2] My advanced student and colleague, Theresa Hernandez, Ph.D., at the University of Colorado, has informed me through personal correspondence that a neurobehavioral research study, "Functional consequences of Jin Shin Tara treatment after stroke," (manuscript in preparation) reveals that in a single-blind crossover design preliminary investigation, Jin Shin Tara treatment results in increased calm, increased vitality and, most importantly, increased communication skills in a group environment for post-stroke aphasia patients. Because of its global, life-changing impact, stroke fits the definition of shock.

[3] Cleary, Thomas. *The Taoist I Ching.* Boston: Shambhala, 1986. p. 192. See also, by the same author, *The Buddhist I Ching.* Boston: Shambhala, 2001. The classic edition of the *I Ching*, with the introduction by Carl Jung, is in the Bollingen series, Princeton University Press, 1950. An excellent commentary on this book is Helmut and Richard Wilhelm's, *Understanding the I Ching*, also in the Bollingen series, with the latest edition being the one from 1956.

[4] Cleary, ibid.

[5] American Psychiatric Association, *Diagnostic and Statistical Manual of Mental Disorders (DSM-IV)*, Washington, DC: 1994. Posttraumatic Stress Disorder, pp. 424–427.

[6] Electroshock therapy is still being used and is sometimes recommended for people with bipolar disorders as well as others struggling with mental illness. Some of these courageous individuals have written stories about their experiences with this intervention. These reports are available from organizations serving people with bipolar disorder on the Internet as well as in a variety of books, including those by Kay Redfield Jamison, a psychiatrist who has bipolar disorder, and *The Bipolar Child* by Demitri and Janice Papolos. In addition, various Websites contain the candid and deeply moving accounts of people who have experience with electroshock therapy, including the Websites of organizations serving the mentally ill such as the National Alliance for the Mentally Ill, the National Depressive and Manic-Depressive Association, and the National Alliance for Research on Schizophrenia and Depression. These references provide a broad spectrum of evaluative perspectives.

[7] Bourke, Joanna. *Shellshock During World War I.* March 2002. Professor Bourke's research was part of a BBC broadcast and is available on line at the BBC homepage. Dr. Bourke is also the author of *An Intimate History of Killing* (London: Granta, 1998) and *The Second World War: A People's History* (Oxford: Oxford University Press, 2001), containing additional information on shell shock.

[8] Bourke, ibid.

Chapter 2

[1] In his book, *The Biology of Transcendence* (Rochester, Vermont: Park Street Press, 2002), Joseph Chilton Pearce guides us artfully through the developmental sequences of the brain so we can see how this neurochemistry can be supported. Arthur Janov's book, *The Biology of Love* (New York: Prometheus Books, 2000), is also devoted to this subject.

[2] Moore, Keith, Ph.D. and Persaud, T.V.M, M.D., *The Developing Human, (6th Edition)* Philadelphia: W.B. Saunders Co., 1998, and Larsen, William J., *Human Embryology,* New York: Churchill Livingstone, 1997. For the most recent information on the development of the prefrontal cortex, see Elkohonon Goldberg's, *The Executive Brain,* Oxford University Press, 2001 and Joseph Chilton Pearce's *The Biology of Transcendence.*

[3] See Allen Schore's *Affect Regulation and the Origins of Self.* New Jersey: Lawrence Erlbaum Associates, 1994 for extremely precise information on post-natal neurological sequencing.

[4] Pearce, Goldberg. ibid

[5] Schwartz, Jeffrey M., M.D. and Begley, Sharon, *The Mind and the Brain.* New York: Regan Books, 2002. Throughout this book Schwartz and Begley emphasize the ongoing plasticity of the brain's structure and the value of therapeutic interventions in this regard. See especially pp. 196–198. The book also contains references to Schwartz's work with obsessive-compulsive disorder (OCD). This research correlates with the interim findings in the University of Colorado study on the use of Jin Shin Tara for post-stroke aphasia.

[6] While this chapter describes the distinctions between sympathetic and parasympathetic shock dominance, be aware that there are also conditions of "mixed dominance" in which sympathetic and parasympathetic shocks are intricately woven together. Indeed one can have both forms of shock, but in most cases there is a clear dominance. When that clarity is lacking, the mixed dominance assessment usually applies.

[7] Amelia's mother is in the process of writing an article about what she observed during her daughter's recovery. She continues to study Jin Shin Tara and the TARA Approach, and she is incorporating this into her work as a teacher.

[8] Arms, Suzanne. *Immaculate Deception II.* Berkeley: Celestial Arts, 1994, p. 86. Throughout the book you will find references to the long-term impact of various drugs and medications on children. William Emerson's article, "Birth Trauma: The Psychological Effects of Obstetrical Interventions," in the Fall 1998 issue of the *Journal of Prenatal and Perinatal Psychology and Health* (pp. 11–43) provides specific details on the after-effects of pitocin and birth induction (see especially p. 28), which relates directly to Leticia's story.

Chapter 5

[1] Goldberg, pp. 62–68. Dr. Schwartz's research with aphasia and OCD, referenced earlier, is also applicable here.

[2] Ibid.

[3] Schore, p. 23.

[4] Bennett-Goleman, Tara. *Emotional Alchemy: How the Mind Can Heal the Heart.* New York: Harmony Books, 2001, pp. 196–197. Tara Bennett-Goleman presents a view of mindfulness and what she calls "meta-cognition" that closely resembles the concept of the compassionate witness. Overall, *Emotional Alchemy* is a good companion to this book, with its Buddhist-based techniques for dissolving shock-conditioned thinking.

[5] Chodron, Pema. *The Places That Scare You.* Boston: Shambhala, 2002.

[6] Cousins, Norman. *Anatomy of an Illness.* New York: Bantam, 1981.

[7] Ibid.

8 This excerpt from *The Dreaming Child: How Children Can Help Themselves Recover from Illness and Injury,* is used with the permission of the Dom Project.

9 Blanchard, Edward B., Ph.D. and Hickling, Edward J., Psy.D. *After the Crash.* Washington, D.C.: American Psychological Association, 1997. See especially pp. 21–34, which highlight the "large degree of mental and emotional suffering resulting from motor vehicle accidents in this country." Regarding studies of long-term PTSD and autoaccidents, see pp. 233–239. For the relationship between long-term mood disorders and auto accidents, see pp. 59–75, which also contain information about drug use and dependence. Of special interest in the study of shock are the statistics that reveal the frequency of previous trauma, car accidents, and recovery rates. For this, see pp. 48–50. In cases where there are multiple accidents and previous trauma it may be that full recovery is delayed because the situation requires the recognition and treatment of shock. Another good source for this information is Scaer, Robert C., M.D. *The Body Bears the Burden.* New York: Haworth Medical Press, 2001. See especially pp. 63–64 in regard to "trauma conditioning" and p. 159 for the relationship between motor vehicle accident recovery and language.

Chapter 6

1 The books listed here by Drs. Chamberlain and Verny are the notable exceptions in this literature as their writing is intended for a general audience. Schore, ibid. inter alia. Lipton, Bruce. "Nature, Nurture and the Power of Love." *Journal of Prenatal and Perinatal Psychology and Health,* 13(1), Fall 1998, 3–10. Madrid, Antonio. "Maternal Infant Bonding and Asthma." *Journal of Prenatal and Perinatal Psychology and Health,* 14(3–4), 279–289. Chamberlain, David. *The Mind of Your Newborn Baby.* Berkeley: North Atlantic Books, 1998. Verny, Thomas, M.D. *Nurturing the Unborn Child.* Chicago: Olmstead Press, 2000.

2 Steingraber, Sandra. *Having Faith.* Cambridge: Perseus Publishing, 2001, pp. 7–10. I have actually condensed this wonderful discovery story to highlight it, but I highly recommend that it be read in its entirety.

3 See resource list at the end of this chapter that will help you to identify threatening pollutants and what you can do about them.

4 Steingraber, ibid. p. 33.

5 Chamberlain, ibid. p. 207.

6 Chamberlain, personal correspondence. Landy, et al. Ultrasonic Assessment of Fetal Disappearance in the First Trimester," *American Journal of Obstetrics and Gynecology,* 1986, 14(9), p. 155.

7 Pointelli, Alessandra. *From Fetus to Child.* New York: Routledge, 2000, p.110.

8 To find out about Haptonomy, *www.haptonomie.org.*

9   Glynn, Laura, et al. "The Influence of Corticotrophin-Releasing Hormone on Human Fetal Development and Parturition," *Journal of Prenatal and Perinatal Psychology and Health,* 14(3–4), Summer 2000. Barbazanges, Arnaud, et al. "Maternal Glucocorticoid Secretion," *Journal of Neuroscience,* 16(12), June 15, 1996. Steingraber, ibid. inter alia, and *Living Downstream.* New York: Addison Wesley, 1997, inter alia. "New Report Links Chemicals Commonly Found in Industry and Home to Behavioral and Learning Disabilities," *Natural Resources Council of Maine,* May 11, 2000. Polgreen, Lydia, "Pollution Linked to Low Birth Weights in African-Americans," *NY Times,* January 17, 2003. Text of PBS script for Bill Moyers broadcast, "Are We Making Our Children Sick? How Environmental Toxins Affect America's Children." Aired May 10, 2002. Colborn, Theo, et al. *Our Stolen Future.* New York: Dutton, 1996, inter alia.

10   Panthuramphorn, C., M.D., et al. "Environmental Influences on Human Brain Growth and Development."*Journal of Prenatal and Perinatal Psychology and Health,* 12(3–4), Spring 1998, pp.163–174.

11   Schore. "The Neurobiology of Attachment and Early Personality Organization." *Journal of Prenatal and Perinatal Psychology and Health.* 16(3), Spring 2002, p. 250.

12   Raine, Adrian. "Biosocial Studies of Antisocial and Violent Behavior in Children." *Journal of Abnormal Child Psychology,* August 2002.

13   Dr. Peter Levine's Website: *http://www.traumahealing.com.* Michel Odent, M.D.: *http://www.birthworks.org/bwodent.html.*

14   Van de Carr, F., M.D., et al. "Prenatal University: Commitment to Fetal-Family Bonding." *Journal of Prenatal and Perinatal Psychology and Health.* 12(3–4), Spring 1998, pp. 119–134.

15   Napierala, Susanna. *Water Birth.* Westport, CT.: Bergin and Garvey, 1994. This book contains the fascinating report of what may well have been the first medically advised and supervised water birth in France in 1805. The doctor prescribed a water birth as an intuitive inspiration, and successfully encouraged an otherwise recalcitrant labor.

16   Arms, Suzanne. *Immaculate Deception II.* Berkeley: Celestial Arts, p. 83.

17   Borysenko, Joan. *A Woman's Book of Life.* New York: Riverhead, 1996, 93–94.

18   Leboyer, Frederick, M.D. *Birth Without Violence (revised edition).* Rochester, Vermont: Healing Arts Press, 2002.

Chapter 7

1   Schwartz and Begley, pp. 196–200.

2   Carson, Rachel. *Silent Spring.* New York: Houghton-Mifflin, 1994.

Chapter 8

[1] Laucht, Manfred. "Behavioral Sequelae of Perinatal Insults and Family Adversity." *Journal of the American Academy of Child and Adolescent Psychiatry.* October 2000.

[2] Prescott, James W., Ph.D. "The Origins of Love and Violence." *Journal of Pre- and Perinatal Psychology and Health,* 10(3), pp. 143–188, Spring 1996. Schore, Allan N., "The Effects of Early Relational Trauma on Right Brain Development, Affect Regulation and Infant Mental Health." *Infant Mental Health Journal,* 22, pp. 201–269, 2001.

[3] Iain, Murray, "Juvenile Murder," Christian Science Monitor, March 27, 2000, p. 9. Report of the Children's Defense Fund, 2000. Steingraber. *Having Faith.* inter alia. Also, Steingraber. *Living Downstream.* inter alia. Coburn, Theo. *Our Stolen Future.* inter alia.

[4] Schwartz, ibid. McEwen, Bruce. "Stress and Brain Development." *Journal of the American Academy of Child and Adolescent Psychiatry,* January 1999.

[5] Wilson, John J. Office of Juvenile Justice and Delinquency Prevention, "Safe from the Start." *Report of the National Summit on Preventing and Reducing the Negative Impact of Children's Exposure to Violence,* November 2000.

[6] Ibid.

[7] Report of the Work Group on Quality Issues. "Assessment and Treatment of Children and Adolescents Who Are Sexually Abusive of Others." *Journal of the American Academy of Child and Adolescent Psychiatry,* December 1999.

[8] Ibid.

[9] Ibid.

[10] Safe from the Start. ibid.

[11] Karr-Morse, Robin and Wiley, Meredith S. *Ghosts from the Nursery.* New York: Atlantic Monthly Press, 1997, p. 285.

[12] Somé, Sobonfu E. *Welcoming Spirit Home.* Novato, Calif.: New World Library, 1999, p. 44.

[13] Morse-Wiley, ibid. p. 291.

[14] Ibid. p. 296.

[15] Miller, Sukie, Ph.D. *Finding Hope when A Child Dies.* New York: Simon and Schuster, 1999, p. 117.

[16] Somé, ibid. p. 80.

[17] "Assessment and Treatment of Adolescents Who Are Sexually Abusive." ibid.

Bibliography

Abbott, Roberta. *From Shell Shock to Post-Traumatic Stress Disorder*. Conference of Defense Associations Institute, 2000 Symposium.

Abraido-Lanza, Ana F. "Psychological Thriving Among Latinas with Chronic Illness." *Journal of Social Issues* (Summer 1998): 405–424.

Amen, Daniel G. *Change Your Brain, Change Your Life*. New York: Three Rivers Press, 1998.

Arms, Suzanne. *Immaculate Deception*. Berkeley, Calif.: Celestial Arts, 1996.

Barkow, Jerome, et al. *The Adapted Mind: Evolutionary Psychology and the Creation of Culture*. New York: Oxford University Press, 1992.

Bass, Ellen and Laura Davis. *The Courage to Heal*. New York: Harper & Row, 1988.

Beinfield, Harriet and Efrem Korngold. *Between Heaven and Earth*. New York: Ballantine, 1991.

Bennett-Goleman, Tara. *Emotional Alchemy: How the Mind Can Heal the Heart*. New York: Harmony Books, 2001.

Blanchard, Edward B, Ph.D. and Edward J. Hickling, Psy.D. *After the Crash: Assessment and Treatment of Motor Vehicle Accident Survivors*. Washington, DC: American Psychological Association, 1997.

Blankenship, Kim M. "A Race, Class, and Gender Analysis of Thriving." *Journal of Social Issues* 54(2) Summer 1998, 393–404.

Bourke, Joanna. *Shell Shock During World War One*. BBC History Homepage, 2002.

Breuer, J. and S. Freud. *Studies on Hysteria*. London: Hogarth Press, 1955.

Brower, B. "A Tip of the Tongue to the Brain." *Science News*, 160(10), p. 155, 2001.

———. "Babies Show an Eye for Faces." *Science News*, 160(21), p. 331, 2001.

———. "Certain Mental Illnesses May be Tied to Violence." *Science News*, 158(18), p. 279, 2000.

Bruch, Hilda. *Golden Cage*. New York: Vintage, 1979.

Burmeister, Alice. *The Touch of Healing*. New York: Bantam, 1997.

Caduto, Michael J. and Joseph Bruchac. *Keepers of the Night: Native American Stories*. Golden: Colo., Fulcrum Publishing, 1994.

Carson, Rachel. *Silent Spring*. New York: Houghton Mifflin, 1962.

Cassou, Michell and Stuart Cubley. *Life, Paint and Passion*. New York: Tarcher, 1995.

Castellino, Raymond. "The Stress Matrix: Implications for Prenatal and Birth Therapy." *Journal of Prenatal and Perinatal Psychology and Health*, 15(1), Fall 2000, 31–62.

Chamberlain, David B., Ph.D. *The Mind of Your Newborn Baby*. Berkeley: Calif., North Atlantic Books, 1998.

———. "Prenatal Receptivity and Intelligence." *Journal of Prenatal and Perinatal Psychology and Health*, Volume 12, Nos. 3–4, Spring 1998.

Chard, Philip. *The Healing Earth*. Wisc.: NorthWord, 1994.

Cleary, Thomas, tr. *The Taoist I Ching*. Boston: Shambhala Press, 1986.

Colborn, Theo, et al. *Our Stolen Future*. New York: Dutton, 1996.

Colodzin, Benjamin. *How to Survive Trauma*. New York: Station Hill, 1993.

Connelly, Dianne M., Ph.D. *Traditional Acupuncture and the Law of the Five Elements*. Columbia, Maryland: Traditional Acupuncture Institute, Second Edition, 1994.

———. All Sickness is Homesickness. Columbia, Maryland: Traditional Acupuncture Institute, 1986.

Cousins, Norman. *Anatomy of an Illness: Reflections on Healing and Regeneration*. New York: Bantam Books, 1979.

Cowan, Eliot. *Plant Spirit Medicine: The Healing Power of Plants*. Columbus, NC.: Swan, Raven and Co., 1991.

Crow, David. *In Search of the Medicine Buddha: A Himalayan Journey*. New York: J. P.Tarcher, 2001.

Csikszentmihalyi, M. *Flow: The Psychology of Optimal Experience*. New York: Harper Perennial. 1990.

———. *The Evolving Self: A psychology for the third millennium*. New York: Harper Perennial, 1993.

———. *Creativity: Flow and the psychology of discovery and invention*. New York: Harper Perennial, 1996.

Dacey, John S., and Kathleen H. Lennon. *Understanding Creativity: The Interplay of Biological, Psychological and Social Factors*. San Francisco: Jossey-Bass, 1998.

Damasio, Antonio R. *Descartes' Error: Emotion, Reason and the Human Brain*. New York: Avon, 1994.

————. Antonio R. *The Feeling of What Happens*. New York: Harcourt Inc., 1996.

De Beauport, Elaine, et al. *The Three Faces of Mind: Developing Your Mental, Emotional and Behavioral Intelligences*. Wheaton, Ill: Quest Books, 1996.

Donden, Yeshe. *Health through Balance*. New York: Snow Lion, 1986.

Emerson, William R., Ph.D. *Shock: A Universal Malady—Prenatal and Perinatal Origins of Suffering*. Six Audiotapes. Emerson Training Seminars, Petaluma, Calif., 1999.

————. "Birth Trauma: The Psychological Effects of Obstetrical Interventions." *Journal of Prenatal and Perinatal Psychology and Health*, 13(1), Fall 1998, 11–44.

England, Marjorie A. *Before We Are Born*. London: Mosby-Wolfe, 1996.

————. *Life Before Birth*. London: Mosby-Wolfe, 1996.

Epel, Elissa S. "Embodying Psychological thriving: physical thriving in response to stress." *Journal of Social Issues*, Summer 1998.

Essex, Marilyn J., et al. *Maternal Stress in Infancy May Sensitize Children to Later Stress Exposure: Effects on Cortisol Behavior*. Health-Emotions Research Institute, Dept. of Psychiatry, University of Wisconsin, February 2002.

Field, Tiffany. *Touch*. Cambridge, Mass.: MIT Press, 2001.

Finnegan, John. *The Vital Role of Essential Fatty Acids For Pregnant and Nursing Women*. excerpt from *The Facts About Fats*. Berkeley, Calif.: Celestial Arts, 1993.

Ford, Julian D. "Disorders of Extreme Stress Following War-zone Military Trauma." *Journal of Consulting and Clinical Psychology*, 1999, vol 67, iss 1, pp. 3–12.

Freud, S. *The Complete Psychological Works of Sigmund Freud* (On the Psychological Mechanism of Hysterical Phenomena: A Lecture, Heredity and the Etiology of Hysteria, The Etiology of Hysteria) London: Hogarth Press, 1962.

Friedman, et al. *Neurobiological and Clinical Consequences of Stress: From Normal Adaption to PTSD*. Smithville, Tex.: Runa-Raven Press, 1995.

Gelb, Michael J. *How to Think Like Leonardo Da Vinci*. New York: Dell Publishing, 1998.

Gershon, Michael D. *The Second Brain*. New York: Harper Collins, 1998.

Gilliland and Verny. "The Effects of Domestic Abuse on the Unborn Child." *Journal of Prenatal and Perinatal Psychology and Health*, Volume 13, Nos. 3–4, Spring/Summer 1990.

Glendinning, Chellis. *My Name is Chellis and I'm in Recovery from Western Civilization*. Boston: Shambhala Publications, 1994.

Glynn, Laura, Ph.D., et al. "The Influence of Corticotropin-Releasing Hormone on Human Fetal Development and Parturition." *Journal of Prenatal and Perinatal Psychology and Health*, 14(3–4), Spring/Summer 2000, pp. 243–256.

Goldberg, Elkhonon. *The Executive Brain: Frontal Lobes and the Civilized Mind*. New York: Oxford University Press, 2001.

Goleman, Daniel. *Emotional Intelligence*. New York: Bantam, 1995.

Gordner-Gordon, Joy. *The Healing Voice*. Calif.: Freedom, 1993.

Grasso Fitzpatrick, Jean. *Once Upon A Family: Read Aloud Stories that Nurture Healthy Kids*. New York: Penguin Putnam, 1998.

Griffin, Kawanza L. *Herbicides are linked to miscarriages*. Milwaukee Journal Sentinel, September 23, 2002.

Hammer, Leon. *Dragon Rises, Red Bird Flies*. New York: Station Hill, 1990.

Herman, Judith. *Father-Daughter Incest*. Cambridge: Harvard University Press, 1981.

———. *Trauma and Recovery*. New York: Harper, 1992.

Horowitz, Mardi. *Stress Response Syndromes*. NJ.: Aronson, 1986.

Irving, Michael, Ph.D. "Sexual Assault and Birth Trauma: Interrelated Issues." *Journal of Prenatal and Perinatal Psychology and Health*, Volume 11, No. 4, Summer 1997, pp. 215–250.

Janov, Arthur. *The Biology of Love*. Amherst, NY: Prometheus Books, 2000.

Janus, Ludwig, M.D. "The Impact of Prenatal Psychology on Society and Culture." *Journal of Prenatal and Perinatal Psychology and Health*, Volume 11, No. 4, Summer 1997.

Judith, Anodea. *Eastern Body Western Mind*. Berkeley, CA: Celestial Arts, 1996.

Kaptchuk, Ted. *The Web That Has No Weaver: Understanding Chinese Medicine*. New York: McGraw-Hill/Contemporary Books, 2000.

Karagulla, Shafica, and Dora Kunz. *The Chakras and the Human Energy Fields*. Wheaton, Ill.: Theosophical Publishing House, 1989.

Karagulla, Shafica. *Breakthrough to Creativity*. Calif.: DeVorss, 1985.

Karr-Morse, Robin and Meredith S. Wiley. *Ghosts from the Nursery: Tracing the Roots of Violence*. New York: Atlantic Monthly Press, 1997.

Larre and de la Vallee. *Rooted in Spirit*. New York: Station Hill, 1995.

Larsen, William J. *Human Embryology*. New York: Churchill Livingstone, 1997.

Laucht, Manfred. "Behavioral Sequelae of Perinatal Insults and Early Family Adversity at 8 Years of Age." *Journal of the American Academy of Child and Adolescent Psychiatry*, Oct. 2000.

Leboyer, Frederick, M.D. *Birth Without Violence*. Rochester, Vt: Healing Arts Press, 2002.

LeDoux, Joseph: *Synaptic Self: How Our Brains Become Who We Are*. New York: Viking Press, 2002.

———. *The Emotional Brain: The Mysterious Underpinnings of Emotional Life*. New York: Simon and Schuster, 1996.

Lee, John. *Writing from the Body*. New York: St. Martin's Press, 1994.

Levine, Peter. *Waking the Tiger*. Berkeley, Calif.: North Atlantic Books, 1997.

Lipson, Tony, M.D. *From Conception to Birth: Our Most Important Journey*. Newton, NSW, Australia: Millennium Books, 1994.

Lipton, Bruce, Ph.D. "Nature, Nurture and Human Development." *Journal of Prenatal and Perinatal Psychology and Health*, 16(2), Winter 2001, pp. 167–180.

MacLean, Paul, "A Mind of Three Minds: Educating the Triune Brain," in Cahill, J.S., ed. *Education and the Brain*. Chicago: University of Chicago Press, 1978, pp. 308–42.

Madrid, Antonio, M.D. and Dale Pennington, Ph.D. "Maternal Infant Bonding and Asthma." *Journal of Prenatal and Perinatal Psychology and Health*, 14(3–4), Spring/Summer 2000, pp. 279–288.

Mahler, Margaret, et al. *The Psychological Birth of the Human Infant: Symbiosis and Individuation*. New York: Basic Books, 1975.

Maiden, Anne Hubbell and Edie Farwell. *The Tibetan Art of Parenting* from *Before Conception through Early Childhood*. Boston: Wisdom Publications, 1997.

Maltz, Wendy, and B. Holman. *Incest and Sexuality*. Lexington, Mass.: Heath, 1991.

Marlow, David H. *Psychological and Psychosocial Consequences of Combat and Deployment with Special Emphasis on the Gulf War*. RAND Institution, 2000.

Masterson, James. *Psychotherapy of the Borderline Adult*. New York: Brunner/Mazel, 1976.

Masunaga, Shizuto. *Meridian Exercises*. Japan Publications, 1987.

McEwen, Bruce S., Ph.D. "Allostasis and Allostatic Load: Implications for Neuropsychopharmacology." *Neuropsychopharmacology*, Vol. 22(2)(2000), pp. 108–124.

———. "Stress and Brain Development." *Journal of the American Academy of Child and Adolescent Psychiatry*, Jan. 1999.

McLaren, Karla. *Emotional Genius*. Columbia, Calif.: Laughing Tree Press, 2001.

McNeill, M. Evelyn. *Neuroanatomy Primer*. Baltimore: Williams & Willkins, 1997.

Menzam, Cherionna. *An Authentic Birth*, Masters Thesis available from author, 1996.

———. *Dancing Our Birth: Prenatal and Birth Themes and Symbols*. Unpublished doctoral thesis.

Michaels, Melissa. "Surfing the Creative" and "Birth" (two videos), available from Melissa Michaels, P.O. Box 7478, Boulder, CO 80306. 1-877-Bdanced, *surf@bdanced.com*

Miller, Alice. *Banished Knowledge: Facing Childhood Injuries*. New York: Doubleday, 1988.

————. *Breaking Down the Wall of Silence*. New York: Dutton, 1991.

————. *For Your Own Good*. New York: Farrar Strauss Giroux, 1983.

————. *The Drama of the Gifted Child*. New York: Basic Books, 1981.

————. *The Untouched Key: Treating Childhood Trauma*. New York: Doubleday, 1990.

————. *Thou Shalt Not Be Aware*. New York: New American Library, 1986.

Miller, Sukie, Ph.D. *Finding Hope When A Child Dies: What Other Cultures Can Teach Us*. New York: Simon and Schuster, 1999.

Mines, Stephanie, Ph.D. *Jin Shin Tara: A Tool for Titrating Trauma* (Self Care, Book 1, Book 2, Book 3 and The Energetic Pathways), Boulder, Colo.: Dom Project.

————. *Sexual Abuse/Sacred Wound: Transforming Deep Trauma*. New York: Station Hill, 1996.

————. *The Dreaming Child: How Children Can Help Themselves Recover from Illness and Injury*. Boulder, CO.: The Dom Project, 1998.

————. *Two Births*. New York: Random House, 1972.

Monahon, Cynthia. *Children and Trauma*. New York: Lexington Books, 1993.

Moore, Keith, Ph.D. and T.V.N. Persaud, M.D. *The Developing Human: Clinically Oriented Embryology*. Philadelphia: W.B. Saunders Company, 6th Edition, 1998.

————. *Before We Are Born: Essentials of Embryology and Birth Defects*. Philadelphia: W.B. Saunders, 1993.

Murray, Iain. "Juvenile Murders." *Christian Science Monitor*. March 27, 2000, p. 9.

Napierala, Susanna. *Water Birth*. London: Bergin and Garvey, 1994.

Nathanielsz, Peter W., M.D. *Life in the Womb: The Origin of Health and Disease*, New York, Promethean Press, 1999.

————. *Life Before Birth*. New York: Promethean Press, 1992.

National Center for Children Exposed to Violence Statistical Report. Yale University, 2001.

Newham, Paul. *The Singing Cure*. Boston: Shambhala, 1994.

Neumann, Erich. *The Child*. New York: Harper, 1996.

Ni, Maoshing, trans. *The Yellow Emperor's Classic*. Shambhala, 1995.

Nilsson, Lennart. *A Child is Born*. New York: Delacorte Press, 1976.

No author given—"Practice Parameters for the Assessment and Treatment of Children and Adolescents Who Are Sexually Abusive," *Journal of the American Academy of Child and Adolescent Psychiatry*, December 1999.

No author given—"Violent Behavior in Children and Youth: preventive interventions from a psychiatric perspective," *Journal of the American Academy of Child and Adolescent Psychiatry*, March 1999.

Nuland, Sherwin. *How We Die*. New York: Vintage, 1995.

———. *The Wisdom of the Body*. New York: Knopf, 1997.

Ochberg, Frank, ed. *Post Traumatic Therapy and Victims of Violence*. New York: Brunner/Mazel, 1988.

Ou-i, Chich-hsu, and Thomas Cleary, trans. *The Buddhist I Ching*. Boston: Shambhala Press, 2001.

Papolos, Demitri F., MD and Janice Papolos. *The Bipolar Child*. New York: Broadway Books, 2002.

Pearce, Joseph Chilton. *The Biology of Transcendence*. Rochester, Vt: Park Street Press, 2002.

———. *Magical Child*. Bergenfield, NJ: NAL Dutton, 1992.

Pert, Candace. *Molecules of Emotion*, New York: Scribner, 1997.

Phillippi, Donald. *Kojiki*, Tokyo: University of Tokyo Press, 1985.

Physicians for Social Responsibility. *New Report Links Chemicals Commonly Found in Industry and Home to Behavioral and Learning Disabilities*, May 11, 2000.

Piontelli, Alessandra. *From Fetus to Child: An Observational and Psychoanalytic Study*. London: Routledge, Chapman and Hall, 2000.

Radin, Dean, Ph.D. *The Conscious Universe*. San Francisco: Harper Collins, 1997.

Rainer, Tristine. *The New Diary*. Los Angeles: Tarcher, 1978.

———. *Your Life as Story*. New York: Tarcher, 1997.

Raloff, Janet. "Coming to Terms with Death." *Science News*, 159(24), pp. 378–380.

———. "Prenatal Exposures Effect Sperm Later." *Science News*, 158(19), p. 303.

Redfield Jamison, Kay. *Touched With Fire*. New York: Touchstone Books, 1996.

———. *An Unquiet Mind*. New York: Random House, 1997.

Rodriguez, Luis J. *It Doesn't Have to be this Way: A Barrio Story*. San Francisco: Children's Book Press, 1999.

Rossi, Ernest. *The Psychobiology of Mind-Body Healing*. New York: Norton, 1993.

Roszak, Theodore. et al. *Ecopsychology*. San Francisco: Sierra Club, 1995.

———. *The Voice of the Earth*. San Francisco: Sierra Club, 1990.

Sapolsky, Robert. *Stress, The Aging Brain, and the Mechanism of Neuron Death*. New York: Freeman, 1994.

———. *The Trouble with Testosterone*. New York: Touchstone, 1998.

———. *Why Zebras Don't Get Ulcers*. New York: Freeman, 1998.

Sawyer, David, M.A. *Birthing the Self: Water Based Methods for Healing Prenatal and Birth Trauma*. Available from David Sawyer, 2455 Broadway, Boulder, CO 80304. 303-440- 9725, *davidsawyer@ibm.net*

Scaer, Robert C, M.D. *The Body Bears the Burden: Trauma, Dissociation and Disease*. New York: Haworth Medical Press, 2001.

Schore, Allan N. " The Effects of Early Relational Trauma on Right Brain Development, Affect Regulation, and Infant Mental Health." *Infant Mental Health Journal*, 2001, Vol. 22, pp. 201–269.

Schore, Allan N. *Affect Regulation and the Origins of the Self: The Neurobiology of Emotional Development*. Hillsdale, NJ: Lawrence Erlbaum Associates, Inc., 1994.

Schwartz, Jeffrey, M.D. and Sharon Begley. *The Mind and the Brain: Neuroplasticity and the Power of Mental Force*. New York: Harper Collins, 2002.

Schwartz, Leni. *The World of the Unborn*. New York: Marek, 1980.

Seem, Mark, Ph.D. *Bodymind Energetics* Rochester, Vt: Healing Arts Press, 1989.

Seligson, Fred Jeremy. *Queen Jin's Handbook of Pregnancy*. Berkeley, Calif.: North Atlantic Books, 2002.

Sewall, Laura, Ph.D. *Sight and Sensibility: The Ecopsychology of Perception*. New York: Tacher-Putnam, 1999.

Sheldrake, Rupert. *A New Science of Life: Morphic Resonance*. Vt: Park Street Press, 1995.

———. *Seven Experiments That Could Change the World*. London: Fourth Estate, 1994.

Sheldrake, Rupert, and Matthew Fox. *Natural Grace*. New York: Doubleday, 1997.

Shepard, Paul. *Nature and Madness*. University of Georgia Press, 1998.

Somé, Sobonfu E. *Welcoming Spirit Home*. Novato, Calif.: New World Library, 1999.

Somerville, Richard. *The Forgiving Air*. Berkeley: University of California Press, 1996.

Sonne, John C., MD. "Interpreting the Dread of Being Aborted in Therapy." *Journal of Prenatal and Perinatal Psychology*, Volume 11, No. 4, Summer 1997.

Steingraber, Sandra, Ph.D. *Living Downstream*. Reading, Mass: Addison-Wesley, 1997.

———. *Having Faith*. Cambridge, Mass: Persons Publishing, 2001.

Sternberg, Esther, M.D. *The Balance Within: The Science Connecting Health and Emotions*. New York: WH Freeman and Company, 2000.

Swerdlow, Joel. "Unmasking Skin." *National Geographic*: Nov. 2002. p. 36–63.

Tedeschi, Richard G. et al. "Posttraumatic Growth: A New Focus in Psychotraumatology." *Newsletter of the British Psychological Society*, April 2000.

Teeguarden, Iona Marsaa, et al. *A Complete Guide to Acupressure*. Tokyo: Japan Publications, 1996.

————. *The Joy of Feeling*. Tokyo: Japan Publications, 1987.

————. *Acupressure Way of Health: Jin Shin Do*. Tokyo: Japan Publications, 1978.

Terr, Lenore. *Too Scared to Cry*. New York: Harper, 1990.

————. *Unchained Memory*. New York: Harper, 1994.

Travis, John. "Sizing Up the Brain." *Science News*, 162(20), pp. 312–314.

Upledger and Vredevoogd. *Craniosacral Therapy*, Seattle: Eastland, 1983.

Upledger. *Craniosacral Therapy II: Beyond the Dura*. Seattle: Eastland, 1987.

US Department of Justice, Office of Justice Programs, Office of Juvenile Justice and Delinquency Prevention. *"Safe from the Start: Taking Action on Children Exposed to Violence."* Washington, DC. November 2000.

van der Kolk, Bessel, et al. *Traumatic Stress*. New York: Guilford Press, 1996.

Verny, Thomas, M.D. *Nurturing the Unborn Child*. New York: Dell Publishing, 1991.

————. *The Secret Life of the Unborn Child*. New York: Delta, 1994.

Volpe, Joseph S., Ph.D. *Effects of Domestic Violence on Children and Adolescents*. New York: Medam, Inc. 2001.

Wangyal, Tenzin, Rinpoche. *Healing with Form, Energy and Light*. Ithaca, NY: Snow Lion Publications, 2002.

Wauters, Ambika. *Chakras and their Archetypes*. Freedom, Calif.: Crossing Press, 1997.

Wilbur, Ken. *A Theory of Everything*. Boston: Shambhala, 2001.

Wilhelm, Helmut and Richard Wilhelm. *Understanding the I Ching*. Princeton, N. J.: Princeton University Press, 1995.

Wilhelm, Richard, trans. *The I Ching or Book of Changes*. Princeton, NJ: Princeton University Press, Bollingen Series, 1950.

Wisechild, Louise. *She Who Was Lost is Remembered*. Seattle: Seal Press, 1991.

Zerbe, Kathryn. *The Body Betrayed*. Carlsbad, Calif.: Gurze Books, 1995.

About the Author

STEPHANIE MINES, PH.D., is the founder and director of an international training program, the TARA Approach for the Resolution of Shock and Trauma. She conducts seminars and workshops world wide with the purpose of ending the lineage of shock and trauma. She is the author of *Sexual Abuse/Sacred Wound: Transforming Deep Trauma* and *The Dreaming Child: How Children Can Help Themselves Recover from Illness and Injury.* Dr. Mines is a living embodiment of the power of identifying shock and overcoming its pervasive impact on everyday life.

Dr. Mines lives in Eldorado Springs, Colorado with her husband, environmental attorney, Robert E. Yuhnke, and her youngest daughter, Rachel Sofia.

Please visit *www.Tara-Approach.org* for a complete listing of classes in the TARA Approach and to find a teacher representative of the TARA Approach in your area.